THRIVE ON STRESS

THRIVE ON STRESS

How to make it work to your advantage

by

Dr ROBERT SHARPE
and
DAVID LEWIS

SOUVENIR PRESS

Contents

Introduction

This is a book about stress. But it is almost certainly unlike any other book on the subject you have ever read. Most authors emphasise how dangerous and damaging stress can be and suggest ways in which you can avoid it. We are going to tell you exactly the opposite. We are going to show you how to control and use stress to help you lead a healthier and happier life. Once you have learned this control you will see how stress can be a powerful creative force which can transform your future.

As with our earlier book, *The Success Factor,* the Five Stage Programme of explanation, analysis and training has been prepared according to the principles of behavioural psychology. This means that it is a structured Programme which should be absorbed as directed in the text. It is for this reason that we have divided it into Stages, rather than conventional chapters. If you are to derive maximum benefit from the procedures contained in these Stages, it is important to proceed through the Programme in the order in which it has been set down.

In this short introduction we want to describe a little of the scientific and clinical background to the Programme in order to set the procedures which you will be learning in a clinical as well as an historical perspective.

Over the last two decades the approach to dealing with responses to stress situations has developed and evolved dramatically. As recently as twenty years ago stress-based problems, along with many other types of interpersonal, behavioural and even metaphysical difficulties, were treated along classical psychiatric or interpretive psychotherapeutic lines. In the wake of the Freudian era and with the rise to prestige of the medically orientated psychiatrist, the nature of the professional help offered to those suffering in such problem areas was both rigid and repressive. Extremes of treatment dogma prevailed. Brain surgery was held by many to be the ultimate answer for the alleviation of psychiatric problems; in some institutions pre-frontal lobotomy (leucotomy) became almost fashionable. According to certain psychodynamic theorising, such behaviours as homosexuality were to be held as infantile fixations and, consequently, undesirable characteristics. Dogmatically, such disciplines would require their clients to change sexual orientation as a necessary requisite of a treatment programme. We could continue to enumerate a great many more attitudes and approaches which now seem to most people, and certainly to modern behavioural psychologists, had they not been such serious invasions of personal liberty, to have bordered on the ludicrous. At this point, however, it is sufficient to say that such professional disciplines probably succeeded in holding back the course of productive behavioural change and mental welfare by a factor of generations; and that they successfully gathered about themselves a cloak of professionalism which confined their activities to those relatively few individuals who had the patience, inclination or income to find their way into their consulting rooms. The trappings and distinguishing marks of the professional cloak included such incontrovertibles as the diagnosis sheet, the drug regime, the voluntary or involuntary inpatient period, the lengthy time commitment, the 'pay now be treated later' contract, the cloistered consultations, the white linen coat and the black leather couch.

During the last few years of the half-century-long stranglehold exerted by these disciplines, experimental psychologists had begun to give practical demonstrations of their discontent with the prevailing psychiatric gospel.

Studies of the results produced by the then popular psychiatric and psychotherapeutic interventions revealed that, statistically, there was no more advantage in spending a number of years in treatment than there was in remaining untreated! Approximately 60 per cent of those who underwent therapy made some alleged progress while almost exactly the same percentage of people who did not enjoy the benefit of a professional intervention reported a decrease or a removal of their problems over the same time period. Furthermore the progress made by those in treatment was frequently expressed by the professional helper in such unquantifiable and indefinable terms as 'a strengthening of ego boundaries', 'a stronger personality' or 'worked through Oedipal conflicts'.

A second major finding was that the currently popular approaches tended to look at any 'mental process' other than the actual problem which was being presented and that these specific difficulties were left to solve themselves in the course of interpretative insight therapy.

This situation gave rise to considerable opposition among the more scientifically based experimental behavioural psychologists of about thirty years ago. They gradually evolved an approach to dealing with psychological problems whose major criteria were:

a. That it should be rapid – lasting for weeks rather than for years.
b. That it should be self-manageable by the client who could therefore leave the therapist quickly and continue to make progress alone.
c. That it should work, in the sense that the problem or problems which the client actually presented should either be considerably decreased or completely removed by the end of the therapy.
d. That the programmes used in therapy should be so based upon scientifically proven principles that they could be replicated with other clients.

By about the mid-fifties they were well on the way to achieving these goals and the new discipline of behaviour therapy had come into being.

A*

The last twenty years has seen behaviour therapy and applied behavioural psychology become extremely successful and widely sought after in hospitals, institutions and privately. The approaches used in behaviour therapy have themselves gradually developed from being mostly consulting room based to, nowadays, consisting largely of educational or training programmes which the therapist either teaches *in vivo* (in real life situations) or gives as structured homework assignments to the client to carry out himself or herself.

It is in this area of self-regulated programmes that we have been particularly concerned. The research and clinical experience of Dr Robert Sharpe has repeatedly validated the general assessment of applied behavioural psychology as having powerful therapeutic value. Having organised training workshops for both members of the psychiatric professions and the general public, he had shown that it was possible for the principles underlying behavioural change to be used to help large numbers of people to solve a wide range of problems and overcome all sorts of difficulties by developing self-regulated programmes. After lengthy research and validation, this teaching of behavioural self-management principles by means of workshops was refined to a stage where the training could be made widely available through books, tape cassette courses and other techniques of mass communication. In collaboration with David Lewis, an expert in these techniques, programmes were created which can be understood and implemented by anyone with an interest in changing their lives for the better. These programmes have been extensively tested and shown to be rapid and effective with large numbers of people and across a wide spectrum of problem areas. The skills which the programmes teach have been termed – **Response Control Procedures** (RCPs).

Response Control Procedures are currently available in Great Britain, Europe and America through an international organisation called **Stresswatch**. The functions of **Stresswatch** are to research, develop and provide programmes based upon applied behavioural psychology principles which can be used singly or in combinations, in written or audio form, by the general public. In the majority of situations, training programmes in RCPs will completely remove the psychological problems which are obstructing performance in and enjoyment of life. There may be some very severe difficulties where personal, medical or psychological help is also advisable but even in these instances the effect of the RCP Programmes is to diminish considerably the number of sessions required in the consulting room.

In the ten RCP Programmes described in Stage Four you will discover all the major skills and strategies necessary to control the effects of stress and strain in every area of life.

Stage One

Understanding Stress

CONTENTS

Stage One

Understanding Stress

INTRODUCTION

What does the word *stress* suggest to you? The chances are it conjures up ideas of something unpleasant and potentially harmful which it is best to try and avoid. Most people regard stress in this way, as a prime threat to their health and a major obstacle to their happiness. We tend to associate *stress* with *distress* and describe it in terms of all the bad things that can happen to us. This generally negative approach to stress is well illustrated by these comments taken from our case history files.

'Stress is worrying about money' – housewife and mother of two children.

'Stress is living in a noisy, dirty and dangerous city' – New York cab driver.

'Stress is not being able to cope with the demands of living' – business executive, aged 45.

'Stress is being afraid of growing old and getting sick' – accountant, aged 60.

'Stress is too much work chasing too little time' – salesman, aged 30.

The popular press often describe stress in graphic terms as 'the space age sickness' or 'the curse of the consumer society' and such dramatic phrases accurately reflect the widespread pessimism about the nature and effects of increasing stress. There are countless books which warn of the dangers of stress-related diseases and any number of experts prepared to read off the latest casualty figures in mankind's war against stress – so many middle-aged men and women struck down with heart diseases, so many more people turning to drugs such as Valium to help them survive the stress of life, so many more suicides in the affluent, stressful West.

The message of this book is very different.

We want you to forget all the bad, gloomy things you have been told about stress.

We want you to stop fearing stress and start using stress. To stop trying to avoid stress and start learning to control stress.

Why?

Because, properly controlled and used, stress can be the best thing that ever happens to you. Once you have learned the procedures which enable you to master stress you will find that it is no threat to your survival and success but a powerful creative force which can transform your life for the better.

Perhaps you find these claims hard to believe? Such a reaction is perfectly natural because it probably contradicts everything which you have seen, heard or thought about stress. However, our claims are made on the basis of extensive research and clinical experience and the knowledge gained through years of practical application of the procedures which you will learn in our Five Stage Programme. These findings leave no room for doubt. Stress can harm you when it runs riot in your life. Learn to control and use it and you will be able to live a healthier, happier, more successful and more fulfilled life. In short – **You Can Thrive on Stress**.

The procedures required to control and use stress creatively are neither especially complex nor particularly hard to learn. They require training in certain skills and strategies developed from behavioural psychology. How you can acquire them and how you can put them to work for you is the subject of this book.

The majority of people never learn these procedures. As a result they spend their lives trying to cope with damagingly high levels of uncontrolled stress or they devote much of their time and energy in trying to escape from stress. As we will explain in a moment, you cannot adapt to uncontrolled stress in the long term without suffering mental or physical damage nor can you ever avoid stress. There are, in fact, only these choices:

We can become the masters of stress or we must become its victims.

We must make it clear at this point that everybody needs a different level of stress in order to live a healthy, happy and successful life. Later in this Stage we will describe how this optimum level of stress varies not only between one person and another but within ourselves from one day to the next and from one area of activity to another. What we are talking about here are the dangers of living at a stress level which is out of phase with our natural requirements. In the long term exposure to this sort of uncontrolled stress can lead to severe health damage from a wide range of stress-related diseases: for example coronary attacks, hypertension, ulcers, a nervous breakdown or exhaustion. Whatever price our minds and bodies eventually exact for prolonged exposure to such stress, we can be sure it will be very unpleasant. It may be fatal.

Even short term encounters with uncontrolled stress can be painful and demoralising as most people know only too well. We have probably all suffered, at one time or another, from the discomfort of a churning stomach, a dry mouth, a thumping heart and uneven breathing. In very stressful situations we may find it hard even to perform at all. Although we may manage to appear physically calm and collected, our minds are racing and confused. In such circumstances it is hardly surprising if we fail to make a good impression on those we most want to think well of us.

'I wanted to get the job but stress during the interview spoiled my chances.'

'I want to pass the examination for which I have studied but stress in the exam room will ruin it for me.'

'I want to shine socially and impress people but stress turns me into an uninformative, tongue-tied dummy.'

'I want to work creatively but stress from a deadline makes me panic.'

'I want to enjoy sex and give my partner pleasure but stress prevents me from performing as I would like.'

We blame stress for our troubles time and again. What we should do is blame our inability to control and use that stress.

Stress – The Fire of Life

The usual approach to stress is to regard it as primitive man looked on fire. Because he could not control the flames which swept through the forests, he feared it and shunned it. He felt he had good reason for his terror. He could see the destruction the fire caused and knew the sharp pain of an incautious encounter. But that same fire which terrified our ancestors gives light and power to our cities. The chemical reaction has not changed. The potential for destruction has not altered. The inherent danger remains the same. But we are confident of our ability to control and use that fire for our own good. We know that we can contain it.

Stress is the fire of life. It can bring destruction. It can cause untold misery and pain. But with the skills and strategies taught in our Five Stage Programme you can learn to contain it. The methods we use to exercise this mastery are called **Response Control Procedures**.

Response Control Procedures (RCPs)

These are the procedures taught in Stages Four and Five of this book. They have been developed from the clinical and research experience of one of the authors of this programme of control, Dr Robert Sharpe.

Dr Sharpe is a behavioural psychologist and one of the foremost authorities on stress. As director of a large, London based practice he heads a team of therapists which annually treats hundreds of victims of uncontrolled stress.

The procedures which Robert Sharpe created to help these clients have been refined and simplified so that they are easy to learn and both safe and effective when self-administered. It is the first time that the powerful procedures of the psychologist's consulting room have been made available to the general public in a programmed form.

The Five Stage Programme

In the first Stage we will explain what *Stress* is, how it occurs and how we commonly try to escape from it. In the second Stage we will look at *Strain,* which is the internalised consequence of exposure to stress.

In Stage Three we will show you how to analyse your own responses to stress and to distinguish between the different types of stress which may be influencing you at this moment. From the results of this analysis you will immediately be able to plug into those **Response Control Procedures** described in Stage Four which can help you most quickly and most effectively.

In Stage Five you will be shown how to use the selected RCPs in a structured programme of learning which will help you to establish them swiftly and surely.

Finally, in Stage Six, we will look at the social and economic problems of uncontrolled stress and suggest ways in which group stress control programmes might be introduced to benefit institutions, communities and industry.

THE FLIGHT FROM UNCONTROLLED STRESS

Let us look now at the way in which people attempt to handle stress. Most of us have evolved a number of strategies either for increasing the amount of stress in our lives or for escaping from it. Men and women who find the pace of life too slow for them may spend their spare time in hazardous and stress-inducing leisure pursuits. Young people bored and frustrated with dead-end life in the city may turn to vandalism or crime, largely as a means of making their environments more stimulating. For most people, however, stress is something to be avoided and a whole industry has grown up to provide 'escapes' from the stress of life. As we will explain, all of these escapes are more apparent than real, but this does not prevent them from being very popular.

Diversions

These include the cinema, theatre and television, spectator sports and amusement parks. Increasingly these offer stressful situations in a controlled, safe and socially acceptable setting. Audiences watching violent films with their high-speed action, slow-motion destruction and carefully choreographed blood-letting are able to become physically aroused in the safety of their seats. The more stressed and anxious about everyday life members of an audience feel, the more likely they are to seek escape through such vicarious exposure to artificial stress. Indeed a measure of the amount of social stress present at any time is the level of violence present in these forms of escape. The trouble with such diversions as a form of escape is that the release from stress which they provide is temporary and we return to the real world with none of the stress problems in our own lives resolved.

Removals

These may be quite drastic and physical or fairly minor and mental. For many young people the flight from stress involves dropping out into a sub-culture which rejects the values of conventional society. For others escape lies in some form of spiritual commitment, either to an established religion or by way of gurus, yoga or meditation. We are not saying that this way is wrong or that there is not a great deal of good to be derived from many of these mental practices. But they are not likely to offer direct solutions to specific stress problems to the majority of people.

The more affluent members of society buy cottages in the

country or villas by the sea. Annual holidays provide temporary escape for millions and, again, there are positive benefits to be derived from such periodic retreats. The change of environment is often psychologically helpful and rest, cleaner air and more relaxed eating habits help restore the body. But once the holiday is over we usually return, like parolees, to the prison of everyday stress. Within a couple of days the holiday is forgotten and the mental and physical benefits are being rapidly eroded through exposure to the old levels of uncontrolled stress.

Addictions

These range from medically prescribed tranquillisers to illegal drugs, and include tobacco, drink and food. Perhaps the most significant gauge of people's increasing fear of stress is the rise in the numbers taking some form of tranquilliser to help them ride through the day. More than one million people in Britain, and 15 per cent of the population of the United States, are now taking Librium or Valium regularly and the latter has become the most prescribed drug in the world. Tranquillisers act on the central nervous system and inhibit the conduction of nerve impulses. Pep pills – amphetamines, dexedrine or benzedrine – are also widely used and have an opposite effect to tranquillisers in stimulating part of the nervous system. A survey carried out amongst the 14 million residents of New York State aged more than fourteen years revealed that 110,000 regularly used this type of 'escape' to overcome their stress difficulties. The same survey showed that there was a wide use of illegal drugs, especially marijuana, with 485,000 admitting to its regular use. There were also 41,000 heroin addicts and 50,000 regular users of LSD.

Alcohol and tobacco are not only perfectly legal 'escape' routes from stress; they are both socially acceptable and easily obtainable. As a result the United States now has five million alcoholics. Research which linked cigarette smoking to lung and heart diseases had only a minimal effect on sales, an indication of how much pleasure and relief smokers derive from this form of 'escape'.

Food is not usually regarded as being addictive, except in the sense that we must eat to live, but it can be. It provides relief from stress, soothes anxiety and reduces tension – all three major factors in obesity problems. People eat because it makes them feel less stressed and a weight problem is born.

Therapy

This comes in many guises and is practised by a vast range of specialists, from priests to psychoanalysts and gurus to spiritual revivalists and growth therapists. Lying on a couch, for years in most cases, and talking about your problems may or may not help reduce stress. It will certainly diminish your bank balance. The self-knowledge gained through such procedures may be very valuable; philosophical insights can enrich your life in many ways and therapies of many different kinds may provide comfort in the face of difficulties. But they are unlikely to provide practical or effective solutions. What you need are specific procedures for bringing the stress in your life under control so that you can utilise it constructively.

To return to our earlier analogy about fire, let us imagine that your house has caught alight. The *diversions* escape route offers you a chance to forget all about your problems for a little while and hope that the fire will go out in the meanwhile. Of course it does not do so! The *removal* philosophy says, in effect, never mind about that house, we'll find another. The trouble is that we carry the destructive flames around with us and rapidly set alight to the next residence, and the next. The *addiction* approach does not attempt to put out the flames but it does dull the pain of living in a burning building. The *therapy* escape route, when effective, is undoubtedly the best approach. A concerted effort by all concerned and the flames are quenched. The trouble is that the fire might reignite spontaneously at any time, putting you right back in the same danger and difficulties as before. Even if it does not catch alight again your house may be permanently condemned to darkness and cold. You dare not reintroduce the fire which could light and warm it because you still have no knowledge of how to keep the flames under control.

The Five Stage Programme in this book will teach you how to extinguish the flames and locate the most inflammatory parts of your house so that you can be on the alert for any further uncontrolled outbreak. You will then learn how to reintroduce the fire of stress into your life but on your own terms and under your complete control.

You Cannot Escape From Stress

You cannot escape from stress even if you run away from the rat race and live in a grass hut on a South Sea island.

You cannot escape from stress by joining a monastic order or by moving to a cave in the mountains of Tibet.

You cannot escape from stress by taking drugs or drink.

You cannot escape from stress in sleep, in meditation or in the deepest state of relaxation of which the body is capable.

There is only one time when you will be free from stress. The technical term for that state is *dead*!

To paraphrase the Book of Common Prayer: 'In the midst of life we are in stress!'

We can best illustrate this point by reference to two case histories on our files. As with all such histories quoted in this book, the names have been changed in order to ensure confidentiality.

CASE ONE

Peter Browne was a 42-year-old marketing director with an advertising agency. He had been married for twenty years and had two children in their teens. He liked to describe himself as a 'one ulcer man in a two ulcer job' but his physical health was actually good. He had managed to give up smoking, watched his diet and played squash regularly. Every summer he and his family spent three weeks in the country and enjoyed themselves tremendously. When they were in their quiet cottage surrounded by fields and trees Peter and his wife would often talk about the wretchedness of the city rat race compared with the tranquillity of the 'stress-free' country. For years they had talked only half-jokingly about selling up their city apartment and buying a small market garden. But when he was 42 Peter finally took the plunge. Deciding he could no longer tolerate the stress of his work and his urban lifestyle, he persuaded his wife that they should sell up and make their dream of a rural existence finally become reality. He gave up his well paid, stressful job and purchased a small market garden in the depths of the country. Peter knew little about agriculture but he had some capital and was prepared to work hard and learn from his mistakes. For a few months all went well. But soon the novelty of living in the country began to wear off and when winter came the landscape took on an increasingly bleak and hostile appearance. His wife found that she had little in common with the country women and making friends was difficult. The boys, moved to new schools at a critical period in their education, found it hard to settle and disliked the long bus journey to college.

Peter had realised he must make mistakes but he was unprepared for the number he did perpetrate. The physical work, in all weathers, was far tougher than he had imagined. In the city Peter and his wife had been active socialisers. Now their nearest acquaintance was two miles away. There were no more parties and visits to the theatre and cinema. After work there was little to do but go to bed exhausted. Peter and his family stood their new life for a year and then moved thankfully back to the city. He had aged 'ten years my wife says' in those twelve months and used up most of his savings. That 'stress free' interlude in the country had given him the ulcer which he had managed to avoid in more than twenty years of stressful city dwelling.

Peter Browne *volunteered* himself into a lifestyle which he believed would be more relaxing and agreeable. But every year millions of active men and women are *forced* to change their way of life – on retirement. Many look forward to being liberated from the discipline of office or factory routine. After years of hard work they savour the idea of being their own masters and devoting all their time to themselves. Few realise just how difficult the adjustment can be or how much they needed the stresses of their familiar life. Unable to control the new stresses of their retirement they can suffer physically and mentally until they make the necessary changes of attitude and behaviour. For some this is fairly easy, but for others it can present a real difficulty as our second case history shows.

CASE TWO

Anne Kay retired from her job as an administrator at the age of 66 after more than thirty years at the same busy hospital. She had enjoyed her job although it meant working long hours, often under considerable pressure. But she had no regrets when the time came to leave the hospital. She was looking forward to having an easier time and being able to devote herself to her hobbies of gardening and painting.

For the first few months Anne's retirement was all that she hoped for. But gradually the lack of routine in her day became wearying. She had soon tidied her small garden into shape and with nothing else left to do except paint, her enthusiasm for the hobby began to pall. While she was working Anne had always been an early riser, but now with nothing which she considered 'worthwhile' to fill her day she stayed in bed later and later. She grew depressed and soon even making meals and keeping the house in order became a chore she often skipped. Everything seemed a monumental effort. Even invitations, for coffee mornings and lunches, from neighbours and friends were too much trouble. She began to make excuses and, inevitably, the invitations were not repeated. After a year Anne hardly ever went outside the house. One day, when she had forced herself to go down to the shops, she collapsed in the street and was taken to hospital. The doctors could find nothing physically wrong with her but the incident preyed on her mind. She started to believe she was seriously ill. Every minor ache and pain, the normal consequences of growing old, became magnified into the symptoms of a terminal illness. She started to plague her GP for pills and sympathy. He listened with as much patience as time allowed and prescribed tranquillisers. He also suggested that she might have become agoraphobic – that is, she had acquired a terror of going out – and gave her the name of a psychologist. For weeks Anne put off going to see him but finally she gathered enough courage to make an appointment.

The journey to his consulting room was a nightmare but Anne forced herself to make the effort. Once there she found her luck had changed. The psychologist not only gave her the professional help she needed to treat her phobic condition – but he also found her a job. He had known her several years earlier at the hospital and was aware of how highly they had valued her hard work and attention to detail. A colleague of his was in need of a receptionist and the psychologist put Anne in touch with him. Anne went for an interview deeply pessimistic about her chances of success. But she got the job and agreed to work there 'until' in her words 'he could find somebody younger'. That was three years ago and Anne is still in her job. She is under stress again, more than in her old position because the work is more varied and, at seventy, she has to take a little more time over everything. But her mental and physical health are excellent and she finds plenty of time for her hobbies and her friends.

Anne Kay and Peter Browne thought they were getting rid of their stresses when they left their regular jobs. But what happened was that they swopped the stresses of a lifestyle with which they were familiar for the stresses of a new and unfamiliar way of life. All their old strategies for coping with and controlling stress, which they had used successfully in the past, now became ineffective.

Research in Europe and America has shown that this need for familiar stress is very widespread. When men are thrown out of work in an economic depression their mental and physical health is almost certain to suffer, even though their unemployment pay is sufficient to live in reasonable comfort. As the unemployment figures mount, doctors in the worst affected areas know that their surgeries will soon be crowded with out-of-work patients complaining of a wide range of complaints, most of which will have a psychological basis.

In one recent investigation French researchers studied 12,000 office workers who had just been made redundant. After only three months of enforced idleness 40 per cent of them had become too sick to have started a new job even if employment had been available. White collar workers are not the only ones affected. In another study 377 manual workers who had been laid off were given a medical examination immediately after dismissal and 78 per cent of them were found to be in excellent health. At the second check up, only a week later, doctors found that 89 per cent of the previously healthy group now complained of feeling depressed and anxious. As the weeks of enforced idleness slipped past they began to develop various ailments most of which had a psychological basis. By the time the investigation ended 31 per cent of them had heart trouble.

This is not to suggest that it is impossible to switch from an active urban existence to a busy country life, or the other way around. Not everyone who retires becomes the victim of depression and phobias. Many men and women do make the transformation from one lifestyle to another completely successfully. But when you examine such changes you invariably find that a considerable amount of luck or a great deal of realistic planning has been involved. Usually such people succeed because they do not delude themselves that they can escape from stress or even that such an attempt to escape would be the best course for them. They understand that they are merely changing one type of stress for another and that this new set of stresses must be controlled and used constructively.

WHAT IS STRESS?

Stress, as we explained at the start of this Stage, is usually associated with the less pleasant aspects of life.

Stress is too much work and too little relaxation.

Stress is hostility from others.

Stress is too little income chasing too many outgoings.

Stress is noise and dirt, being too hot or too cold, too tired or too depressed.

All the descriptions of stress in general use have one thing in common. They imply that *stress* must be equated with *distress* and that it is something which we encounter in patches on the journey through life. It is thought to increase as we get older and to be worse in the present than it was in the past. In a typical scenario for mounting stress problems, compiled from hundreds of questionnaires in our files, childhood and early youth are usually seen – in retrospect – as being relatively stress free. People admit to occasional periods of minor stress such as important examinations, clashes with authority and arguments with boy- or girl-friends when young, but by and large, they generally feel that these were the happiest and least stressful years of life. Then came adulthood and with it new responsibilities and pressures. There was a career and the struggle for promotion and higher pay. There was an increasing realisation of the political and social injustices in the world. With material success came increasing financial obligations, rates and taxes to be paid, mortgages and hire purchase agreements to be settled at regular intervals. With age came the stresses of trying to compete with younger men, of trying to remain physically and sexually attractive, of retaining the respect of sons and daughters and of approaching senility and death.

As stresses mount our minds and bodies come under increasing pressure. We risk 'nervous breakdown', ulcers, heart trouble and high blood pressure. Doctors advise us to take things easy. If we reject their advice our bodies may protest to such an extent that we get an enforced rest in hospital. In the ultimate and most irreversible revolt of which it is capable the body simply stops working. 'Death', it has been observed, 'is nature's way of telling you to slow down!'

This popular view of stress is both inaccurate and misleading. It is inaccurate because it implies that only certain aspects of our lives produce stress. It is misleading because it suggests that if we were to avoid those specifically stressful situations we would automatically be better off. The practical consequence of this popular view has been the flight from stress which we discussed earlier.

Our definition of stress is more comprehensive and avoids this dangerous misconception:

Stress = An individual's perception and assessment of the environment.

Let us examine exactly what this definition involves.

First of all it means that everything we see, hear, feel, taste and smell is a source of stress, whether it involves a quiet country lane in summer or a congested city street in the middle of a winter storm. It also means, since we ourselves are part of our own environment, that the way we think, our memories, ambitions and dreams are also sources of stress. Even when we are deeply asleep, therefore, we are experiencing stress from that part of our environment enclosed in our skull and skin as well as from the external environment.

But the definition implies more than a passive perception of the world around us. The fact that we *assess* the environment with a cerebral cortex which contains a unique collection of memories and learned responses means that our view of that environment is equally unique. All living things share the same world only in a limited physical sense. Because external stimuli are filtered by different senses and by individual minds we each inhabit a distinct and personal environment. It can be said that there are as many worlds as there are 'I's' to see them.

Let us take an everyday example to illustrate this point. Imagine a quiet city street. There are some cars parked beside the kerb and a few people out strolling. A casually dressed, long-haired boy is staring into a store window where a pretty girl is setting out a display. An old lady is sitting on a bench and watching a labrador dog sniff along a pavement towards her. A policeman is on patrol.

On the basis of common sense we might imagine that all these people are perceiving and assessing the scene in a similar way, but this is not so. Each will be filtering the environment through their senses and their brains and colouring them with all the accumulated opinions, attitudes and prejudices of their individual minds. Let us imagine what some of these different views might be. The old lady may be watching the labrador dog and remembering nostalgically her childhood when she had a similar pet dog. The boy, eyeing the pretty girl, may be seeing the scene in sexual terms. The girl may be concentrating on the effectiveness of her window display. The policeman's perceptions will have been greatly influenced by his training, as a detailed study by Professor Jerome Skolnick of California has shown. Law enforcement officers are taught to recognise certain types of people and situations as potentially dangerous and, because of this, our policeman may be seeing the cars in terms of traffic violations or stolen vehicles and looking at the casually dressed boy with suspicion.

The same scene may be perceived in four different ways and at four different levels of stress. The old lady may become nervous as the dog approaches for fear it will jump up on her. The girl may be worrying that she will not finish the display before it is time to go home. The boy might be thinking how nice it would be to ask the girl out and feeling his stomach churn anxiously as he anticipates a rejection. We have already seen the policeman may be viewing the apparently innocent street with suspicion.

It could be that some of the people in this imaginary scene were perceiving and assessing the street at very high levels of stress. If the old woman was a dog phobic the approach of even a small, friendly animal could make her extremely frightened. If the girl had been threatened with the sack for slack work she might become increasingly anxious over the effectiveness of her display. The boy, if he had been brought up to regard sex as sinful, could be feeling guilty and tense as he watched the pretty girl and found himself aroused. As for the policeman – it would only need him to recognise one of the cars as a vehicle used in a recent crime for his level of stress to rise sharply.

In other words the amount of stress present for each individual in that scene depended entirely on how each perceived and assessed it. This is true of each and every situation in life. Even at night when we are asleep, the way we assess the world through our dreams will determine the level of stress involved.

The behavioural psychologist's view is that these differences in perception and assessment can be accounted for largely by learning.

The old woman had *learned* to become phobic about dogs.

The boy had *learned* to feel guilty about sex.

The girl had *learned* that shoddy work resulted in a threat of dismissal.

The policeman *learned* that danger could lurk even in an apparently tranquil environment.

This concept of learning is an important one. Clearly if it is possible to learn to regard certain situations or objects as sources of chronic stress, then we can learn *not* to regard them in this way just as effectively. The way in which we have learned to respond to our environment, together with other factors such as physical health, age and temperament, influences the amount of stress which we need to perform happily, healthily and efficiently. It is a matter of common observation that this level varies from person to person. Sources of stress which somebody born and brought up in a big city can use productively, might be sufficiently alien to send somebody raised in an isolated part of the country into a nervous collapse. In the same way a type of stress which a countryman might find stimulating and constructive could be regarded by the city dweller as dull and wearying.

Optimum Stress Level (OSL)

The amount of stress at which each individual functions most effectively we have termed the *Optimum Stress Level* (OSL). As we will explain in Stage Three of this programme, where we ask you to analyse your own lives in order to determine how you are reacting to different forms of stress, the OSL can vary from one area of life to the next. A man who needs a very high level of stress in his recreation, and meets it by doing some dangerous sport such as sky-diving or mountain climbing, may function best at work on a lower optimum level of stress.

It is impossible to set any figure for the OSL because one can only determine it in a subjective way. *You* are the only person who can satisfactorily fix your OSL for any particular area of your life. You do so by assessing how efficiently, happily and enthusiastically you are carrying out some particular task. So long as you are performing any piece of behaviour in a successful and effective manner, without feeling any mental or physical ill effects, then your OSL is being realised. A helpful analogy may be to compare the OSL with the capacity of a car's fuel tank. Every vehicle has its own fuel need which varies with the capacity of the tank and the quantity of petrol already present when refuelling starts. If just sufficient petrol is poured into the tank to fill it then the car can travel as far and as fast as it is capable. If too much fuel is poured in there is an overflow with risk of fire. If there is too little fuel in the tank then the car cannot travel as far as it would otherwise be capable.

The OSL is the capacity of the tank. The fuel is every aspect of the environment which the individual perceives and assesses. In other words the total stress impinging on that individual. So long as that stress is maintained close to the optimum level it is valuable and motivating. If it rises too high or falls too low then performance, health and happiness will be increasingly affected.

Negative Stress Responses

Stress levels which either fall below an individual's particular OSL or rise drastically above it produce responses which make it more difficult or less pleasant to perform a desired piece of behaviour. We have termed these *Negative Stress Responses.*

Negative Stress Response = Any response, mental or physical, which adversely affects performance.

Let us look at a number of situations in which Negative Stress Responses can arise.

Suppose that you are attending an important interview. Your desired piece of behaviour is to make a good impression, to put over your views and qualifications in an effective and convincing manner. It is natural under these circumstances to feel some anxiety. Up to your OSL the stresses produced by this situation can help you. They will key up the whole system, making you more alert and efficient. In fact if the stress levels fell below your OSL under such circumstances, you might give the impression of being rather lethargic, unenthusiastic and unresponsive. But if the stress level rises sharply above your OSL then you will experience extreme physical anxiety perhaps combined with mental confusion. Your heart will start to thump wildly, you may fidget and be unable to sit still. Perhaps your mouth will go dry and your uneven breathing will make it difficult to speak clearly and convincingly. You may perspire or feel slightly sick as your stomach churns. The key points which you wanted to bring out will simply disappear from your panic stricken mind only to reappear ten minutes after the interview is all over. These Negative Stress Responses will have proved damaging to your ability to perform the desired behaviour.

B

Take a very different situation, such as a young man making love. His desired behaviour is to enjoy the sex act in a relaxed way which will enable him to share the maximum amount of pleasure with his partner. Clearly if the stresses produced by the situation fall below his OSL for that particular activity then neither he nor his partner are likely to gain much enjoyment from it. He will be unresponsive, bored and disinterested. But if the stresses rise sharply above his OSL then mental and physical anxiety will make it very difficult to perform effectively. He may find it hard to achieve or sustain an erection. His ejaculation may be premature. Perhaps he will be so anxious and concerned about performing satisfactorily that even though he does cope physically there will be very little mental enjoyment.

Finally let us look at the kind of situation which arises when we go into a room full of strangers at a party. Our desired behaviour will probably be to create a good impression, to enjoy ourselves and to make new friends and acquaintances. To do this we need sufficient stress to be alert, bright and sparkling. Too little and we appear bored and boring. Too much and our anxiety may be such that we cannot really respond to the situation in a relaxed and interested manner.

Perhaps at this point you begin to see how we can go about controlling stress and using it productively.

First of all it is necessary to discover your own OSL's in different areas of life. As we have explained these can vary from activity to activity. Once these OSLs have been determined you must learn to use certain procedures to maintain them. In some situations this will mean reducing the overall stresses in the environment so as to reduce the level of stress to an optimum. But at other times it will be necessary to *increase* the amount of stress, by adjustments to your environment, so as to raise your stress level to the optimum.

In Stage Three of this book we will show you how to analyse the stresses in your own life to determine your OSL.

In Stages Four and Five we will explain the procedures by which this optimum level can be maintained.

In the first Stage of this programme we have introduced some basic concepts about stress. These are summarised below. It is important that you understand them fully before reading Stage Two.

SUMMARY

Stress = An individual's perception and assessment of the environment

This definition implies that we each see the world around us in a unique way. Because of this, some aspects of the environment may be regarded as significant and stressful by one individual whilst producing hardly any response from another.

Because stress consists of everything in our environment, including the thoughts and memories in our brains and the physical responses of our bodies, we cannot escape from stress. Even when we are deeply asleep or very relaxed we are under stress. This means that it is pointless to try and flee from stress. What we *can* do is learn to control it and make it work for us.

Uncontrolled stress can cripple us mentally and physically. Controlled stress is a creative force which allows us to lead a happier, healthier and more successful life.

Anybody can learn how to harness stress and make it work for them. The procedure is first to determine the level of stress at which we function most happily and most efficiently and then to maintain that level. We have termed this the Optimum Stress Level (OSL).

The OSL varies between individuals and each individual is likely to have a different OSL in different areas of activity. The OSL for each individual and every activity which that individual attempts can only be determined subjectively by that individual. It can be defined as follows:

OSL = The level of stress at which we can perform a desired piece of behaviour most easily, efficiently and happily.

Negative Stress Response = Any response, mental or physical, which adversely affects performance.

When the level of stress falls below our OSL we perform in an inefficient and unrewarding way. Everything seems to be an effort. We feel bored, lethargic and under-stimulated. We may make mistakes because we find it hard to concentrate. We will feel no enthusiasm for the task in hand and little inclination to start on anything new.

When the level of stress rises above our OSL we become anxious and uncomfortable. Performing a piece of desired behaviour is difficult due to physical tension and mental confusion. We may experience a rapidly beating heart, trembling, nausea or poor digestion, a dry mouth and uneven breathing. Our minds will be unable to concentrate on the key issues and we may forget training and instructions. (See Table One.)

Stress is often thought of as a mysterious and immeasurable internal state of mind and body. As we have seen it is actually an external force, even though it includes such internal factors as thoughts and physical responses.

Stress acting on an organism produces Strain.

Strain is the internal response to Stress.

In Stage Two of the programme we will examine Strain to see how it arises and how it affects us.

Table One – OSL and Negative Stress Responses

Stress Level	Effect on Behaviour
Higher than OSL	Physical anxiety and mental confusion. An inability to think effectively, to remember instructions or training or to work out problems clearly and objectively. At high levels panic may occur causing dangerous choices and decisions to be made. Bodily tension may include rapidly beating heart, high blood pressure, excessive perspiration, trembling and feeling faint, churning stomach and indigestion, dry mouth and uneven breathing. Co-ordination may be impaired and reflexes slowed down. These are all Negative Stress Responses.
Optimum Stress Level (OSL)	A feeling of alertness and self-confidence is created. We think and respond quickly and effectively. We perform well and have a feeling of enthusiasm and well being. We are interested and involved in the task which we can carry out in an energetic and easy manner.
Lower than OSL	A lack of interest or enthusiasm for the task in hand. A feeling of depression and futility. A belief that nothing matters any more and that even the simplest job is a monumental chore. We feel bored and lacking in energy. The world looks drab and grey. We find it very hard to summon up the energy to start new jobs or create fresh interests. These are all Negative Stress Responses.

Stage Two

Understanding Strain

CONTENTS

Stage Two

Understanding Strain

INTRODUCTION

We have explained that stress is *everything* in our environment as perceived and assessed by us. It is things which are physically outside our bodies, such as traffic congestion and mountain landscapes, an unexpected bill or a letter bringing good news. But it is equally processes and responses taking place within ourselves, a cut thumb or an aching leg, an upset stomach or a cold in the head. It involves our memories, expectations and imaginations as well. If we recall a humiliating experience, start to worry that a minor stomach upset might be something more serious, or look ahead to an unpleasant appointment we are producing internal stressers.

It may strike you as odd that we have included mountain landscapes and good news in our list of stressers because, as we said in the First Stage, most people equate stress with distress. But the stress from pleasant and agreeable situations can be just as intense and often trigger off the same kind of behaviour. Dr Hans Selye in his classic study *The Stress of Life* uses the term *eustress* (from the Greek word 'good') to describe this kind of stresser. Teenage girls at a pop concert will often scream, hold their heads in their hands and move agitatedly from the *eustress* of joy and excitement at seeing their idols. Very similar responses can be seen in some cultures at times of great grief and mourning.

Of course the categorising of an internal or external experience as pleasant or unpleasant is, as we discussed earlier, a highly subjective matter. To a painter an angry sky, vivid with colour and dramatic banks of dark, tumbled clouds may appear as beautiful and majestic. A sailor looking at the same scene may

B*

fear the bad weather it portends. An empty expanse of beach, sea and sky might seem romantic to a young couple but a nightmare to an agoraphobic. Even our assessment of situations which we would normally consider distressing may alter with circumstances. The sight of an aircraft crashing in flames, condemning the crew to an agonising death would normally be regarded with horror. But in times of war the downing of an enemy aircraft in this way can bring cheers and tears of joy from the watching population who have just been bombed by it. Being attacked in the street by a mugger or caught in air turbulence whilst flying would be considered stressful by most people. Yet the amount of stress they present is likely to vary from person to person. A young, fit judo expert might be less stressed by the thought of crime in the street than an elderly woman. A qualified pilot would be better able to cope with the stress of unexpected turbulence than his untrained and in-experienced passengers. On the other hand he might still be as stressed as they are because his training would enable him to understand the hazards facing them all.

Assessment of the situation is obviously of critical importance when it comes to the amount of internal strain generated by an external or internal stresser. It is this internal strain which produces the complex neuro-chemical changes in our bodies which result in feelings of tension, mental confusion and physical discomfort. How and why this happens will be explained in a moment.

The relationship between environment and stress and between stress and strain can be summarised as follows:

STRESS (An individual's perception and assessment of the environment)

→ results in →

STRAIN (The consequence of that unique perception and assessment on the mental and physical state of the individual concerned).

RECOGNISING STRAIN

There are many commonly accepted strain effects which can be experienced to greater or lesser degrees by different individuals. If we were to ask a large number of people to describe their own experiences of strain they might use words and phrases such as: 'Sweating, tension, rapid heartbeat, nausea, dizziness, fainting, indigestion, high blood pressure, uneven breathing, headache, lethargy, crying, depression, drowsiness, aches, lack of concentration, difficulty with mental processes such as recalling facts and figures, computation, grammatical construction and ordering of data.' These are, of course, all valid terms by which an individual might assess a strain level at a certain point in time and we shall refer to combinations of these experiences when we later develop the Response Control Procedures (RCPs) with which to deal with them. But often strain is recognised and described through its effects on the way the individual performs those learned activities and skills by which their life is organised and run. A typical description might be: 'I felt so upset that I couldn't work all afternoon' or 'I was so bored that I just sat and said nothing'. Often, when people consider stress they tend to miss out the stage of strain in the chain of events, the end of which is some performance impairment. Correctly stated this chain goes:

STRESS → STRAIN → Change in Performance →
Further STRESS → Further STRAIN . . . and so on.
(See Diagram One)

Examples of fully stated STRAIN chains can be seen in the boxed extracts from the case studies on pages 45 and 46.

Diagram One: The Stress Spiral
showing the way in which each wave of strain and performance breakdown adds itself to the preceding level of stress
and leads to further strain and performance breakdown.

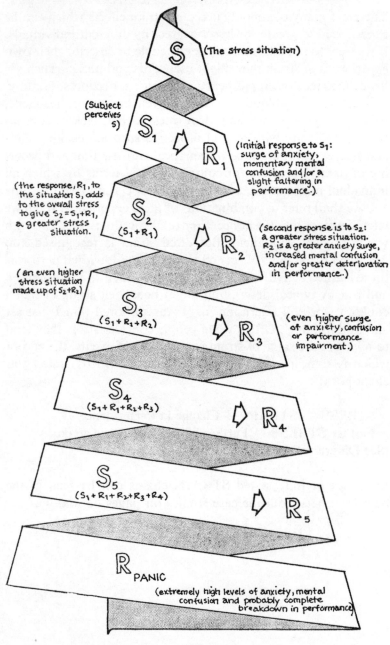

S (The stress situation)

(Subject perceives S)

S_1 ⟹ R_1 (Initial response to S_1: surge of anxiety, momentary mental confusion and/or a slight faltering in performance.)

(the response, R_1, to the situation S, adds to the overall stress to give $S_2 = S_1 + R_1$, a greater stress situation.

S_2 ($S_1 + R_1$) ⟹ R_2 (Second response is to S_2: a greater stress situation. R_2 is a greater anxiety surge, increased mental confusion and/or greater deterioration in performance.)

(an even higher stress situation made up of $S_2 + R_2$)

S_3 ($S_1 + R_1 + R_2$) ⟹ R_3 (even higher surge of anxiety, confusion or performance impairment.)

S_4 ($S_1 + R_1 + R_2 + R_3$) ⟹ R_4

S_5 ($S_1 + R_1 + R_2 + R_3 + R_4$) ⟹ R_5

R PANIC (extremely high levels of anxiety, mental confusion and probably complete breakdown in performance)

CASE THREE

Housewife. Aged 27.

'. . . I was at home with my two young children preparing tea to entertain my mother-in-law. I was keyed up for the occasion but quite looking forward to showing her what a competent woman her son had married. Half an hour before she was due to arrive one of the neighbour's children came around to play with mine. I told them that they could play together but that they must be good as I was expecting a visitor. Five minutes after they arrived one of them had upset the tea tray onto the carpet. I thought immediately of the mess that my mother-in-law would be confronted with and my stomach turned over. I broke into a sweat, became tense and as I rushed to clear up the damage I tripped and fell myself. I felt even more tense and burst into tears. My mother-in-law arrived to find me weeping and clearing up the mess. . . .'

CASE FOUR

Sales Executive. Aged 42.

'. . . I was in a meeting with an important client and about to present the results of a market research programme. A large and important contract rested on my presentation. I felt confident when I started because I had done the work well. But, soon after I started, the client's accountant, a young and aggressive individual, started to attack me over the statistics. This really threw me because I couldn't seem to get him to grasp the true position. I suddenly felt my mind go blank of any more rational argument to present. I began to have difficulty in remembering the most obvious of basic points to refute his contentions as he kept hammering away at me with details irrelevant to the major decision. I felt myself becoming dizzy and my face broke into a sweat as I realised that I was not putting any effective argument forward in favour of my proposals. I began to stammer slightly and my heart began to pound. Finally I made a concession to his argument and agreed with something he said even though I knew it was completely wrong. From that moment on there was no point in sticking to my well worked out presentation and we lost the contract. . . .'

	Case Study Three	*Case Study Four*
STRESS	Accident caused by child	Unexpected and aggressive attack
STRAIN	Internal feelings of stomach turning over, tension and later crying	Mind going blank, impairment of memory, dizziness, sweating and rapid heart rate
CHANGE IN PERFORMANCE	From cheerfully carrying out preparations to tearfully being resigned to not impressing mother-in-law	From confidently presenting sale proposals to surrender to opposing and incorrect point of view

Often, though, we would hear these accounts expressed in the following way:

'. . . one of the children overturned the tea tray. I broke down and rushed around weeping and making even more of a mess. I was still doing so when my mother-in-law arrived. . . .'

'. . . the client's accountant attacked me very aggressively on irrelevant details. His views were wrong but within seconds he had me agreeing with him and I lost all hope of winning the contract. . . .'

In these versions of the accounts we only have information relating to the stress and the changes in performance which are, of course, the same as in the more fully expressed accounts. In order to use our Response Control Procedures (RCPs) it is essential that such accounts should be given as in the fully detailed boxed examples, since in order to control the strain response it is necessary first to recognise and describe it. This is an important point to which we shall return in Stage Four.

STRAIN AND PERFORMANCE

While it is important to be able to describe the strain responses in detail, they have very little relevance for most people unless they are considered in relation to the performance of major activities in life. These activities, as we shall explain later, are found in the four Life Areas – A. Work and Study; B. Family, Marriage, Sex and Intimacy; C. Social and Interpersonal Relationships; D. Leisure and Sport; and consist of either *mental* activities, such as planning, calculating, concentrating, ordering of data, explaining, remembering; or *physical activities*, such as muscular effort, and co-ordination; or an integrated mixture of these two.

These Life Area skills and learned activities provide their own sources of stress. The amount of stress which they present depends upon how complex they are to perform and how well trained we are in their performance. For example a novice typist working against a deadline is likely to be under more stress than an experienced secretary. A young housewife preparing an evening meal for her husband may be under more stress than a more experienced married woman who is used to cooking and running a home. In other words the stress produced by daily life activities is largely a product of how practised we are in their performance.

Many of the skills and activities in the four Life Areas, together with strategies for increasing their performance, are described in our earlier book *The Success Factor*. In this present book our major area of concern will be those sources of stress which are not produced directly from Life Area activities but which originate from other unsought sources and have a bearing on the performance of our desired life activities. These stress sources may be an addition to or a subtraction from the stress level associated with a particular life activity and can therefore generate a high or low total strain response.

We have called the sources from which stress and therefore strain can be generated the **Lifestyle Stressers**. We can group the **Lifestyle Stressers** under six major headings.

THE LIFESTYLE STRESSERS

Performance Stressers

These are the sources of stress inherent in the actual accomplishment of a piece of mental or physical behaviour. The usual features by which such behaviour is recognised are that it involves a desire to carry out a particular activity or attain a particular goal; a planning phase; an operational phase where an attempt is made to perform in the desired way; a feedback phase where the performance is assessed; and a continuation phase where the next attempts are modified in the light of previous performance. In general all of these behaviours respond to practise and the stress and strain which they produce diminish with time as the behaviour is practised more and more frequently. Good examples are driving a car, speaking in public, and playing a sport. In these and many other cases the behaviour will be difficult and laborious in the early stages but will become progressively easier as the skill is established.

Threat Stressers

These are situations which are perceived and assessed as dangerous. They may involve objective and actual risk to the bodily welfare of the individual, such as those implicit in a physically aggressive confrontation, a battle, riot or war, a high risk sport or involvement in a physical accident. They may equally include encounters which are not objectively harmful but which are assessed as such by a particular individual. These latter occur primarily in phobic situations.

Boredom Stressers

These are situations which are perceived and assessed as lacking in physical or mental stimulation. Typically these may be situations which are so familiar to an individual that they need no active thought to deal with. They are often found in production line work, household chores and similar routine physical activities. They may also be seen in situations where people are not employed to their full capacity either physically or mentally.

Frustration Stressers

These are situations which are perceived and assessed as being undesirable but beyond one's power to control. They can take many forms. One is the classic *double bind* situation where a person is placed in such a position that whatever response he or she makes it is bound to have an unpleasant or humiliating result. This may be seen in sexual situations where a partner is frequently rejected. If he or she decides simply to stop making advances then the unpleasant consequence is sexual deprivation. On the other hand if a sexual advance *is* made the unpleasant consequence is that of being ridiculed, humiliated and rejected. Any situation in which there are large numbers of unpleasant consequences contingent on any of the alternative responses available can be termed a *double bind* frustration situation. Another source of this type of stress is any form of imprisonment, either by the State or by such factors as confinement to bed, entrapment due to poverty or family pressures. Frustration stresses also originate from bureaucracy, as in governmental taxation and other constraints, which gradually produce more and more forms and an increasing number of rules and regulations for controlling private and business life. In short the more subordinate clauses there are in a governmental edict or sanction the greater will be the level of frustration stress produced. This is a socially significant factor which we will discuss at greater length in Stage Six.

Bereavement Stressers

These are situations which are perceived and assessed as resulting in a loss of any kind. It is fairly obvious that one major source of bereavement stress is that due to the death of a close relative or friend. But it can also occur with the loss of a relationship, moving away from an area where one has had many friends, losing a job or even a treasured possession. Loss of reputation, whether real or imagined, or of a personal sense of value, such as dignity or usefulness to others, also comes into this category.

Physical Stressers

These are a different type of stresser since they involve actual physical damage to the person. For example breaking limbs, suffering from a disease or infection, and working in conditions of pollution or extremes of temperature where precautions cannot be taken.

FACTORS AFFECTING STRAIN LEVELS
These six Lifestyle Stressers all produce strain ranging from the tolerable to the acute depending on three factors:

The intensity of the Lifestyle Stresser

The intensity factor can best be illustrated by looking at the response of a phobic sufferer to a situation perceived and assessed as dangerous. Consider a man who has claustrophobia. If he is taken into a large, well-lit public hall with plenty of clearly marked exits and sufficient space to move around, he will probably be able to cope without much difficulty. Now lead him into a smaller side room. There are still a number of exits and, although he starts to feel uncomfortable and to show signs of physical tension, there is no panic. The intensity of the stress has increased but it is still manageable. From the side room we proceed into a small office. The walls are dark and the ceiling low. There is only one window and it is closed. The man begins to tremble and sweat, his mouth is dry and his stomach churns. He can only tolerate the situation with difficulty. From the office we proceed to an elevator. This is a small, totally enclosed box. The man forces himself to step inside but as the door slides shut he panics. The intensity of the stress has now resulted in such strain that his coping strategies and his fear of being made to look foolish in public are no longer powerful enough to hold back the physical terror which engulfs him.

The duration of exposure to the Lifestyle Stresser

Duration of exposure to a Lifestyle Stresser does not always work in quite the way one might expect. The strain experienced does not go on rising and rising but, after reaching a certain peak, levels off. This is known as adaptation to stress (see Diagram Two). During the First World War such adaptation was a regular feature of life in the trenches. The initial exposure to the hazards of shellfire, bombing, sniper and machine-gun fire produced a high level of stress. But most of the men who survived the first few weeks soon adapted to the death and the dangers. While newcomers would fling themselves into the mud as a shell whistled overhead, the more experienced trench hands

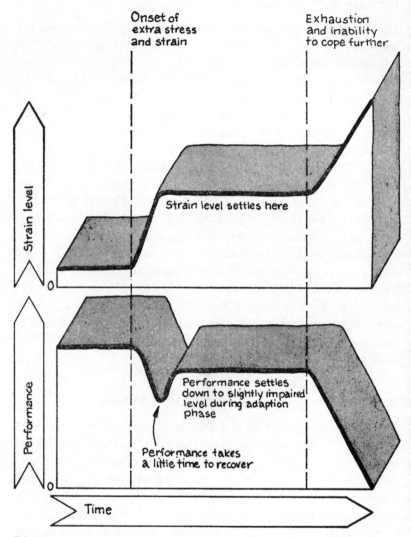

Onset of
extra stress
and strain

Exhaustion
and inability
to cope further

Strain level

Strain level settles here

0

Performance

Performance settles
down to slightly impaired
level during adaption
phase

Performance takes
a little time to recover

0

Time

Diagram Two: Showing adaptation to stressers in the presence
of which a constant state of strain arousal must be maintained
in order to survive. The end point, exhaustion, is shown with
the inevitable rise in strain levels.

remained unmoved and unmoving. They had learned to judge by the sound of a shell how close to them it would land. But such adaptation does not last for ever and takes a severe toll on the individuals concerned. High levels of strain, even where they are coped with through adaptation, cause such wear and tear to the system that mental or physical breakdown is almost inevitable. It often happened that some minor additional stress, perhaps being subjected to a slightly heavier than normal bombardment, precipitated a collapse due to shell-shock. Those who managed to sustain adaptation to the stress throughout the war were still likely to show the effects even years later. During the Second World War some of the bitterest fighting on the Eastern Front took place around the ruined and beleagured city of Stalingrad. In the bitterness of a Russian winter Soviet and Nazi troops fought savagely for every square yard of rubble-strewn territory. The closing weeks of the battle involved close-range combat as men hunted one another to death in the gutted, smouldering buildings and through the pitch black cellars. The rate of hypertension recorded by medical teams amongst the Soviet troops rose from an average of 4·1 per cent found in a civilian population to 64 per cent! Most of those who survived the campaign were dead by the early 1960s at relatively early ages.

The busy executive who works long hours at high pressure and never seems to rest or relax is another example of the adaptation response. But such people are very likely to snap, mentally or physically, with very little warning. After carrying out a major investigation into the nature and causes of heart diseases, Dr Ray Rosenman, a San Francisco cardiologist, and Dr Meyer Friedman postulated that there were two sorts of people: Type A's and Type B's. Type A's are ambitious, competitive and aggressive. They have an intense urge to get things done, to achieve and succeed. Type A's drive themselves, and others, hard. They seldom feel the need for medical help and rarely go to a doctor. They take little exercise, perhaps the occasional game of golf, and like to go on holiday to places where there is 'something happening all the time'.

Type B's are easy going, less competitive and not so achieve-ment orientated. They are gentle, non-aggressive people who like to relax quietly with a book or listening to a piece of music. Of course not everybody is a clear cut Type A or Type B; most of us are mixtures of both. But the genuine Type A, and probably we know at least one person who seems to fit into this category, is an excellent example of the person adapted to a high level of strain. The Type A is also a dreadful warning about the toll such adaptation finally takes. They are far more likely to suffer a coronary attack than Type B's. Out of 3,500 males, aged from thirty-one to fifty-nine, examined by Dr Rosenman and Dr Friedman, 257 of them later succumbed to heart attacks. Of these, 70 per cent were Type A's.

The number of other Lifestyle Stressers already present in the individual's environment

The third factor involved in determining the level of strain produced by the Lifestyle Stressers is the number of those and other stressers present in the environment at any one time.

In Stage One we talked about the *Optimum Stress Level* and compared this to petrol in the tank of a car. The capacity of the 'stress tank' represented the total amount of stress which could be usefully accepted. If too much or too little stress is present then Negative Stress Responses occur.

We can now see that the 'tank' is filled from six different sources, the Lifestyle Stressers, as well as from the actual task we are undertaking at a particular time. The flow of stress from these sources varies from a steady trickle to a gusher, producing levels of strain from the tolerable to the severely damaging. When our environment is producing too little stress the resulting level of strain is too low and does not key up the system to give the best possible performance. When the Lifestyle Stressers are in full flood high levels of strain result. Both these conditions lead to Negative Stress Responses. An optimum level of stress produces an optimum level of strain and leads to peak performances.

The situation can be summed up like this:

High Level of Stress → High Level of Strain → Negative Stress Responses.
Low Level of Stress → Low Level of Strain → Negative Stress Responses.
Optimum Stress Level → Optimum Strain Level → Ideal mental and physical responses.

The best way of illustrating how the Lifestyle Stressers combine to fill the 'stress tank' and how the flow of stress can be controlled in order to maintain the OSL is to imagine a container standing beneath six taps. The capacity of the container represents the OSL, the taps the source of stress from the six Lifestyle Stressers (see Diagram Three).

These taps are constantly producing a flow of stress into the tank, some at a greater rate than others. On occasions the volume of stress produced from all six of the taps is so low that the 'stress tank' never fills to anywhere near the OSL. When this happens a lack of interest and stimulation occurs leading to Negative Stress Responses. Sometimes one or more of the taps starts to pour out stress. The tank rapidly fills and may overflow beyond the OSL unless steps are taken to regulate the inputs of stress. This control can be exercised in two ways. We can bail out the stress from the tank as it fills or we can adjust valves on the taps to limit the input. To do this requires knowledge of the specialist procedures needed to control each of the six taps.

Let us further imagine that the flow to these taps is also controlled by six distant valves which we cannot easily and quickly adjust. All we can do, if we are observant enough, is to watch for the signals which alert us to the fact that these distant valves are about to be turned on or off causing the flow from the taps to increase or diminish. By doing this we will be able to anticipate moments when the taps will either start to gush with

Stage Two:
Diagram Three: Representation of flow from six Lifestyle Stressers into Stress Tank.

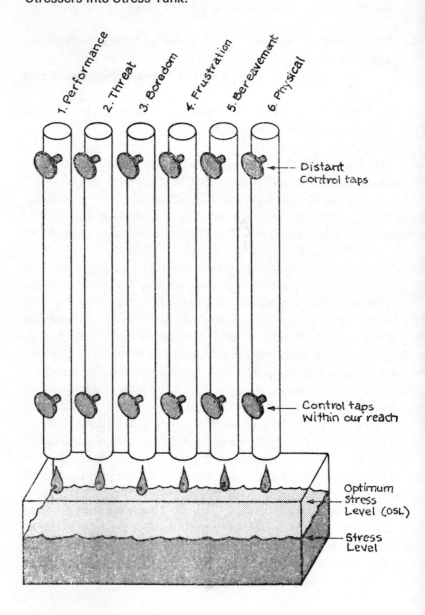

stress or will dry to a trickle. Such early warnings will enable us to prepare strategies for controlling the supply in the most appropriate way. That is, by increased 'bailing' and by operating the controls immediately to hand to prevent an overflowing of the stress tank or to allow the level of stress to build up in order to see us through a stress 'drought'. There is one other important fact about the way these taps operate. They very seldom work as single units. Cross-linking of the controls ensures that when one starts to flow rapidly at least one or two others will also start to gush out stress. At the same time, because of this cross-linking, adjusting one very often, although not invariably, reduces the flow from the others.

Now let us see how the different parts of this analogy relate to real life experiences. The remote valves controlling the flow of stress are events outside our immediate control; a redundancy, a bereavement, a period of tedious work, a humiliating experience, rising crime figures, the ending of an important relationship. If we have been observant these stressers probably will not come as a complete surprise since most events inducing Lifestyle Stresses build up over a period of time, and can be anticipated if we are prepared to make the necessary effort. By anticipating them we can take steps to control the inevitable increase or decrease in stress.

The procedures by which the stress tank can be bailed out and the taps of the six Lifestyle Stressers controlled form part of the RCP programme. They will be taught in Stage Five of this programme.

Remember that since:

Optimum Level of Stress → Optimum Level of Strain

it is possible to regulate the Optimum Level of Strain by controlling the stress inputs.

It is also important to bear in mind that stress reaching us from the six different Lifestyle Stresser taps accumulates in the stress tank. This accumulation of stress explains why quite trivial events can sometimes produce responses out of all proportion to the nature of the irritation. A few months ago one of us, Robert Sharpe, dealt with a case (see Case Study Five) which well illustrates this point.

CASE FIVE

A man in his thirties had attacked and caused bodily harm to a young couple who were playing a transistor radio, too loudly in his opinion, on a public common. The courts were baffled that he should have responded in such a violent way to such a petty irritation. An investigation into his background revealed that at the time he had been under considerable stress from a number of Lifestyle Stressers. His wife had recently left him (Bereavement Stresser) and he was in dispute with the authorities who wanted him to move out of his council-owned property to make way for a family. He felt they were being unreasonable but that he had no chance of winning against anonymous bureaucracy (Frustration Stresser). He believed that if he lost his house he would have to leave the area and give up a well paid job which he enjoyed (Threat Stresser). These three Chronic Stressers, all of which were at a high intensity, had brought his stress level way over the OSL. The playing of the radio annoyed him and he asked the couple to switch it off. They refused and his level of stress went over the top. He responded with a violent outburst of anger directed at the only objects in his life which it was then physically possible for him to attack.

A similar situation is often encountered in the all too common battered baby syndrome. The mother may be inputting several Lifestyle Stressers, especially physical exhaustion. The child cries once too often for her to cope and she strikes out, often with tragic consequences for the whole family.

Eustress: the Stress of Happiness

So far we have said nothing about *eustress*, the pleasant and desirable stressers in our environment. In physiological terms the response to *eustress* and other, unpleasant forms of stress, are often very similar. The same types of neurochemical responses produce much the same state of physical arousal. People will cry and shake from joy as much as from grief, and people will laugh out of misery as loudly as they will from happiness. Indeed it may be difficult to tell on occasions exactly what emotion is being expressed. We have already mentioned the behaviour of young fans at a pop concert. To take another illustration, a man's wife is seriously ill in hospital and he is waiting by the telephone for news of the operation. He paces the floor restlessly, his face is pale and his muscles tense. He breathes unevenly and starts at every sound anticipating the ring of the phone. Then the call comes through. His wife will be all right. He replaces the receiver, but continues to pace, too excited and relieved to relax. His breathing is unsteady, tears of relief flow down his cheeks which are still pale from the relief of the good news.

Intense *eustress* can be as mentally confusing and physically disturbing as distress caused by the Lifestyle Stressers – ask any big lottery winner or new father! But despite the physical effects frequently being similar in appearance and as internally disorientating, for the purposes of RCP programmes we do not consider *eustress* as one of the Lifestyle Stressers. This is because the psychological consequences are so obviously different and the beneficial effects so pronounced. *Eustress* can be used to help combat the effects of the Lifestyle Stressers and maintain the OSL even in times of great difficulty.

LIFESTYLE STRESSERS IN ACTION

Case History Six shows how at one stage in a person's life stresses from all the Lifestyle Stressers can result in a positive approach to life's challenges; but how when left to run out of control, they result in a deterioration in performance due to highly damaging Negative Stress Responses.

CASE SIX

John started his business career at the age of twenty-two after attending university and taking an arts degree. By the time he was twenty-eight he was married with a child aged four and found his work as a sales manager for a supermarket chain to be interesting, financially rewarding and offering every prospect of rapid promotion. There were patches of boredom in his life and times when he felt frustrated both at work and with his family. But generally John functioned at his OSL for most of the time. As a result he was happy, cheerful and easy to get along with at work and at home. He worked with enthusiasm and was in good health, all of which resulted in his giving his best performance most of the time. John was faced with a fairly bright situation at this stage of his life with stress being no real problem to him because all the inputs were useful and he had acquired commonsense strategies to keep their total at his OSL. (Some of these will be found in the main body of this text.) But five years after this extremely promising position was achieved a very different situation had emerged. John had always tried hard and given his best in his job. He had been anticipating promotion when the department chief retired and indeed, perhaps unwisely, he had so counted on this promotion he had allowed himself to get into debt on the assumption that the increased pay would enable him to afford a higher standard of living. But the expected promotion did not take place. When the chief retired another man, whom John considered his inferior, was promoted. John tried to rationalise the situation by telling himself that his turn would come, but his main feeling was one of anger and resentment. This remained unassuaged by the apologies of his immediate superior who told him that the order for promotion had come from head office.

There was an immediate rise in two Lifestyle Stressers at this point for John – Bereavement and Frustration. The bereavement came from the loss of self-esteem, loss of confidence and loss of reputation within his office. It also came from the loss of a rashly anticipated income. The frustration came from the fact that there was nobody he could blame or from whom he could claim redress. Head office was remote and could not be hurt as he had been. The man directly in his line of attack, his superior, was sympathetic and clearly on his side – a fact which only added to his frustration.

As a result of both of these Lifestyle Stressers John started to drink more heavily, which increased his performance stresses at work and at home. He lost his enthusiasm for work – 'what's the point when so little notice is taken of effort?' – and the boring patches which he previously skimmed over now seemed to have increased until they filled his whole working day. His financial position was much less secure and he felt himself threatened by too little income chasing too many outgoings. Circumstances he failed to anticipate turned on two of the Lifestyle stress taps and now all six were spurting dangerously away. At this point, with his work and marital relationships steadily deteriorating, John sought professional help and was effectively guided towards those RCPs which enabled him to regain a positive approach to his life through the control of his stress input.

At around the age of twenty-eight John can be seen to have managed his life effectively and enjoyably by the use of his own commonsense stress control strategies.

Performance stresses had reached an optimal level since continued practice at his job had made it easy for him to perform whilst still challenging his skills with the occasional new task or problem for him to solve.

Threat stresses had been kept low through a realistic appraisal of the risks from redundancy and ill-health making it impossible to work. Fears of these and other possible disasters were coped with by taking out insurances and having regular health checks.

Boredom stresses were kept at a minimum by ensuring that the humdrum work at the office was counterbalanced by seeking out fresh challenges and the routine of family life was offset by a relationship with his wife which was ever experimental and expanding.

Frustration stresses, involving national and international tension, the steady expansion of taxation and the general rush of life had been minimised by his decision not to waste his energy in worrying about situations over which he had no control and by taking an interest in his neighbourhood community and local politics.

Bereavement stresses, due to the loss of friends or self-esteem, were not present at this point in his life and his basic attitude was that they happened to other people rather than to him.

Physical stresses were present to some extent in his life as a poor diet, too little exercise and smoking took their toll. But in general his youth and health allowed him to cope with them with no obvious deterioration at that point.

By about the age of thirty-three, however, we can see a very different picture of the effects of the Lifestyle Stressers and a clear inability on John's part to control their effect by his earlier commonsense approach.

Performance stresses had risen sharply as his physical condition deteriorated through drinking bouts and resulted in a lowering of his ability to perform efficiently.

Threat stresses had multiplied as a result of his growing inability to meet his debts or to maintain a successful interaction with his wife and child which would be likely to keep them by him during a time of crisis.

Boredom stresses had increased because he was no longer performing so well at work, and had stopped taking on challenging tasks since there was no pay off for achieving them in terms of promotion and recognition.

Frustration stresses increased as he found his personal efforts thwarted by the faceless machine of 'head office', which seemed to have no regard for his true worth. As more of his time was spent in drinking he no longer had any available for local politics. Instead of taking an active part in neighbourhood affairs he joined the mass of people who merely complain bitterly about their lot.

Bereavement stresses soared with his loss of self-esteem and expected income. He was soon caught in a vicious circle. The more he drank the less efficient he became and the less respect he enjoyed from his colleagues and superiors at work and his wife and child at home.

Physical stresses rose dramatically due to his drinking, heavier smoking, lack of exercise and bad diet.

As each of these Lifestyle Stressers resulted in a deterioration of performance, so another Lifestyle Stresser would become involved and increase the negative spiral.

If this sounds all too familiar it's because it is! It's the old, old story of the way most people attempt to cope with the stresses and strains of modern life.

What might John have done if he had learned RCPs and been able to master stress instead of becoming its victim? The programme taught in Stages Four and Five of this book would have trained him to do the following:

(1) He could have anticipated a sudden rise in any of the Lifestyle Stressers so that the change in situation did not take him by surprise.

(2) He would quickly have replaced the anger and resentment which led to a Frustration stress by seeking out positive elements in his position and capitalising on them.

(3) He would have worked through the Bereavement Stresser in the correct way, still not enjoying the experience but remaining in control of the situation because he knew exactly why he felt as he did and what would happen next. This would have enabled him to compress the Negative Stress Responses into a few hours instead of months.

(4) He would have been able to limit the inflow of additional stress from these two Lifestyle Stressers so that the other stress taps did not start flowing at an excessive rate.

(5) While controlling the input of stress from the two Lifestyle Stressers he would have been able to use bailing procedures to bring the amount of stress already present back to his OSL.

As a result of implementing this programme he would have emerged from the setback stronger than he had been before it happened. He would have dealt with the increased stresses quickly and efficiently, while learning useful lessons from the experience. He would have been able to identify objectively the reasons why the expected promotion had not materialised and corrected them. Instead of losing his enthusiasm for the work the disappointment would have acted as a stimulus making him work more effectively towards promotion in the future. He would have thrived on stress.

OSL AND THE LIFE AREAS

In Stage One we explained that OSLs may vary quite widely according to the activities involved. A man who prefers a quiet time at work, and operates best at a low stress level, may spend the weekend climbing mountains and require a considerable degree of stress before his recreational OSL is reached and he functions at peak efficiency. An actress who needs a strong stress stimulation to give her best performance on stage, and therefore has a high OSL in her work, may like nothing better than to go home to a quiet family life. Only in the privacy of her home, surrounded by her children, does she feel truly relaxed and happy when away from the theatre. In this case her private life demands a low OSL.

For the sake of convenience we have divided all human activity into four Life Areas. These are:

A. **Work and Study.**
B. **Family, Marriage, Sex and Intimacy.**
C. **Social and Interpersonal Relationships.**
D. **Leisure and Sport.**

We have already seen that the Lifestyle Stresser taps are interconnected so that an increased flow from one of them may well result in several stressers being increased. The same kind of generalisation of stress almost always takes place between the four Life Areas. A rise in the Lifestyle Stressers at work usually increases the level of stress at home, in social situations and in recreation. A man who is suffering from Negative Stress Responses in his job is likely to be irritable with his family, less effective sexually, less socially competent and more easily put off a game or sport. After a time the stress levels may be so high in all the Life Areas that it is difficult to disentangle one problem from the next. The threads of Negative Stress Responses become intertwined, twisting into a confused and apparently hopeless maze of setbacks, arguments, frustrations and disappointments. Fortunately it is not necessary to disentangle these threads in order to make RCPs work for you. What happens in our programme is that the four Life Areas are first compartmentalised, so that no further seepage of stress can take place between them, and then the level of stress in each Area is reduced to the Optimum by using control procedures.

NEGATIVE STRESS RESPONSES: HOW YOU RECOGNISE THEM AND WHY THEY OCCUR

We have already explained that Negative Stress Responses arise when the amount of stress present either falls below or rises above the OSL. Now we must examine these Negative Stress Responses in more detail to see what they are and why they occur.

c

Negative Stress Responses come in four types:

High Level Negative Mental ⎱ **Both these are caused by**
High Level Negative Physical ⎰ **excessive stress**

Low Level Negative Mental ⎱ **Both these are caused by**
                               ⎬ **inadequate amounts of stress**
Low Level Negative Physical ⎰ **being present**

High Level Negative Mental

These are typified by mental confusion. The victim of High Level Negative Stress Responses finds it hard to think and, therefore, to act effectively. Prior instructions and previous ideas about how the problem should be tackled are forgotten as the brain stumbles through a confusion of conflicting thoughts and ideas. As the intensity of Negative Mental Responses rises, confusion may give way to blind panic and the victim can often act in a foolish and self-destructive manner. A person being rescued from drowning may struggle and fight with rescuers. A pedestrian caught in the path of a speeding car may stand transfixed in terror and make no effort to leap to safety. The danger does not always have to be as obvious as in these two examples to induce High Level Negative Mental Stress Responses in some people. A spider phobic, for example, might begin to think wildly of how they could run from a room at the sight of a small and perfectly harmless spider. A person suffering examination stress may be unable to sort out ideas and write coherently even though he has learned the necessary facts.

To explain this breakdown in mental processing it is simplest to compare the mind to a telephone switchboard. However complex the board, however many billions of connections there may be, there can always come a time when too many messages are being received for the board to deal with them all effectively. Unless the flow of messages is controlled and spaced out and unless there is some method of establishing priority of one type of message over another, none of them can be properly handled. This, in very crude terms, is what happens when an individual responds with High Level Negative Mental behaviour. Too many messages are flooding into the cerebral cortex for them to be sorted out, considered and dealt with efficiently. When a High Level Negative Mental Response is coupled to a High Level Negative Physical Response, a large proportion of those messages may be due to bodily conditions. With such a jumble of conflicting messages there is inevitable confusion which, in turn, creates even more confusion and physical anxiety until panic sets in.

High Level Negative Physical

These responses include a racing heart, uneven breathing, a dry mouth, high perspiration, giddiness, nausea, churning stomach, blushing, fainting and increase in urination or defecation. These symptoms can occur in mild forms without corresponding Negative Mental Responses. What usually happens, however, is that High Level Negative Physical and Mental responses either occur together or follow very closely on one another. For instance a person may experience a high level of Negative Physical Responses yet manage to remain mentally calm and ordered for a short while. Then, quite quickly, as the mind receives messages of distress from the body, these signals generate an increasing amount of mental confusion. Before long what may have started as a low level of physical anxiety has soared into total panic.

Earlier in this Stage we explained the Strain Chain and described how stress led to strain which produced a change in performance. This change, when it is a negative one, will result in further stress, more strain and a decreasing ability to perform effectively. The victim is trapped, unless control measures are applied, in a spiral of negative responses as shown in Diagram One.

The reasons for these often bewildering and frightening bodily responses are to be found in the working of a particular part of our nervous system which has been adapted to take care of the body's basic needs. This is called the Autonomic Nervous System (ANS) and it is through the activities of this part of the nervous system that most of the mechanical and automatic behaviours which we carry out are regulated. If we eat a meal, begin sexual relationships with an attractive partner, drift off to sleep or flop exhausted into an armchair after work we do not usually have to think actively of the exact processes of digestion, of showing obvious sexual arousal, of dropping to sleep or of relaxing our muscles. This is all done for us by one of the two branches of the ANS called the **parasympathetic branch**. Similarly if we are suddenly faced with a situation involving bodily danger, such as an aggressive attack, a snarling dog or the enemy in warfare, we do not have to think about tensing our muscles, speeding up the heart so as to rush energy-bearing blood to the muscles and brain, breathing more rapidly to get more oxygen into the blood and sweating so as to cool the body as the energy is being burned in the muscles, in order to fight to our maximum ability or flee as fast as we can. This is done for us by the other branch of the ANS called the **sympathetic branch**. These two branches take away all the effort that would be involved in producing these complex, and necessarily speedy responses to the situations which we have described.

We can see then that the **sympathetic branch** of the ANS is responsible for making the body tense, energy-burning and ready to fight or flee.

The **parasympathetic branch** of the ANS is responsible for recuperating the body, building up energy, and enjoying relaxed behaviour.

Having understood that these parts of the nervous system exist and what they are responsible for, it is now important to remember two other key features of them.

The first of these is that the two branches of the ANS work antagonistically. In other words if one of the branches is producing its effects on the body, the other branch is in a quiescent or inoperative state. This will be more obvious when we point out that it is impossible for the body to be both anxious, ready to flee and energy burning at the same time as it is relaxed, enjoying pleasant sexual or eating responses or asleep. We can only be in one or other of these states – that is either sympathetically or parasympathetically dominated – and we will always be in the state which is initially stronger. For example if a person is relaxing after a good meal but suddenly encounters an object of which he or she is phobic and feels a high level of anxiety surge through the body, then this high level of anxiety may well swamp out the parasympathetic feelings of relaxed digestion and produce, instead, the high level physical responses which we detailed above.

The second point to remember is that the parasympathetic and sympathetic activities are not normally under our conscious control. When in a state of physical tension and panic it is usually impossible simply to *tell* the sympathetic nervous system to stop functioning. This is why it is no use for people to exhort a phobic or stress sufferer to 'pull yourself together'. The fact is that the person is incapable of switching off the sympathetic activity unless they have learned, through RCPs, to do so. We shall be teaching methods of controlling the ANS in Stages Four and Five.

How then do High Level Negative Physical Responses occur? The answer is that while the ANS acts in a quite appropriate way for most of the time, it is nonetheless subject to learning principles which can result in inappropriate responses. It is obvious that if we perceive and assess a situation as involving a definite risk of physical injury, then the sympathetic branch of the ANS will speed into action to help us to escape from it. But, of course, as we said earlier, some situations which are not actually harmful may be perceived as such, and because of this trigger that same protective function of the ANS provided by the sympathetic branch. This is due to the fact that the sympathetic branch is 'only following orders' from our cerebral cortex which has perceived a situation which it considers to be dangerous. Under these circumstances the sympathetic branch does not wait to hear long-drawn-out arguments as to whether the situation really *is* dangerous or not (that might well prove totally inefficient if the situation was somebody approaching with a knife!) but springs into action by energising the body to fight or flee. In this way the sympathetic branch of the ANS will be triggered off by any stimulus perceived as dangerous. The phobic sufferer as much as a sportsman under stress may respond with just the same reaction as if they were faced by a ferocious animal. It is as difficult for that phobic or that sportsman to switch off the sympathetic activity as it would be to stand calm and unaffected in the face of deadly danger. Such a control over this learned sympathetic responding to situations which are not really dangerous can only be gained through a structured retraining of the ANS, as we shall later describe.

Now that we have explained the basic mechanics of, and reasons for the ANS, let us next look at the ways its functioning can go wrong and cause us distress in modern civilisation.

When a threat to survival is perceived the ANS swings into action. Like a destroyer preparing for action the sympathetic branch of the ANS puts the body into a state of maximum readiness. To fight or flee the organism must be alert and energetic. Blood is diverted away from such temporarily less essential areas as the skin and digestive tract and pumped to the muscles of the limbs and to the brain; the rate of perspiration is increased; digestion is stopped or slowed down; and the production of saliva ceases, making the mouth dry. There are less obvious effects too – for instance the rate at which the blood clots is increased so that in the event of an injury damage will be minimised.

Stone age man had real threats to life and limb. When the 'fight or flight' system switched on it was usually followed by one of these energy burning consequences. The individual fought and won, ran away and escaped, or was killed. With much of the released energy burned up, the parasympathetic branch of the ANS had little difficulty in bringing the system back to normal. The heart rate gradually slowed down and the blood pressure was reduced. The rapid breathing was brought back under control, digestion returned to normal. The mouth was once again lubricated with saliva. After a few moments rest everything was tranquil again, until the next emergency.

But modern man has managed to alter the environment to such an extent that our direct threats to survival have been largely reduced. Today there are irate bosses to placate and angry spouses to pacify rather than encounters with sabre-toothed tigers to survive. But the ANS is still set up for the 'fight or flight' responses which worked so well a million years ago.

Consider what happens in a confrontation between an employee and an angry boss. As the dressing down starts the ANS responds to a stress situation which has been assessed as a threat to survival. At once the whole system is keyed up for action. But action never materialises. Instead the employee must usually just endure the verbal attack. When nothing happens to use up the released energy the parasympathetic branch of the ANS tries to restore the body to normal running. It attempts to slow down the heart, lower blood pressure, restart the digestion, return the blood to the skin, slow the rapid breathing. The sympathetic branch, still on the alert, opposes these changes. The result is distinctly uncomfortable. His mouth goes dry; he perspires; as blood is diverted to and then away from the brain he may feel giddy or faint; his stomach will churn and he may feel sick; his heart will pound and his breathing will be irregular making it difficult to speak clearly and firmly. At the end of such a confrontation the continuing conflict within the body, which has not been resolved by any vigorous action, continues leaving him weak and ill. There has been no satisfactory outlet for the anxiety response as physical danger did not really exist. But the ANS reacted as though it did.

Low Level Negative Mental

These responses include depression and a feeling that the world is a bleak, black place which offers nothing of interest. There is no enthusiasm to pursue current tasks or to develop new ones. The victim of Low Level Negative Mental Responses typically feels miserable and without hope. Everything seems too much of an effort. A housewife suffering from the effects of Low Level Negative Mental Stress may sit at home all day, half reading magazines, watching television without really absorbing what is being shown or just sitting around. Meanwhile a whole lot of urgent household tasks will accumulate but she can find no energy to start on them. Any suggestions for new interests or activities outside the home will probably be met with the response that it is too much effort, or that she will be bored. A man working on a production line who experiences Low Level Negative Mental Stress Responses will be unable to think constructively about anything. He will function like a rather ineffective piece of machinery and take no interest or pride in his task. This type of response is all too common in industrial society and the fault lies not with the individuals – although there are procedures which they can adopt to help themselves – but with the philosophy of mass production and the conveyor belt society. In Stage Six we will be looking at the problems of stress as a social condition and suggesting ways in which management and workers could collaborate to improve the quality and quantity of output by controlling stress.

Just as High Level Negative Mental Responses can occur when too many messages are being received and dealt with by the cerebral cortex, so too can too few messages result in an under use of the system. If an intelligent person is forced into a task which is routine or a very bright child made to follow a curriculum which is humdrum, then there will be a lack of stimulation resulting in boredom and probably depression. The prospect of a challenge is motivating to most people. If the challenge is too great they may fail so often that they will abandon the attempt. But if the challenge is too small, if success is certain, there will be very little reason to have a go. The consequences of success under such circumstances will not be sufficiently rewarding or, in the language of behavioural psychology, the activity will be insufficiently reinforcing.

The concept of *reinforcement* is an important one because an absence of suitable reinforcers in the environment is the prime cause of depression and Low Level Negative Mental Responses. Reinforcers can be described as anything and everything which gives an individual pleasure. They may be physical rewards such as extra pay, a new car, a prize or promotion. Or they may be quite simple: pleasure at a beautiful view or a piece of music, pride at a challenge met, comfort from a friendly smile or satisfaction at a word of praise and encouragement from a colleague or relative. Eating is a very reinforcing piece of behaviour and so is sex. These two are especially valuable in establishing behaviour because the reinforcer is an immediate consequence of that piece of behaviour. Research has shown that the closer a piece of behaviour is followed by a reinforcer, the most quickly and firmly it will be established. The greater the time lag between a piece of behaviour and the reinforcer, the less likely it is to have any effect on the establishment of that piece of behaviour.

When we eat there is immediate pleasure from the taste and smell of food being chewed. When we have sex there is usually an immediate reward from the sensations of touch and sight.

If a child is given a reward, a word of praise or a sum of money, immediately after completing a task then it is very likely that the piece of behaviour which produced that reinforcer will be repeated. If the reinforcer is delayed for a few hours or a few days then it is less likely to have any effect on that piece of behaviour being repeated.

Reinforcers do not have to be a positive response from the environment. A piece of behaviour which brings to an end some punishing or unpleasant response will be equally reinforced. Suppose a girl is crying after a row with her boyfriend. He puts

c*

his arms around her and kisses her. She stops crying. That response will reinforce the behaviour of putting his arms around her. The next time the girl cries it is highly probable that the boy will put his arms around her again. In Stage Five we will be showing you how to use reinforcers to establish RCPs quickly.

Low Level Negative Physical

These responses are typically lethargic and lackadaisical. Sufferers from Low Level Negative Physical Responses often move slowly and without interest or enthusiasm. Co-ordination skills may be impaired making it difficult to perform efficiently. It may happen that the body performs the tasks demanded of it in such a mechanical fashion that quite serious mistakes can be made simply through a misreading of the signals. Because the victim of Low Level Negative Physical Responses expects something to happen in a certain way at a certain time, he or she will respond as though it has happened. In behavioural psychology this is called a *set*. Many industrial accidents for example can be traced back to carelessness which, in turn, is born of lack of physical stimulation because the job has become so routine. On that one, rare occasion when something out of the ordinary happens it is not noticed until too late to take proper preventive measures. Such a state can also occur after extremely high levels of physical stress have been present. For instance most mountaineering accidents occur on the way *down* from a climb because the climbers have relaxed excessively on reaching the summit and are not as keyed up to look for danger when they descend. This is why it is important to keep a good distribution of stress at the OSL rather than to allow the stress level to drop well below the optimum.

Low Level Negative Physical Responses occur because the activities to be carried out have suffered from the consequences of habituation. This means that familiarity with the routine has resulted in clearly defined, deeply cut grooves of communication within the brain. When starting on such a piece of work the messages needed for co-ordinated activity flow swiftly and effortlessly along these well-established neural pathways, allowing us to perform, for most of the time effectively, without much cognitive thought. There are times when habituation is very useful – for example it would be difficult to ride a bicycle if one had to think constantly about maintaining balance, or to read a book if every word had to be separately considered. The danger of habituation is that because we see or hear what we expect to see and hear, inconsistencies and dangers may be overlooked. A man who cycles to work every day may become so used to the route he takes that he fails to notice some new obstacle and has a crash. When reading familiar phrases we may see what we expect to see rather than what is actually there. 'Paris in the the Spring' is an example of a familiar phrase which can be absorbed without actually being read. If you found nothing wrong with the phrase as printed here, for example, we suggest that you re-read it.

Habituation on production lines and in other routine industrial and work settings often leads to shoddy workmanship, disinterest on the part of employees and the risk of accidents. Small errors are simply missed through habituation, inconsistencies ignored until it is too late. Household chores are just as much subject to the risks of habituation as factory work and the statistics show that more accidents occur in the home than in any other situation – a result of habituation coupled with inadequate fail-safe procedures on the equipment used. Low Level Negative Physical Responses can be tackled successfully by individuals using RCPs and the methods for doing so will be described in Stage Five. But they are just as much a social problem. The ways in which they can be dealt with in industrial and business settings for the benefit of employees, employers and society as a whole will be explained in Stage Six.

SUMMARY

In this Stage we have explained the relationship between Stress and Strain as follows:

STRESS (An individual's perception and assessment of the environment)

$\rightarrow$ results in $\rightarrow$

STRAIN (The consequence of that unique perception and assessment on the mental and physical state of that individual).

Strain Chain

STRESS $\rightarrow$ STRAIN $\rightarrow$ Change in Performance $\rightarrow$ Further STRESS $\rightarrow$ Further STRAIN . . . and so on.

Strain leads to change in performance and this may lead to further stress and increasing strain. It is important to state this strain chain fully when describing strain. Frequently only the initial stress and the deterioration in performance are described, but until the strain chain is fully described we are unable to take steps to control it.

Strain is generated by what we have termed Lifestyle Stressers which can be grouped under six major headings:

Performance Stressers – Sources of stress inherent in carrying out a piece of mental or physical behaviour.

Threat Stressers – Arise from situations perceived and assessed as dangerous.

Boredom Stressers – Arise from situations perceived and assessed as lacking in physical or mental stimulation.

Frustration Stressers – Arise from situations perceived and assessed as being undesirable but beyond one's power to control.

Bereavement Stressers – Arise from situations perceived and assessed as resulting in a loss of any kind.

Physical Stressers – These involve actual physical damage to the person.

The level of strain resulting from these stressers depends on three factors.

(1) The intensity of the Lifestyle Stresser.
(2) The duration of exposure to the Lifestyle Stresser.
(3) The number of other Lifestyle Stressers already present in the individual's environment.

We can adapt to strain, even high levels of strain resulting from intense and lengthy exposure to high levels of stress, although there is likely to be a deterioration of performance even in the short term. In the long term such adaptation almost always results in mental or physical breakdown.

High Level of Stress → High Level of Strain → Negative Stress Responses.
Low Level of Stress → Low Level of Strain → Negative Stress Responses.
Optimum Stress Level → Optimum Strain Level → Ideal mental and physical responses.

Eustress is the stress produced by great joy, happiness or other pleasant and desirable emotions. The physiological effects of *eustress* may appear the same as those resulting from *distress* but they are very different psychologically and beneficial. They can be used to regulate the input of stress from other Lifestyle Stressers.

Our levels of stress are seldom equally high in all areas of life and we often need a higher level in one area than in another to perform effectively. We have divided all human activity into four Life Areas for convenience of description:

A. Work and Study.
B. Family, Marriage, Sex and Intimacy.
C. Social and Interpersonal Relationships.
D. Leisure and Sport.

Negative Stress Responses can affect our performance in all these Areas. They can be High or Low Level Physical and High or Low Level Mental. A level of stress higher than the OSL results in either High Level Negative Physical Responses or High Level Negative Mental Responses or, typically, a combination of both.

A level of stress lower than the OSL results in either or both types of Low Level Negative Responses.

High Level Negative Physical Responses result from the activities of the two branches, the parasympathetic and sympathetic, of the autonomic nervous system. This is not normally under our conscious control.

High Level Negative Mental Responses occur when we are trying to process too much information at once.

Low Level Negative Physical and Mental Responses occur when there is too little stimulation from the environment. This leads to boredom, apathy, and a tendency to perform in a routine way which can result in accidents and mistakes.

The first two Stages of this book have examined what is actually involved in those frequently used words 'stress' and 'strain'. We hope that you can already start to relate some of this information to your own life and to see rather more clearly how stress and strain may be affecting your performance of important behaviours.

The next step is to carry out the analysis of your current situation so that you can begin to see exactly the types and intensity of stressers which are present in your life and the ways in which they may be damaging your ability to perform effectively, happily and healthily. This analysis begins in Stage Three.

Stage Three

Analysing Your Own Stress Levels

CONTENTS

Stage Three

Analysing Your Own Stress Levels

INTRODUCTION

The programme of analysis which follows is designed to provide you with insight into your individual stress levels in each of the four Life Areas which we defined in Stage Two.

A. **Work and Study.**
B. **Family, Marriage, Sex and Intimacy.**
C. **Social and Interpersonal Relationships.**
D. **Leisure and Sport.**

It will also enable you to discover which of the six Lifestyle Stressers may be causing you most difficulties at the moment. These two analyses are carried out by using specially devised statement inventories. You can answer them in a few minutes anywhere and at any time. At the end of these analyses you will have gathered personal stress level data which you can use in Stages Four and Five in order to construct your own, unique programme of stress control.

As we have already explained, any assessment of stress usually involves a very subjective value judgement. The Optimum Stress Level is defined as being the level of stress at which you can perform a desired piece of behaviour most happily, healthily and effectively. For this reason any attempt by us to put a numerical value on different types of stress would be both invalid and, if attempted, misleading. It is impossible to say, for example, that fear of death would score 90 out of 100 whilst fear of spiders would only score 30 marks. A spider phobic might be stressed into a state of panic at the sight of even a small spider, whilst coping perfectly easily with abstract concepts of mortality. However, in order to allow you to see the stress effects present in your life in as graphic and helpful way as possible, we have devised a score system for use in the statement inventories. The scores we have set must, however, be seen as relative values rather than our assessment of the merits or demerits of any particular form of stress. In order to make this point clear the scoring system has been arranged so that you finish up not with a particular number but with an ideographic representation of the stress situation present. This type of display enables you to see, at a glance, the relative amounts and types of stress present in your life. These statements have been compiled from information contained in hundreds of case studies. They have been found very effective in helping to identify specific areas of stress even if there was no real insight into the reasons for, and the nature of, these difficulties before the analysis started.

STATEMENT INVENTORY NUMBER ONE: LIFE AREA STRESS RESPONSE ANALYSIS

In the following analysis you will find a total of sixty-four situations, each of which has associated with it five alternative responses. To complete the analysis, tick, or note down, one or more of the alternative responses for each of the situations. It does not matter how many of the alternatives you select for each situation but try to ensure that when you select any alternative it reflects your *usual* or *overall* response in this general kind of situation. It will usually be quite clear to you whether, for example, you are always very bored or always highly anxious in a certain situation. But if genuinely you feel two or more of the alternative responses at a high level for most of the time, then mark them both or all for that situation. If you prefer not to mark the book then note down the letters against each alternative which is relevant for each situation on a sheet of paper. This method has the additional advantage that you need not refer back to the statements when scoring your responses later. You should complete the analysis in all four Life Areas before turning to the scores.

Life Area A – Work and Study

(1) When working against a tight deadline
    a. My thoughts become confused and unproductive.
    b. I feel physically tired and lazy.
    c. I feel tense and anxious.
    d. My mind goes blank on the task.
    e. I usually meet my target efficiently.

(2) At work break times
    a. My mind continues to race about my work.
    b. My muscles are tensed and my heart beats fast.
    c. I feel bored.
    d. I feel physically restless and fidget.
    e. I can enjoy a relaxed rest.

(3) When I arrive at the office
    a. I feel sluggish.
    b. I dread to think of the day's events.
    c. I hope today will bring some interesting events.
    d. I feel my stomach lurch and my heart begin to pound.
    e. I am ready and keen to work.

(4) At office or business functions
    a. I set myself apart from the rest out of boredom.
    b. I feel sleepy and lethargic.
    c. I feel anxious and tense.
    d. I think constantly of how I ought to perform.
    e. I enjoy talking and usually make good contacts.

(5) On the way to, and at home after, work
    a. I fidget or pace around looking for something to do.
    b. I rush home and try to cram in chores for the evening.
    c. I am thinking all the while of the next day's problems.
    d. I can find nothing to occupy my thoughts.
    e. I can put the worries of the day behind me.

(6) When approaching or taking examinations or tests
   a. I become highly anxious and tense.
   b. I become sleepy or succumb to other activities.
   c. I lose concentration and day dream.
   d. Thoughts become jumbled and confused as they race around in my head.
   e. I feel confident that I am well prepared.

(7) Before or during an interview with my superiors or prospective employers
   a. I cannot make the effort to present my points strongly.
   b. My voice is unsteady as I sweat and tremble.
   c. I feel lacking in energy and enthusiasm.
   d. I race through my answers trying to say more than is necessary.
   e. I am relaxed and put myself over well.

(8) When answering my correspondence
   a. I can find no interest in content.
   b. I struggle to find answers and get my points in order.
   c. I soon begin to perspire and feel tense and uncomfortable.
   d. It takes me a great deal of time to get around to opening and reading the letters.
   e. I do so quickly and effectively.

(9) On my way to work in the morning
   a. I am tense and have to rush as I am often late.
   b. I hope desperately that the day will hold something of interest.
   c. I have to drag myself reluctantly from the house.
   d. I find my mind is full of things I must remember to do as soon as I arrive.
   e. I feel alert and look forward to the day ahead.

(10) When settling down to my work projects for the day
    a. I cannot decide which of several pressing problems to tackle first.
    b. I yawn sleepily as I know my talents will not be stretched or my abilities properly used.
    c. I have little enthusiasm as the projects are beneath me.
    d. My heart beats violently and my tension level mounts.
    e. I can immerse myself in them quickly.

(11) When performing repetitive tasks at work
    a. My actions are lazy and lackadaisical.
    b. I feel I couldn't care less about the job or anything else.
    c. My muscles ache through tension and I sweat nervously.
    d. I keep worrying about all sorts of problems, large and small.
    e. I can keep myself occupied mentally and still perform well.

(12) When bombarded by questions and requests from all sides
    a. I become tense and tongue-tied.
    b. My thoughts become confused and I cannot reply.
    c. I feel bored and unable to summon the enthusiasm to answer.
    d. I retreat from the situation by finding some excuse for leaving the office.
    e. I can remain cool and answer calmly.

(13) When demanding my rights at work
    a. I do not try too hard as I convince myself not to feel strongly about anything.
    b. I blush and stammer and speak in an obviously anxious way.

    c. I feel it is too much of an effort to protest seriously.

    d. I confuse the issue by trying to say too much in a clumsy way.

    e. I usually get what I want.

(14) When addressing people on work topics
    a. I am tense and very anxious while talking.
    b. I cannot make clear points as they are not structured adequately.
    c. I do not try as I fear they will be bored.
    d. I speak in a flat, uninspiring way.
    e. I keep my points concise and understandable.

(15) Before or during a confrontation with my subordinates
    a. I worry for days and present my views badly.
    b. I feel detached and unable to generate any enthusiasm.
    c. I have difficulty addressing them and myself to the same point.
    d. I rush about frenetically trying to organise the meeting.
    e. I plan what I am going to say and stick to it.

(16) When planning an important contract or piece of work
    a. I cannot gather together all the relevant facts and materials effectively.
    b. I cannot sort out the key points from the rest.
    c. I am physically uncomfortable, with high heart rate, tension or indigestion.
    d. I cannot find the enthusiasm to begin.
    e. I prepare myself well and carry out the task effectively.

Life Area B – Family, Marriage, Sex and Intimacy

(1) When in a situation where I could ask for a date
   a. I feel that I cannot be bothered.
   b. I feel sure my advance will be rebuffed.
   c. I become tense and tongue-tied.
   d. I do not push myself and let the moment slip by.
   e. I do so without worrying.

(2) When attempting or engaging in coitus
   a. My mind wanders onto other thoughts.
   b. I do not feel a strong sexual urge.
   c. I rush the situation in case things go wrong.
   d. I keep wondering whether I am doing things right.
   e. I enjoy the experience fully.

(3) When I feel upset with my sexual partner
   a. I begin to feel bored and disenchanted.
   b. I tremble with suppressed rage.
   c. I leave the situation as I am too bored to deal with it.
   d. My mind races unproductively with thoughts of what I might say or do.
   e. I am able to express my feelings and talk things over reasonably.

(4) When anticipating a row with my sexual partner
   a. I become highly anxious and tense.
   b. I can think of no constructive points to make.
   c. I cannot work myself up to starting a confrontation.
   d. My thoughts become confused and I panic.
   e. I think about the grievance and do not get sidetracked into petty quarrels.

(5) When making decisions involving my sexual partner
   a. I keep worrying whether I am doing the right thing for both of us.
   b. I cannot summon the energy to talk about things.

c. I feel tense about my role in the situation.

d. I am too bored to think out the situation.

e. I do so fairly and objectively.

(6) When in an intimate situation, which could lead to sex
a. I feel no drive or urge to continue.
b. I feel over-excited and anxious about failure.
c. I find myself thinking that it does not matter whether or not we have sex.
d. I worry about how my advances may appear.
e. I am relaxed and ready for anything that may happen.

(7) When out socially with my partner
a. I worry all the time how people are assessing us.
b. I am constantly on edge as we meet other people.
c. I cannot raise the enthusiasm to make conversation.
d. I stand around bored and look idly on.
e. Our being together enhances my enjoyment.

(8) In conversation with my partner
a. I am unstimulated by the situation.
b. I talk laconically with little energy.
c. We speak rapidly and the conversation is often confused.
d. I am thinking of so many issues that I cannot concentrate on the conversation.
e. I am relaxed and at ease and enjoy the exchange.

(9) When I consider approaching my partner for sex
a. I become anxious about being rejected.
b. I am easily put off if the initial response seems unfavourable.
c. I often hope that things will not progress any further.
d. My eagerness for a favourable response makes me confused and ineffective.
e. I do so without hesitation or fear of rejection.

(10) During rows with my partner
   a. I become sullen, withdrawn and uncommunicative.
   b. I feel tense and perhaps slightly nauseous with suppressed rage.
   c. I cannot think clearly as my mind is completely confused.
   d. I find the whole situation boring and a waste of time.
   e. I put my own point of view reasonably but forcefully.

(11) While caressing and being caressed in a sexual situation
   a. I feel unresponsive and lack enthusiasm.
   b. My mind wanders off to other things.
   c. I worry most of the time whether I will become sexually aroused.
   d. I become very excited and worry about my ability to control my responses.
   e. I get fully involved and enjoy it.

(12) The location and layout of my home
   a. Gives me no enthusiasm or interest for my home life.
   b. Makes me worry considerably about running costs and upkeep.
   c. Encroaches excessively on my free time in travelling and home improvements.
   d. Is so dreary that I just use it as a place to sleep and eat in.
   e. Gives me great pleasure and satisfaction.

(13) When dealing with my children's problems and questions
   a. I dismiss them briefly and tritely.
   b. I am bored and uninterested in them.
   c. I quickly become frustrated and often angry.
   d. I become confused and worry that I may be ineffective as a parent.
   e. I feel I handle them fairly and effectively.

(14) When I see my partner before we part in the morning
    a. I am so concerned with the events of the day ahead that I have little time for us.
    b. I can find nothing interesting for us to do or talk about.
    c. There is little active involvement and I say very little.
    d. I am in a state of nervous tension in case we have an argument.
    e. I feel pleasantly relaxed.

(15) When my children do something which displeases me
    a. My temper flares and I lose control of myself.
    b. I cannot summon the energy to do anything about it.
    c. I am not interested in what they do.
    d. I am confused and at a loss to know how to deal with them.
    e. I tell them calmly how I would prefer them to behave.

(16) When I see my sexual partner in the evening after work
    a. I just slump into a chair and do not want to do anything.
    b. I am bombarded with problems whilst still wound up from the day at work.
    c. I am tense, unable to relax and flit from one activity to another.
    d. My mind goes blank and I switch on the TV, watching it without taking much in.
    e. I feel affectionate and glad we are together.

Life Area C – Social and Interpersonal Relationships

(1) When meeting strangers at a party
  a. I become tense, my heart races and my mouth becomes dry.
  b. I cannot bring myself to join a group who seem to be enjoying themselves.
  c. I am constantly worried about what I shall say when they finish talking.
  d. I cannot summon up interest in the topics of conversation.
  e. I feel relaxed and enjoy myself.

(2) When holding a conversation socially
  a. I feel myself becoming anxious when I have to talk.
  b. My mind wanders quickly from the topic.
  c. I wonder how I appear to others in the group.
  d. I feel myself becoming bored and listless.
  e. I feel relaxed and speak easily.

(3) When arriving late at a social gathering
  a. I cannot find the enthusiasm to approach and talk to others.
  b. I feel worried that every eye will be on me.
  c. I am sure there will not be enough of the evening left to interest me.
  d. I feel tense and anxious of others, criticism.
  e. I apologise and lose no time in mixing and enjoying myself.

(4) When detaching myself from social encounters
  a. I am embarrassed in case I hurt the other person's feelings.
  b. I am anxious because they may think badly of me for leaving.
  c. I feel bored and let the parting conversation drag on and on.

d. I feel too lethargic to make the physical effort of leaving.

e. I can do so easily and without feeling awkward.

(5) When telling a joke or story
   a. I become very anxious in case I spoil the punch line.
   b. I struggle continually to remember the story as I am telling it.
   c. My voice is flat and lacking in vitality.
   d. I feel sure the point of the tale will be missed.
   e. I am confident and relaxed.

(6) When dealing with an unwelcome request from a friend
   a. I agree because I cannot work up the energy to argue.
   b. I agree because I feel sure that I must give in eventually.
   c. I become tense and anxious and talk confusedly about other commitments.
   d. My mind is confused and racing with objections and feelings of obligation.
   e. I can say no without feeling guilty.

(7) When giving a formal or informal talk socially
   a. My delivery is poor and I stumble anxiously over my words.
   b. My voice sounds flat and uninspiring as I talk disinterestedly.
   c. I struggle to bring some order to my confused thoughts.
   d. I present a dull delivery which has received the least amount of preparation possible.
   e. I deliver my material confidently.

(8) When holding an unpopular opinion
   a. I could not care less about others being upset.
   b. I become very anxious and embarrassed about the situation.

    c. I move away from the group and make it clear I think them unworthy of further regard.

    d. I express my confused thoughts badly and fail to argue effectively.

    e. I can express and defend it confidently.

(9) When thinking about an invitation out for the evening
    a. I feel sure that I will be bored throughout the evening.
    b. I make the preparations for going out in a desultory manner.
    c. I am tense and concerned that people will criticise me.
    d. I keep wondering whether I will be a social success.
    e. I feel pleasurable anticipation.

(10) When entertaining at my own home
    a. I spend long hours worrying over details of the arrangements.
    b. I think what a bore it is to have to disturb my usual routine.
    c. I rush around anxiously to cover my concern about the occasion going well.
    d. I become lethargic and cannot make an effort as I am bored by the occasion.
    e. I am relaxed and enjoy myself.

(11) When introducing myself socially
    a. I simply say 'hello' and remain very diffident.
    b. I am highly concerned about how people will respond to me.
    c. I feel no motivation to contribute to the conversation.
    d. I blush and stammer nervously.
    e. I do so in an easy and confident way.

(12) When asked for my views in a social gathering
    a. My stomach turns over and my mouth dries with anxiety.

b. I find the whole issue tedious.

c. I answer laconically, often with half finished sentences.

d. Several things come into my mind at once and my answer is confusing.

e. I express myself concisely and confidently.

(13) When I feel I have had bad service
    a. I cannot be bothered to say anything by way of complaint.
    b. I do not think it is worthwhile giving any more consideration to such a trivial matter.
    c. I become frustrated and anxious because I feel unable to make a complaint.
    d. I become completely confused in wondering how I should approach the situation.
    e. I complain and assert my rights effectively.

(14) When dealing with unwelcome encounters
    a. I sigh inwardly and prepare myself to put up with being bored.
    b. I talk aimlessly giving trite answers.
    c. I become confused while trying to decide which tactic I can employ to get away.
    d. I feel trapped and helpless and become tense and anxious.
    e. I can tell the person that I do not have sufficient time to continue.

(15) When I am criticised in public
    a. I blush and stammer and feel extremely humiliated.
    b. I am so shocked that I cannot find thoughts or words in defence.
    c. I consider the critics so beneath me that I do not bother to respond.

    d. I make deprecatory remarks but do not feel like getting involved.

    e. I can use the positive aspects of the criticism and point out the errors in the rest.

(16) When listening to others talk

    a. I just nod now and again but do little else.

    b. I find I am often disinterested in their conversation.

    c. My thoughts race with witty remarks and comments and I miss the point of their conversation.

    d. I feel my anxiety rising and I wonder how to respond to the situation.

    e. I pay attention to what is being said and easily become interested.

Life Area D – Leisure and Sport

(1) When looking for a leisure pursuit
- a. I usually just jot down a few ideas and then leave them.
- b. I try to spread myself over too many activities at once and do none effectively.
- c. I think all the while of the arguments for and against each activity.
- d. I feel it is all too much of an effort and give up.
- e. I follow each avenue individually and seriously.

(2) When faced with a period of inactivity
- a. I sit around waiting for something to happen.
- b. I become agitated and anxious that I should be doing more.
- c. I cannot be bothered to think of things to do.
- d. I am bombarded with guilty thoughts about things I ought to be doing.
- e. I can occupy myself productively either physically or mentally.

(3) When motoring in heavy traffic
- a. I sit and brood wearily over the waste of time.
- b. I become fidgety and restless but unable to do anything constructive about the situation.
- c. I become more and more confused and my mind races over the things I ought to do.
- d. My heart rate rises and I feel myself begin to perspire as I wrestle with the car.
- e. I remain relaxed, alert and calm.

(4) When taking a holiday
- a. I am constantly thinking of my work which I have left.

D

  b. I try to cram in as many trips and visits as I can.

  c. I moon around without finding anything of interest to do.

  d. My mind goes blank and I am unable to make the smallest decision.

  e. I really relax and enjoy myself.

(5) When choosing a holiday

  a. I cannot be bothered to select a place and leave it to others.

  b. I have so many alternative ideas to consider that I cannot reach a decision.

  c. I become tense and anxious when I consider all the things that could go wrong.

  d. I cannot find the energy to collect brochures or to talk about ideas.

  e. I take a great interest in the choices open to me.

(6) While travelling long distances by aircraft, train or boat

  a. I am constantly anxious and fearful of a disaster or delay.

  b. I keep thinking how bored I am.

  c. My thoughts are in a turmoil as I try to plan the rest of my itinerary.

  d. I fidget aimlessly and do nothing productive.

  e. I am relaxed and can enjoy the journey, working if necessary.

(7) When thinking about a proposed flight

  a. I have a great deal of trouble in deciding between alternative schedules.

  b. I put off making enquiries until the last possible moment.

  c. I feel bored and unenthusiastic about the event.

  d. I become tense and anxious.

e. I look forward to it and choose my schedule efficiently.

(8) When playing my favourite sports
   a. I expend a great deal of energy through anxiety and tension.
   b. I cannot summon the energy for a comeback after a bad spell of play.
   c. I am sure that I will not do well and do not bother to hope for success.
   d. I worry continually about how my performance looks to others.
   e. I do so with confidence and pleasure.

(9) When sitting down to my hobby
   a. I become drowsy and fiddle at it.
   b. I cannot unwind enough to enjoy it.
   c. I soon become bored and my mind starts to wander.
   d. My mind is usually full of thoughts concerning other matters.
   e. I am relaxed and interested.

(10) When considering world events
   a. I become depressed because things are beyond my control.
   b. I become afraid and tense that some catastrophe will occur.
   c. I worry at length about the consequences of all I hear and read.
   d. I avoid the news and make no effort to understand what is happening.
   e. I select areas of interest and follow them closely.

(11) When performing in public
   a. I worry constantly about critical comments being made.
   b. My performance lacks enthusiasm and energy.
   c. I expend a great deal of energy in fruitless tension.
   d. I cannot get interested in what is happening.
   e. I am confident of my ability.

(12) When something goes wrong during leisure time
   a. I just give up and lounge aimlessly around.
   b. I rush around with no well organised plan to correct matters.
   c. I become mentally confused and cannot think effectively.
   d. My first thought is to give up and abandon the situation.
   e. I cope by revising my schedule.

(13) When under pressure during competitive recreation
   a. My muscles tense and I cannot co-ordinate my actions.
   b. I give up all hope of winning.
   c. I feel listless and lacking in energy to make a real effort.
   d. I am so worried about my performance that I cannot work out appropriate strategies.
   e. I find the competition spurs me to greater efforts.

(14) When thinking about retirement
   a. I keep putting off the thought.
   b. I worry a great deal about what will happen to me.
   c. I cannot bring myself to look for alternative interests.
   d. I become tense and afraid for the future.
   e. I look forward to planning a new way of life.

(15) When training for my sport or hobby
   a. I often miss sessions because I feel too lethargic.
   b. I become depressed when I think of the hours of effort ahead.
   c. I am tense and uncomfortable.
   d. I worry about whether I will ever be any good.
   e. I stick to a regular timetable and enjoy the discipline.

(16) When trying to sleep
   a. Thoughts race through my mind and I become more wakeful.
   b. I cannot relax my muscles and toss and turn.
   c. I do not feel tired.
   d. Depression overwhelms me.
   e. I can relax and drift off to sleep easily.

Life Area Analysis – Scores and Scoring Procedure

In Stage Two we explained that there are four Negative Stress Responses which occur when the level of stress perceived and assessed in the environment rises above the OSL. These Negative Stress Responses are:

(1) **High Level Physical.**
(2) **Low Level Physical.**
(3) **High Level Mental.**
(4) **Low Level Mental.**

The statements which came closest to describing your likely reactions to the sixty-four situations listed will enable you to discover whether you are responding with High or Low Level Mental or Physical Responses in the four Life Areas or whether you have achieved your OSL in at least some of these areas. In order to present these results in a way which emphasises the relative rather than the quantitative nature of the scoring, we have created scoring diagrams. Once again you may prefer to copy these out onto a separate sheet of paper rather than mark the book.

How to Use the Scoring Diagrams

Under the statement scores in each of the four Life Areas you will see a diagram consisting of five linked circles. The outer circles represent High and Low Mental, and High and Low Physical Negative Stress Responses – the inner circle the OSL. Each circle is divided into sixteen segments representing a possible answer. Simply note the score given for the statement or statements which you felt most closely described your response to the given situation and using a pen or pencil fill in one segment on the corresponding circle or circles.

For example, if in reply to situation 1 in Life Area **B**: Family, Marriage, Sex and Intimacy you had ticked the statements a.,

c. and d. this would have given you a score of 4;1;2. If in reply to situation 2 you had ticked statement e. this would have given you a score of 5. In this case the first set of scores would have led to one segment being filled in on circles 4, 1 and 2. For situation 2 you would have filled in one segment on circle 5. Fill in consecutive segments to gain the best overall picture of the Stress Responses present.

When all the statements have been scored and the scores transferred to the circles you will have a graphic representation of your stress responses in each of the Life Areas. You will be able to see, at a glance, if you are responding mainly with, say, High Level Negative Mental or Physical Responses or achieving your OSL in each Life Area.

For example of completed score Diagram see below.

Example of Completed Score Diagram in Life Area A – Work and Study

Situation	Statement(s) selected	Segment(s) to be filled in on Circle(s)
(1)	a. and b.	3 and 2
(2)	c.	4
(3)	a. and b.	2 and 3
(4)	b.	2
(5)	d.	4
(6)	b. and c.	2 and 4
(7)	c.	2
(8)	a. and d.	4 and 2
(9)	b. and c.	4 and 2
(10)	c.	4
(11)	b.	4
(12)	c.	4
(13)	a.	4
(14)	Not applicable	No Score
(15)	b.	4
(16)	d.	4

Example of Complete Score Diagram
in Life Area A. Work and Study.

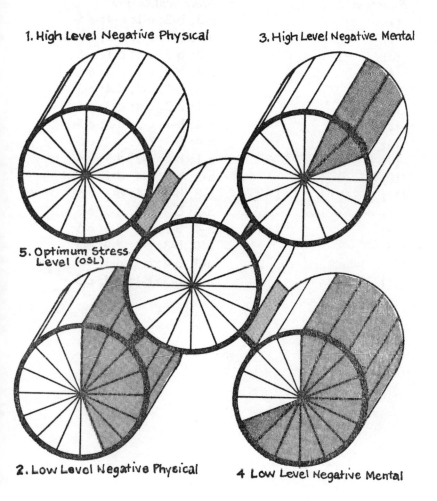

1. High Level Negative Physical

3. High Level Negative Mental

5. Optimum Stress Level (OSL)

2. Low Level Negative Physical

4 Low Level Negative Mental

D*

Life Area A – Work and Study

STATEMENT SCORES

Situation	*Statement Scores*
(1)	a-3; b-2; c-1; d-4; e-5
(2)	a-3; b-1; c-4; d-2; e-5
(3)	a-2; b-3; c-4; d-1; e-5
(4)	a-4; b-2; c-1; d-3; e-5
(5)	a-2; b-1; c-3; d-4; e-5
(6)	a-1; b-2; c-4; d-3; e-5
(7)	a-4; b-1; c-2; d-3; e-5
(8)	a-4; b-3; c-1; d-2; e-5
(9)	a-1; b-4; c-2; d-3; e-5
(10)	a-3; b-2; c-4; d-1; e-5
(11)	a-2; b-4; c-1; d-3; e-5
(12)	a-1; b-3; c-4; d-2; e-5
(13)	a-4; b-1; c-2; d-3; e-5
(14)	a-1; b-3; c-4; d-2; e-5
(15)	a-3; b-4; c-2; d-1; e-5
(16)	a-2; b-3; c-1; d-4; e-5

Life Area A – Work and Study

Score Diagram A

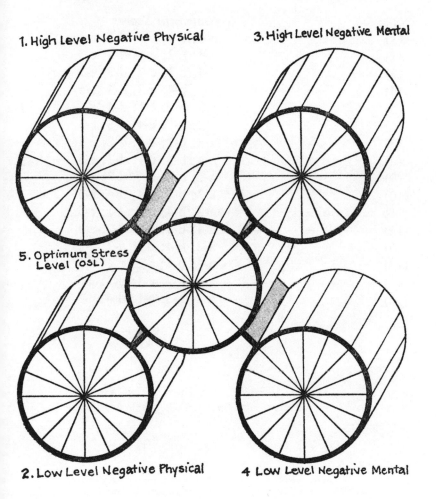

1. High Level Negative Physical

3. High Level Negative Mental

5. Optimum Stress Level (OSL)

2. Low Level Negative Physical

4 Low Level Negative Mental

Life Area B – Family, Marriage, Sex and Intimacy

STATEMENT SCORES

Situation	Statement Scores
(1)	a-4; b-3; c-1; d-2; e-5
(2)	a-4; b-2; c-1; d-3; e-5
(3)	a-4; b-1; c-2; d-3; e-5
(4)	a-1; b-4; c-2; d-3; e-5
(5)	a-3; b-2; c-1; d-4; e-5
(6)	a-2; b-1; c-4; d-3; e-5
(7)	a-3; b-1; c-4; d-2; e-5
(8)	a-4; b-2; c-1; d-3; e-5
(9)	a-1; b-2; c-4; d-3; e-5
(10)	a-2; b-1; c-3; d-4; e-5
(11)	a-2; b-4; c-3; d-1; e-5
(12)	a-4; b-3; c-1; d-2; e-5
(13)	a-2; b-4; c-1; d-3; e-5
(14)	a-3; b-4; c-2; d-1; e-5
(15)	a-1; b-2; c-4; d-3; e-5
(16)	a-2; b-3; c-1; d-4; e-5

Life Area B – Family, Marriage, Sex and Intimacy

Score Diagram B

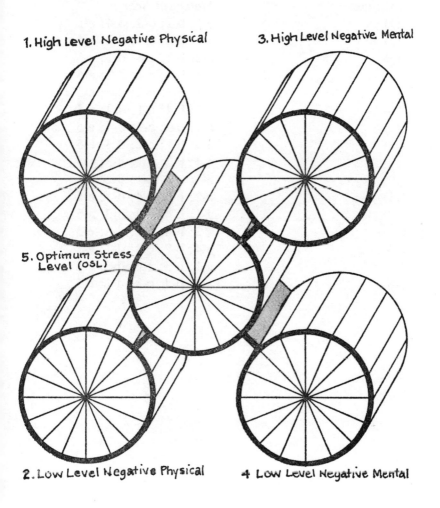

1. High Level Negative Physical

3. High Level Negative Mental

5. Optimum Stress Level (OSL)

2. Low Level Negative Physical

4 Low Level Negative Mental

Life Area C – Social and Interpersonal Relationships

STATEMENT SCORES

Situation	Statement Scores
(1)	a-1; b-2; c-3; d-4; e-5
(2)	a-1; b-4; c-3; d-2; e-5
(3)	a-2; b-3; c-4; d-1; e-5
(4)	a-3; b-1; c-4; d-2; e-5
(5)	a-1; b-3; c-2; d-4; e-5
(6)	a-2; b-4; c-1; d-3; e-5
(7)	a-1; b-2; c-3; d-4; e-5
(8)	a-4; b-1; c-2; d-3; e-5
(9)	a-4; b-2; c-1; d-3; e-5
(10)	a-3; b-4; c-1; d-2; e-5
(11)	a-2; b-3; c-4; d-1; e-5
(12)	a-1; b-4; c-2; d-3; e-5
(13)	a-2; b-4; c-1; d-3; e-5
(14)	a-4; b-2; c-3; d-1; e-5
(15)	a-1; b-3; c-4; d-2; e-5
(16)	a-2; b-4; c-3; d-1; e-5

Life Area C – Social and Interpersonal Relationships

Score Diagram C

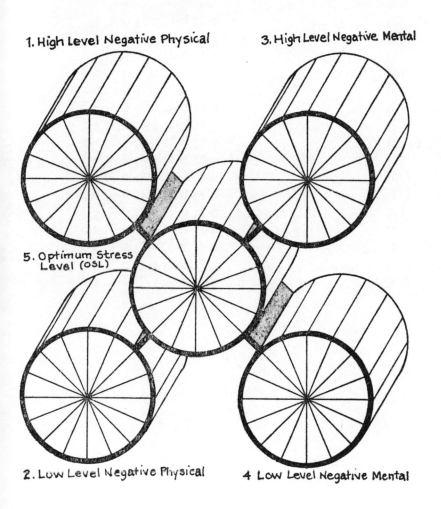

1. High Level Negative Physical

3. High Level Negative Mental

5. Optimum Stress Level (OSL)

2. Low Level Negative Physical

4 Low Level Negative Mental

Life Area D – Leisure and Sport

STATEMENT SCORES

Situation	Statement Scores
(1)	a-2; b-1; c-3; d-4; e-5
(2)	a-2; b-1; c-4; d-3; e-5
(3)	a-4; b-2; c-3; d-1; e-5
(4)	a-3; b-1; c-2; d-4; e-5
(5)	a-4; b-3; c-1; d-2; e-5
(6)	a-1; b-4; c-3; d-2; e-5
(7)	a-3; b-2; c-4; d-1; e-5
(8)	a-1; b-2; c-4; d-3; e-5
(9)	a-2; b-1; c-4; d-3; e-5
(10)	a-4; b-1; c-3; d-2; e-5
(11)	a-3; b-2; c-1; d-4; e-5
(12)	a-2; b-1; c-3; d-4; e-5
(13)	a-1; b-4; c-2; d-3; e-5
(14)	a-4; b-3; c-2; d-1; e-5
(15)	a-2; b-4; c-1; d-3; e-5
(16)	a-3; b-1; c-2; d-4; e-5

Life Area D – Leisure and Sport

Score Diagram D

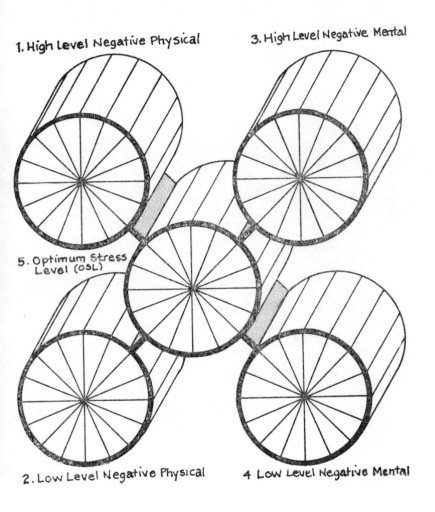

1. High Level Negative Physical

3. High Level Negative Mental

5. Optimum Stress Level (OSL)

2. Low Level Negative Physical

4 Low Level Negative Mental

STATEMENT INVENTORY NUMBER TWO:
LIFESTYLE STRESSERS

In the following analysis you will find a total of sixty situations each of which has associated with it three alternative responses. To complete the analysis tick, or note down, *only one* of the alternative responses for each of the situations. Try to ensure that the alternative which you choose reflects your *usual* or *overall* response in this general kind of situation. If you prefer not to mark the book then note down the letter against the alternative response which is relevant for each situation on a sheet of paper. This method has the additional advantage that you need not refer back to the statements when scoring your responses later. You should complete the analysis in all six Lifestyle Stressers before turning to the scores.

Lifestyle Stresser – Performance

(1) When working to a deadline I find my heart racing or my body perspiring
   a. Almost always.
   b. Quite often.
   c. Very seldom.

(2) When playing a competitive sport under pressure
   a. My whole game breaks down through lack of concentration.
   b. There are periods during the game when my full attention is not directed towards the best playing strategies.
   c. I focus my attention on the game and play to my best advantage.

(3) When in conversation with one or more people
   a. I am frequently struggling for the right thing to say.
   b. I do not like to voice any opinion in case others disagree.
   c. I find no difficulty.

(4) When there are family frictions
   a. I am unable to do anything constructive and usually withdraw from the scene.
   b. I am unable to put my views over effectively.
   c. I am able to state my own position and be responsive to others.

(5) When having sex with my partner
   a. I have very little idea of what to do in order to satisfy him/her or myself.
   b. Our mutual satisfaction occurs, but irregularly.
   c. We usually feel confident that it will be enjoyable.

(6) When carrying out work which is mentally demanding
  a. I frequently lose my concentration and cannot settle down to the job.
  b. I can work only in short bursts with long unproductive periods in between.
  c. I enjoy the challenges and can become involved quickly.

(7) When called upon to make decisions which will affect my family's future
  a. I worry desperately and become highly anxious without coming to a firm decision.
  b. I can usually reach a decision but not without considerable distress.
  c. I usually reach a decision quickly and abide by it.

(8) When involved in situations which may lead to sex
  a. I feel so anxious that I change the subject quickly.
  b. I falter and have difficulty expressing my true feelings.
  c. I can continue with the situation with no discomfort if I wish to do so.

(9) When interviewing or being interviewed
  a. I become tense and mentally confused and perform badly.
  b. I simply state the facts but cannot show much enthusiasm.
  c. I deal with the situation effectively.

(10) When I have to perform in public
  a. I become panic stricken and make every excuse to avoid the situation.
  b. I find it hard to control the feeling of rising tension.
  c. I am not unduly worried by the presence of spectators.

Lifestyle Stresser – Threat

(1) My job involves me in risk of physical danger
   a. Almost always.
   b. Occasionally.
   c. Never.

(2) The frequent car journeys which I make are
   a. Through heavy traffic on busy roads.
   b. On fairly busy suburban roads.
   c. Along quiet or country roads.

(3) I play a sport which involves a risk of physical injury
   a. Frequently.
   b. Now and again.
   c. Never.

(4) My job involves placing other people at risk
   a. As a routine matter.
   b. Now and then.
   c. Never.

(5) I find myself worrying that I may become seriously ill
   a. Frequently.
   b. Now and again.
   c. Never.

(6) When I am involved in a situation which could lead to sex I am
   a. Extremely anxious.
   b. Uncomfortable and embarrassed.
   c. Perfectly relaxed.

(7) Certain objects or situations in life which other people seem to face without anxiety make me
   a. Very tense and anxious.

b. Nervous and uncomfortable.
c. No more anxious.

(8) The likelihood of an international war
a. Keeps me in a continual state of tension.
b. Gives me an uncomfortable feeling quite often.
c. Never bothers me.

(9) When I wish to assert my rights or privileges
a. I feel sure I will come under attack.
b. I feel anxious about encroaching on others' rights.
c. I do not hesitate and continue with ease.

(10) When I have to travel long distances from home, possibly by certain forms of transport
a. I feel very anxious, or panic, and wish I were home again.
b. I approach the journey with trepidation and discomfort.
c. I am not at all concerned.

Lifestyle Stresser – Boredom

(1) On waking up in the morning
    a. I dread the boredom of the day ahead.
    b. I am not particularly moved by thoughts of the day ahead.
    c. I often look forward to my interesting day.

(2) When playing my favourite game or sport
    a. I can find no challenge from my partners or opponents.
    b. I often win without effort.
    c. I am well matched and enjoy the challenge to my skill.

(3) I consider my work to be
    a. Routine, tedious and undemanding.
    b. Generally interesting but accompanied by periods of dull routine.
    c. Frequently challenging and free of excessive routine.

(4) In interactions with my partner at home
    a. I find nothing of common interest to discuss or do.
    b. We have occasional interesting periods with long patches of boredom in between.
    c. We find each other generally stimulating and agreeable.

(5) In my sexual activities
    a. There is little variation and fresh stimulation.
    b. The periods of enjoyment are present but infrequent.
    c. There are frequent enjoyable experiences.

(6) I spend most of my leisure time
    a. At home on my own.
    b. With the few friends I have.
    c. In varied social situations.

(7) I find the area in which I live
   a. Lacking in interest or facilities for doing things.
   b. Presents obstacles to finding interesting activities to pursue.
   c. Provides me with most of the interests which I need.

(8) The mental tasks which I have to perform at work or at leisure
   a. Leave my mind starved for further stimulation.
   b. Exercise my mind gently but never to any great extent.
   c. Challenge me and keep me involved.

(9) In conversations at social functions
   a. I become bored quickly at what I consider to be banal conversations.
   b. I occasionally find something of interest for me.
   c. I usually find something to involve or interest me.

(10) When presented with a novel or demanding situation
   a. I grasp it eagerly as I am starved of challenge in my life.
   b. I am interested and set aside some time for it as soon as I am able.
   c. I assess it carefully to see if I really have time to include it amongst my other activities.

Lifestyle Stresser – Frustration

(1) During interactions with my regular partner or family I find myself in a position where anything I say or do will be wrong
   a. Almost always.
   b. Quite often.
   c. Very seldom.

(2) I feel my abilities at work are
   a. Greatly undervalued and underused.
   b. Often overlooked and under-rated.
   c. Recognised and used to a reasonable level.

(3) My sexual need is
   a. Rarely satisfied.
   b. Irregularly fulfilled.
   c. Met to my satisfaction.

(4) When trying to make my presence felt at home or at work
   a. I always get brushed off.
   b. I feel that people only pay me lip service.
   c. I often make my point.

(5) I feel that bureaucratic machinery is
   a. Fouling my life up almost totally.
   b. Hindering me a lot.
   c. Of no concern to me.

(6) When watching or reading the news I feel
   a. Frequently helpless and manipulated.
   b. Occasionally upset but impotent.
   c. No personal involvement.

(7) When making major decisions in my life I feel that I will
    lose out whichever route I follow
    a. Frequently.
    b. Occasionally.
    c. Never.

(8) When I think about some of the major problems which
    presently confront me
    a. I can see no practical answer to them but only
       ultimate defeat.
    b. I believe that there probably are answers which will
       take a great deal of finding.
    c. I can see that they can be resolved given time and
       careful planning.

(9) I believe that I respond effectively to the challenge of life
    a. Almost never.
    b. Occasionally.
    c. Usually.

(10) I allow the thought that 'since death is inevitable it is
     pointless to achieve anything in life' to impede my
     performance drastically
     a. Frequently.
     b. Sometimes.
     c. Hardly ever.

Lifestyle Stresser – Bereavement

(1) I have lost a close friend or relative
a. Very recently.
b. In the last few weeks.
c. Not for a long time.

(2) Although I lost someone or something dear to me a long time ago
a. The pain of the memory is still sharp.
b. I have times, such as anniversaries, when I feel depressed.
c. I think now and then with fondness of the past.

(3) Having just left a job which greatly interested me
a. I feel distraught and cannot settle down again.
b. I have frequent memories of my previous happiness.
c. I have replaced that interest with another of equal value to me.

(4) Now that I am retired or redundant
a. I become depressed frequently and feel that life has no purpose.
b. I have found one or two things to interest me but I am still very unfulfilled.
c. I find I now have time to do many things which interest me.

(5) Having recently been divorced or lost a meaningful relationship
a. I am desolated and feel I can never replace my loss.
b. It takes a great effort to force myself to look for other relationships.
c. While being sad at my loss I am able to rebuild my life again.

(6) Having just moved to a new area
- a. I miss my old friends greatly and find it difficult to make new friends here.
- b. I keep contact with my old friends and occasionally speak to the people in my new neighbourhood.
- c. I keep contact with my old friends but am making a growing circle of new ones also.

(7) Now that I am getting older
- a. I become panicky that my youth has slipped away and left me unable to cope.
- b. There are times when I resent not being able to perform as well as I used to.
- c. I look forward to a more sedate existence.

(8) Having lost face during a humiliating episode in my life
- a. My confidence has remained very low and I avoid any confrontations.
- b. Occasionally I think about what happened and feel depressed and lacking in self-confidence.
- c. I have put the matter out of my mind and my confidence is growing again.

(9) Having seen my children move away from home
- a. I feel that my life is empty and I have become useless.
- b. I feel I should try to find replacement activities but this is difficult to do.
- c. I am looking forward to planning the rest of my life interestingly.

(10) Having lost my health and been forced to change my lifestyle
- a. I am continually morose and depressed about adjusting to a new set of circumstances.
- b. I am trying to accept the situation but find little that has any real meaning for me.
- c. It is a struggle but I am managing to adapt.

Lifestyle Stresser – Physical

(1) My sleep patterns are
   a. Extremely poor and unreliable.
   b. Occasionally disturbed.
   c. Well regulated and restful.

(2) I find myself spending a lot of time in rooms or work areas which are drab, uncomfortable and depressing
   a. Frequently.
   b. Occasionally.
   c. Seldom.

(3) My eating habits are
   a. Very irregular with hastily chosen food.
   b. Occasionally disturbed by other activities.
   c. Regular and well balanced.

(4) My alcohol intake is
   a. Heavy and frequent.
   b. Frequent but not excessive.
   c. Occasional, light or non-existent.

(5) I travel on congested public transport, or find myself in the fumes of traffic jams
   a. Frequently.
   b. Occasionally.
   c. Seldom.

(6) I make visits to my doctor about minor ailments
   a. Frequently.
   b. Occasionally.
   c. Very seldom.

(7) I experience extended periods of high-level noise, at home or at work
    a. Frequently.
    b. Occasionally.
    c. Very seldom or never.

(8) I have had a major operation or illness
    a. Very recently.
    b. Within the last few weeks.
    c. Very long ago or never.

(9) I feel that my physical appearance or capabilities
    a. Limit my performance severely.
    b. Restrict my achievements to a certain extent.
    c. Are generally satisfactory or helpful.

(10) I suffer discomfort or pain from such complaints as headaches, poor digestion, migraine, asthma, allergic or chronic conditions
    a. Almost constantly.
    b. Frequently.
    c. Very seldom or never.

Scoring

For every Lifestyle Stresser, with the exception of Bereavement, score as follows:

a. responses	...	3 points
b. responses	...	2 points
c. responses	...	0 points
Not applicable	...	0 points

For the Bereavement inventory score as follows:

a. responses	...	10 points
b. responses	...	6 points
c. responses	...	0 points
Not applicable	...	0 points

Scores for Bereavement

By increasing the Stresses we are assuming a value judgement concerning the likely stress resulting from the situations described. There will be circumstances in which this weighting of the answers will be completely invalid. For example it might be that somebody has lost a close friend who died after years of suffering from some incurable disease. In such a situation they might feel unselfishly glad that their friend had escaped from constant pain and would not, therefore, rate the amount of stress produced by the situation as highly as if the loss had been that of a young, active and healthy person. Despite such individual differences, our experience has shown that (a) answers are usually associated with considerable stress levels and that it is rare for a person to answer (a) to more than one or two of the questions. If you are in the position of having to answer (a) to more than three of the questions then your score will take you over the scoring limit on the chart below. If this is the case however, then the level of stress you are currently experiencing in this area will, anyhow, be so high as to be almost certainly well above your *OSL*. In this case we suggest that you dispense with the rest of this analysis and proceed immediately to Stage Four where we will explain the procedures for managing the High Level Mental and Physical Negative Stress Responses resulting from this type of Lifestyle Stresser.

Having added up your scores from each of the six set statements, fill in the chart below or copy this out to avoid marking the book. The most graphic way in which to represent the relative stress is to use the scores to form blocks, as in the case studies below. Because high stress levels are being produced by one or more of the Lifestyle Stressers does not necessarily mean that you are functioning above your *OSL*. What it does suggest is that if you feel under excessive stress then this particular Lifestyle Stresser, or Stressers, is probably the culprit.

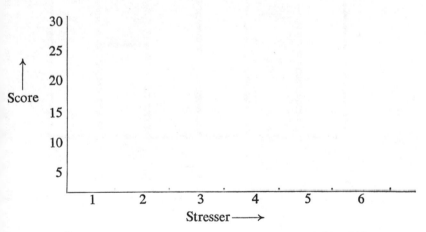

Score Diagram for assessing relative effect of Six Lifestyle Stressers.

E

Case Study Seven
Scores and chart of a client aged 23.
He was a sales clerk who had worked in the same job for three years.

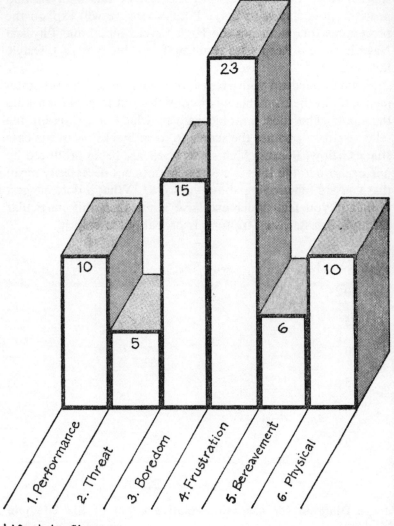

1. Performance 10
2. Threat 5
3. Boredom 15
4. Frustration 23
5. Bereavement 6
6. Physical 10

Lifestyle Stressers

Case Study Eight

Scores and chart of client aged 56.
She was a housewife suffering from agoraphobia. Although she scored high in several areas, the score in the Threat Lifestyle Stresser which resulted from her phobic response suggested that stress in other areas could have generalised from this major area of difficulty.

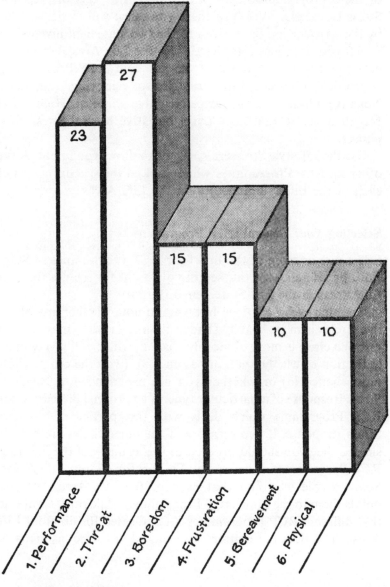

Lifestyle Stressers

HOW TO USE THE ANALYSIS DATA

In Stage Four we shall describe in detail ten RCP Programmes which will enable you to control stress and use it creatively. Each of these Programmes deals with different aspects of Negative Stress Responses. Which of them you select will be determined by the answers you have given to the two statement inventories which you have just completed. Use the Life Area Analysis to direct you to one or more of the first four RCP Programmes which deal in general with strategies for removing High Level Negative Physical, Low Level Negative Physical, High Level Negative Mental and Low Level Negative Mental Stress Responses.

Use the Lifestyle Stressers Analysis to direct you to one of the other six RCP Programmes which look at the specific effects of each of the Lifestyle Stressers on the Life Areas.

Selecting Your General RCP Programme

Select one or more of the first four RCP Programmes in Stage Four by reference to your scoring diagrams for each of the four Life Areas in the first Statement Inventory.

Examine each Life Area in turn and note whether any of the five circles is more heavily shaded than the rest. It may be that just one circle is more obviously shaded, which will give you an indication of whether you are at an OSL (with the centre circle most shaded in) or whether you are experiencing a Negative Stress Response of a particular type. If so proceed directly to the RCP Programme which deals with this particular Negative Stress Response. If two or more of the outer circles are heavily shaded then you should proceed to use as many of the first four RCP Programmes as necessary. Do this for *all* four Life Areas. Some people may find that each of the Life Area Analyses points them to the same RCP Programme, while others will find that different RCP Programmes are indicated for different Life Areas. This does not matter. You should just select as many of the first four RCP Programmes as are necessary for all four Life Areas.

Note down those RCP Programmes which you will be using later but complete the rest of this Stage before turning to them.

Key to Choosing from the First Four General RCP Programmes

Negative Response	RCP Programme/Stage Four
High Level Physical (Heavy shading in circle 1)	Number One
Low Level Physical (Heavy shading in circle 2)	Number Two
High Level Mental (Heavy shading in circle 3)	Number Three
Low Level Mental (Heavy shading in circle 4)	Number Four

Selecting Your Specific RCP Programme

These Programmes are used for controlling the stresses arising in particular Life Areas from specific Lifestyle Stressers. These specific RCP Programmes should be used in conjunction with the general Programmes which you have just selected above.

Examine the block diagram which you drew after completing the second Statement Inventory on Lifestyle Stressers. By inspection, select those Lifestyle Stressers which appear to be exerting considerable influence on your stress levels at this present time. Note these down. Now select from the Key below the appropriate RCP Programmes which correspond to the Lifestyle Stressers which you have noted down.

Key to Choosing From the Six Specific RCP Programmes in Stage Four

Lifestyle Stresser	RCP Programme/Stage Four
Performance	Number Five
Threat	Number Six
Boredom	Number Seven
Frustration	Number Eight
Bereavement	Number Nine
Physical	Number Ten

How to Use the RCP Programmes

At this stage you will have gained considerable understanding of the way in which Lifestyle Stressers affect your ability to perform to your satisfaction in the four Life Areas. It may be that you are not excessively stressed in any of these Areas but wish to take preventive measures against possible uncontrolled stress responses. In this case you will probably find that the general principles taught in the RCP Programmes in Stage Four will be sufficiently helpful in bringing your stress levels to the OSL. Simply understanding the principles and putting them into operation in your own way may, in this case, be all you need.

However, if you feel yourself to be under considerable amounts of uncontrolled stress and strain or if you are the sort of person who needs a more structured programme by which to implement the RCPs then you should first read the strategies and skills described in the appropriate Programmes in Stage Four and then implement them by using the Ten Day Stress Control Training Course to be found in Stage Five. This Training Course is designed to start you off in a scientific way implementing RCPs. It uses learning principles from behavioural psychology to help you build up motivation and establish the Programmes necessary to control stress quickly and effectively.

At the end of the ten days you should find that you are using the RCPs far more easily and, thereafter, it is just a matter of practising consistently.

Your Three Month Stress Check

Just as every sensible person has a regular physical health check, we strongly suggest that you repeat this analysis about every three months. This should protect you against spiralling stress levels as you will tend to catch Lifestyle Stressers before they can get out of hand. Repeat the analysis also at any crisis point to help you quickly bail out excessive levels of stress.

Stage Four

Response Control Programmes

E*

Stage Four

Response Control Procedures

INTRODUCTION

In this Stage you will find ten RCP programmes which have been created to enable you to gain control of stress and Negative Stress Responses in all four Life Areas. These Programmes are:

Programme One – RCPs for – High Level Negative **Physical** Responses.

Programme Two – RCPs for – Low Level Negative **Physical** Responses.

Programme Three – RCPs for – High Level Negative **Mental** Responses.

Programme Four – RCPs for – Low Level Negative **Mental** Responses.

Programme Five – RCPs for – **Performance** Lifestyle Stressers.

Programme Six – RCPs for – **Threat** Lifestyle Stressers.

Programme Seven – RCPs for – **Boredom** Lifestyle Stressers.

Programme Eight – RCPs for – **Frustration** Lifestyle Stressers.

Programme Nine – RCPs for – **Bereavement** Lifestyle Stressers.

Programme Ten – RCPs for – **Physical** Lifestyle Stressers.

PROGRAMME ONE – RCPs FOR – HIGH LEVEL
NEGATIVE PHYSICAL RESPONSES

In Stage Three we talked about the Autonomic Nervous System
and explained how the arousal triggered by the sympathetic
branch of the ANS caused wide-ranging bodily changes to which
we give the general title of anxiety. Typical among the obvious
characteristics of uncontrolled anxiety arousal are:

Muscular tension.
Increased heart rate (tachycardia).
Increased blood pressure (hypertension).
Increased perspiration, blushing and hotness.
Increased respiration and uneven or laboured breathing.
Stomach turning over.
Mouth drying.
Nausea.
Light headedness.
Trembling and loss of muscular control.
Blurring of vision and dizziness.

We also pointed out that the sympathetic branch of the ANS
has a reciprocal branch called the parasympathetic nervous
system and that these two branches compete for ultimate
supremacy in the nervous system. Herein lies the essential basic
building block for the control of anxiety responses. If we can
train the ANS to produce very high levels of parasympathetic
responses whenever we feel the sympathetic nervous system
about to take over inappropriately, then these high levels of
parasympathetic responding can be used to eradicate the anxiety
spiral.

The parasympathetic responses which could be used for this
purpose include:

Sexual arousal.
Digestion and eating.
Relaxation response.

These three activities provide behaviours which are easiest to implement for the purposes of RCPs. While sexual arousal is a useful and powerful response to be incorporated into RCPs, we shall make more obvious use of it when dealing with sexually based stress problems (see Programmes Five, Seven and Eight). Digestion and eating are useful responses when dealing with children's anxiety problems and we shall deal with these more fully in the programme involving family difficulties (see Programme Eight).

For the purposes of RCP Programme Number One we shall concentrate on the most flexible of the parasympathetic responses – the Relaxation Response.

Eliciting and using the relaxation response on self-command is a skill. Like every other skill it is most easily learned through a structured programme which is practised regularly. In this RCP Programme we shall explain and teach the three components involved in learning to relax completely and quickly in whatever situation is necessary, and give an indication of how long this skill might take to acquire, although obviously there will be some individual variation. We shall also examine how this RCP should be used as a preventive measure to stop excessive levels of tension and anxiety from arising at all.

1. Deep Muscle Relaxation

When and Where

During the first few days the best time to practise is in the evening or just before you go to sleep. Choose a quiet comfortably heated room with the curtains drawn and dim lighting. Take off your shoes and loosen any tight clothing. Lie flat on a couch or bed or lie back in a comfortable armchair which provides adequate support for the spine and the neck.

How

First read through this section on deep relaxation and become familiar with the methods and the muscle groups which you are

going to learn to relax. Initially this may seem a little complicated but, by the end of the first practice session, you should be
well on the way to mastering the procedure. To help you to
remember the order of the exercises we have divided the muscle
groups into six main body areas. These are:

(1) *A*rms and hands.
(2) *N*eck and shoulders.
(3) *E*yes, eyebrows and forehead.
(4) *M*outh and throat.
(5) *T*runk and chest.
(6) *L*egs and hips.

You may find it easier to remember the order of these muscle
groups by memorising the mnemonic:

*A*ll *N*ew *E*xercises *M*ust *T*ake *L*onger.

In this the first letter of each word identifies one of the six
main body areas. This mnemonic together with the muscle
groups diagram (see Diagram Four) and the instructions which
we give below should enable you to undertake the first few
practice sessions quite easily.

Alternatively you may prefer to tape record the instructions
from the text and play these back to yourself as you relax. Leave
plenty of time between each set of instructions so that you can
relax fully. A special training cassette which teaches the RCP of
the relaxation response has been developed and recorded by
Dr Robert Sharpe and is one of the range of RCP Programmes
on tape which are available through *Stresswatch*, the organisation described in our introduction.

The Muscle Group Exercises

Read through these exercises and learn them as well as you can
using the mnemonic phrase *All New Exercises Must Take Longer*
in your mind to help you remember the muscle groups.

MUSCLE TENSION AND RELAXATION

Fists
clenched
tenses the
hands

Fist
relaxed

Biceps tensed
arms bent
at elbow

Biceps
relaxed

Triceps
tensed
straightens
the
arm

Triceps
relaxed
let
arms
flop

Grit the teeth
tenses the
jaw

Part the teeth
relaxes the
jaw

Press the lips
together tenses
lips and the
facial muscles

Rest lips lightly
together relaxes
lips and facial
muscles

Press tip of tongue
against roof of mouth
tenses tongue & throat

Let tongue flop
relaxes tongue
and throat

Press head
back,
tenses neck

Let head
rest back
relaxes neck

Shrug
shoulders

Relax
shoulders

Straighten
legs and point
toes down
tenses legs
and toes

Let
legs flop
and feel legs
and toes relax

Breathe in
deeply
tenses the
chest

Breathe out
feel the
chest
relax

Pull stomach
muscles in.
Tenses
stomach

Let stomach
muscles out.
Relaxes
stomach

Tense the
buttocks
together

Let the
buttocks
relax

(A Group) Hands and Lower Arms: Clench both fists as tightly as you can for about five seconds and feel the tension. Now relax them completely and note the difference between tension and relaxation in your hands and lower arms. Carry on letting the muscles unwind for about a minute.

(A Group) Front Upper Arms: Bend your arms at the elbows, trying to touch your wrists to your shoulders, to tighten the muscles at the front of the upper arms, the biceps. Hold this position for about five seconds, then relax and let your arms straighten by your sides. Continue to let the muscles unwind and relax and concentrate on the feeling of letting go for about a minute.

(A Group) Back Upper Arms: Straighten your arms as rigidly as you can. Feel the tension in the back of your upper arms, your triceps muscles, for about five seconds and then let go. Let your arms relax completely and continue to let your triceps unwind for about a minute.

Now take an extra minute and concentrate on all the muscles in the hands and arms, letting them feel more and more deeply relaxed.

(N Group) Neck: Press your head back hard against the couch, bed or armchair so as to tense your neck muscles and hold that position for about five seconds. Feel the tension and then relax your neck and simply let your head rest back gently. Concentrate on the feeling of letting go for about a minute.

(N Group) Shoulders: Shrug your shoulders, drawing them up into your neck as tightly as you can. Notice the tension in your shoulders, hold that position for about five seconds and then relax. Let your shoulders flop and unwind and carry on this feeling of letting go for about a minute.

Now take an extra minute to let the muscles of your neck, shoulders and arms relax completely.

(E Group) Eyes and Eyebrows: Frown as hard as you can and squeeze your eyes tightly shut in order to tense the area around your eyes. Hold that position for about five seconds and then

relax. Feel the relief of letting go and continue to relax the area around your eyes for the next minute.

(E Group) Forehead and Scalp: Raise your eyebrows as high as you can as though enquiring. Feel the tension in your forehead and scalp and hold that position for about five seconds. Feel the tension and then relax. Notice the difference between tension and relaxation and continue the feeling of letting go. Keep your eyes still and looking straight ahead and carry on the feeling of unwinding for about a minute.

Now for another minute let the muscles around your eyes, forehead, neck, shoulders and arms relax completely.

(M Group) Mouth: Press your lips tightly together and tense the muscles in your lips and face. Hold this position for about five seconds and then relax. Let your lips rest lightly together and continue the feeling of letting go for about a minute.

(M Group) Jaw: Bite your teeth together for about five seconds and feel the tension in your jaw. Then relax the muscles in your jaw by parting your teeth slightly so there is no tension in your jaw. Concentrate on the feeling of letting go for about a minute.

(M Group) Throat: Press the tip of your tongue against the roof of your mouth and press upwards as hard as you can. Feel the tension in your tongue and throat and hold that position for about five seconds. Then let go and allow your tongue to flop down into the bottom of your mouth. Feel the relief of letting go and continue to relax your tongue and throat for about a minute.

Now for another minute let the muscles around your mouth, throat, eyes, forehead, neck, shoulders and arms relax completely.

(T Group) Chest: Take in a deep breath and feel the tension in your chest. Hold your breath for about five seconds. Now breathe out and concentrate on the feeling of relaxation. Now take another deep breath and feel the tension again. Hold it for five seconds then breathe out and relax. Now keep your breathing shallow and relaxed but every time you breathe out feel the relief of letting go. Continue to practise this for the next minute.

(T Group) Stomach: Tighten the muscles around your stomach area as though you were preparing to receive a blow. Feel the tension and hold this position for about five seconds. Now relax and let your stomach muscles loosen and unwind. Continue the feeling of letting go and concentrate on the feeling of relaxation for about a minute.

Now take another minute to relax the muscles around your stomach, chest, mouth, throat, eyes, forehead, neck, shoulders, arms and hands completely.

(L Group) Legs and Hips: Squeeze your thighs and buttocks together, straighten your legs and point your toes downwards. Hold that position for about five seconds and note the tension in your legs and hips then relax completely and feel the tension ease away from your legs and hips. Continue to unwind for the next minute.

For the next two or three minutes concentrate on relaxing all the major muscle groups: legs, buttocks, stomach, chest, mouth, throat, eyes, forehead, neck, shoulders, arms and hands.

Feel yourself sinking deeper and deeper into the couch, bed or chair as your body becomes heavier and heavier, more and more deeply relaxed.

General Instructions to be carried out during the above exercises

(1) At the beginning of the exercises, close your eyes and keep them closed until you have completed the last period of total relaxation. This will reduce any unwanted distractions from the environment around you.

(2) While you are dealing with a particular set of muscles try to concentrate completely on those muscles and do not let your mind wander onto anything else.

(3) Make sure that you practise for the first few occasions in a quiet and comfortable environment.

(4) Adopt an attitude of *passive concentration* while letting the muscles unwind and relax after each exercise. Do not try to force yourself to relax as this will simply have the effect of

making you tense up. Instead allow the relaxation to come naturally and once this process has started concentrate your attention on the feeling of letting go as you relax more and more.

(5) Each time you relax a muscle group after it has been in tension mentally repeat the word '*Relax*'. When you have gone through the chest muscle exercises you should then begin to concentrate on the relaxing effects of exhaling. Keep your breathing shallow and every time you breathe out mentally repeat the word '*Relax*' while relaxing your body a little more. Keep your breathing regular and even.

(6) Do not become concerned if you feel cold during the exercises as this is a perfectly normal occurrence and a positive sign that parasympathetic responses are becoming more predominant. It means that your blood circulation is no longer being rushed in the direction of your skin surface for emergency energy supplies but that, instead, it is being diverted to the more recuperative activities such as digestion.

(7) During the last few minutes when you are simply relaxing your whole body, try to keep other thoughts or worries out of your mind by concentrating on your key word 'Relax'. However, if you have difficulty in doing this for the first few days you may find it useful to let your thoughts dwell upon a pleasant image such as sunshine on a beach, a country scene or some tranquil colour and use this image to exclude any discomforting thoughts.

(8) At the end of your relaxation session open your eyes and move your body around slowly. Sit up slowly and return to your normal routine while trying to maintain the feeling of relaxation which you have developed.

You should try to practise Deep Relaxation training at least once a day for about thirty minutes. It will do you a great deal of good if you can manage to practise for two such periods – say one during the middle of the day and one in the evening. After about five days you should find that you are able to relax quite quickly and easily. When you feel confident about your ability to produce Deep Relaxation you should move on to the next set of exercises.

2. Quick Relaxation

Now that you are able to achieve Deep Relaxation you can speed up this process by leaving out the tension exercises and simply allowing your body to relax by remembering the feeling of letting go. Practise this sitting in an armchair and just concentrate on each of the major muscle groups in turn and allow them to relax more and more deeply. You will probably find that, within about ten minutes, you will reach the stage that you usually experience when you have gone through the Deep Relaxation exercises.

If this step, however, is a little too big for you to take, an intermediate stage to lead on to Quick Relaxation is to proceed as follows. Sit in a comfortable armchair and tense your entire body all at once. Clench your fists, bend your arms at the elbows as though trying to touch your wrists to your shoulders, shrug your shoulders, press your head back against the chair and tense your neck, squeeze your eyes tightly shut, clench your teeth and press your lips together, straighten your legs and lift your heels slightly off the floor to tense your stomach muscles and take in a deep breath. Hold all this for about five seconds and then flop out, letting everything relax as quickly and deeply as you can. Stay like this, concentrating on your relaxing image and the key word 'Relax' for about ten minutes.

If you use this intermediate procedure you will quickly find that you can drop the full body tension exercise and go straight on to relax. You should carry out the training frequently during the day for five or ten minute periods and continue to practise for about five more days.

For both the above relaxation procedures you must lie or sit down for the duration of the exercise. However, it is extremely valuable to be able to remain in a relaxed and controlled state while walking around and performing active pieces of behaviour, such as carrying out a job of work, playing a sport and so on. This can be achieved by using a procedure known as Differential Relaxation.

3. Differential Relaxation

In Differential Relaxation you carry out the technique while moving around. It can be used for any piece of behaviour where you need to stay cool and collected while involved in physical effort. You should move onto it when you are confident of your ability to relax quickly, that is within a matter of one or two minutes.

After one of the Quick Relaxation sessions *open your eyes* but keep the rest of your body relaxed and motionless. Notice what it feels like to be able to sit completely relaxed while still processing information received through your eyes. It is important that you concentrate on the different bodily feelings associated with relaxation and visual activities.

While keeping the rest of your body relaxed, *move your head and neck* by *looking around the room*. Take in every detail of your surroundings and once again notice how it feels to move your head and neck while keeping the rest of your body completely relaxed.

Now keep your head still and *slowly start talking to yourself*. It does not matter what you say but get used to the feeling of speaking while keeping the rest of your body completely relaxed and notice the difference between those muscles which are relaxed and those in use.

Stop talking and relax your body completely. After a few moments begin to *move your arms*. Feel the new sensation of moving some of your muscles while the rest of your body remains relaxed. Ensure that your legs and torso stay relaxed and comfortable while you move your arms as though slowly conducting an orchestra.

Now relax your arms and, after a few moments, *stand up*. Start to walk very slowly around the room and keep those muscles which are not essential to walking in a relaxed state. Notice the sensation of walking with your body almost completely relaxed. After a couple of minutes go back to the chair or couch and carry out an all over Quick Relaxation period for a few more minutes.

Do this series of exercises for about five more days and during this time, as you become confident of your ability to relax differentially, gradually attempt more and more complex behaviours while keeping yourself differentially relaxed. At the end of this time you should be able to induce a feeling of relaxation while carrying out almost any everyday activity.

These RCPs have been found to be of great benefit to people who suffer from high levels of tension or insomnia. By taking regular Stress Control breaks during the day, perhaps coinciding with more conventional breaks from work, a person is able to keep a generally low level of muscular tension. This gradually becomes a habit which the body performs without really having to think about it. In this way High Level Negative Physical Responses are banished permanently and you are able to cope coolly and effectively with situations which would otherwise have proved too impossibly anxiety-producing for you even to consider.

Relaxation is a pleasant, rewarding occupation and the benefits which result from it, combined with the enjoyment most people derive from carrying out this RCP, usually provides sufficient motivation to stick to the training programme. If, however, you find it hard to carry out these exercises you may need the more structured framework which can be found in Stage Five to support and guide you in the early stages of training.

PROGRAMME TWO – RCPs FOR – LOW LEVEL
NEGATIVE PHYSICAL RESPONSES

These responses occur when the environment provides insufficient physical stress or demands on physical capabilities. Typical situations in which Low Level Negative Physical Responses are found include:

Repetitious or routine work in the home, or office, or on a factory production line.

After retirement from an active life.

After a broken relationship with a regular sex partner or in the absence of a sex partner at all.

In the absence of a taxing sporting competitor.

In a personal relationship which provides no new excitements or interests.

In an isolated or unfriendly living environment such as in a big city or a remote country area.

Where there are insufficient structured outlets for physical activity, for example playgrounds, playing fields, sports centres.

The usual consequences of this lack of physical stimulation are:

Lethargy.

Lassitude.

An inability to have any great interest in or enthusiasm for the work being tackled.

An inability to start on new projects.

Depression.

Sexual frustration.

A careless attitude to work being done.

Some types of vandalism and petty crime.

The strategies which have to be adopted in situations of underuse of physical capabilities fall into two major categories.

The first is concerned with augmenting the physical stress in the existing Area of concern such as Work and Study, Family, Marriage, Sex and Intimacy, Social and Interpersonal Relationships or Leisure and Sport. The second group of strategies are used when it is impossible to add stresses to the Area directly under consideration, and instead, stress levels have to be built up in alternative Life Areas so that the overall general level of stress is increased. For example, a man working on a production line is faced with two alternatives. The first is to leave his job and find another one which will offer more stimulation. However, this may well prove unrealistic at a time of high unemployment or because of family or financial circumstances. The other option is to find alternative inputs for stress in some of the other Life Areas, perhaps by taking up a Leisure activity which offers the chance to take some risks and expend a lot of physical energy.

Whichever method is chosen, the actual principles of establishing the extra stresses will be very similar. It will depend largely on the Area in question as to which one of the alternatives is taken, although sometimes, as in our example, there will be no effective alternative. Usually it is most beneficial to try to input stress into the actual situation concerned but this frequently requires social or industrial changes of attitude beyond the power of most individuals to instigate. These alternatives will be discussed in Stage Six.

1. The Positive Payoff

We have described some of the situations which produce Low Level Negative Physical Responses. Probably you can think of many others, some of which may affect you personally at this moment. But what all the situations leading to this type of Negative Stress Response have in common is that they lack rewards.

The way in which any piece of behaviour starts and gradually becomes part of our repertoire is by being followed by some positive payoff. The value of these payoffs will vary from one individual to the next. Children may work very hard for a small payoff while others, for instance film stars and tycoons, will work comparatively just as hard only when there is a large number of noughts on their pay check. Whatever the value of the payoff the behaviour which it follows will only continue as long as that payoff remains at least a probability. A general level of motivation and lack of depression is directly related to how much payoff we get from the Life Areas. If the payoff is very low then our motivation is low and we tend not to bother so much about carrying out major pieces of behaviour because there is little or no reward. This, of course, produces a negative spiral because the less behaviour is carried out the less reward there can be anyway. With this in mind, the major strategy which has to be adopted by a person suffering from such Low Level Negative Physical Responses as lack of enthusiasm, lethargy and a careless way of approaching life, is to increase the payoffs which, in turn, increases the desire to carry out more and more behaviour and again builds up the payoff. When we talk about increasing activity, as we shall in this RCP Programme, we intend it to be an increase *not* for its own sake but for the almost inevitable rewards and payoffs which come in its wake. Just as you cannot have payoffs without behaviour so it is almost impossible not to have payoffs if you do have behaviour.

We have used the word payoff, we have used the word reward. In most circumstances these terms would apply primarily to money or some other material benefit. It would be a mistake, however, immediately to assume that if production line workers suffering from depression were given an enormous increase in wages at the end of each week they would then become happy, cheerful and more productive. Experience has confirmed what could have been anticipated from results of laboratory research. The power of payoffs, or 'reinforcers' as they are technically known, is only apparent if they are given in a certain way. Reinforcers only work if they *immediately* follow a piece of behaviour. If a person carries out a piece of behaviour and several hours or days later is given money for his labours this will have no effect on how well or cheerfully the behaviour was carried out. If, on the other hand, the behaviour is followed immediately by a reward of some kind then this will have the result of making it much more likely that the behaviour will recur. This important learning principle and its more complex applications to industrial and business productivity will be discussed in Stage Six.

Let us look at what happens when you are carrying out a series of routine chores at home or in the office. Suppose you complete some washing up or empty one overladen In-Tray. There is a limited payoff from having got rid of one tedious task. But this small reward is usually overshadowed by the daunting collection of equally boring tasks awaiting your attention. It is not surprising under those circumstances that your enthusiasm for the work and the speed and efficiency with which you perform each succeeding task may sharply decline. The behaviours are not receiving any positive payoffs. After a time, this sort of situation may deteriorate to a point where very little activity occurs at all. Now that we can see how this deterioration started, it gives us a strategy by which to regenerate motivation and in doing so help to eliminate Low Level Negative Physical Responses.

The first part of this strategy involves the person in seeking out payoffs which are valuable to them. Anything can be used as a reinforcer provided it is assessed as such by the individual concerned. Because of this you should not, when compiling lists of payoffs, omit any activity because you think that other people might not approve. Remember that in addition to such payoffs as money, food, reading your favourite book or magazine, seeing a film you enjoy and so on, sex is a very powerful source of reinforcement. Especially when the low stress problem is being generated in the sexual Life Area, orgasm and sexual arousal should be used to reinforce further attempts.

In order to obtain your payoffs you must assess your behaviour for four or five days and note down any activity which you enjoy doing and feel pleased about afterwards. In Stage Five we offer a structured, day-by-day Programme for collecting reinforcers, but we will give you some examples here, taken from case histories, to show the range of payoffs used by different people.

> Coffee, reading newspaper or magazine, looking at pornographic books, switching on TV, listening to classical music, masturbating, going for a walk, buying a paperback book, going to the cinema, having sex, buying new clothes, treating oneself to a massage, having hair styled, phoning a friend . . .

are all examples of the positive payoff.

Having collected payoffs which are personally meaningful it is then necessary to select, say, six convenient ones which can easily be carried out, and make a contract with yourself not to allow any of those payoffs unless you have carried out a piece of behaviour as specified by you. In this case it would be a piece of behaviour or RCP adding extra stress to your particular Life Area, or Areas, where it is needed. For another two weeks you should carry out this new piece of behaviour to generate extra stress and, on every occasion, follow it immediately by one of the positive payoffs. It is very important always to follow the behaviour immediately as, if you do not, you may be reinforcing the wrong behaviour! For example, if a lethargic young housewife successfully adds extra stress to her life by using one of the RCPs but before reinforcing that behaviour sits and daydreams for ten minutes in an aimless and negative way about her bleak life, the behaviour which she will be establishing will not be the introduction of needed stress but of miserably doing nothing! Instead she should have her reinforcement, which might be drinking a cup of coffee, phoning a friend or going through some holiday brochures, *ready*, so that she can use it immediately after the piece of behaviour recently incorporated in her life to produce a higher stress level.

Besides these small, immediate, pleasures, reinforcers can also be given in much larger forms, such as going out for dinner or away for the weekend, by using a points or token system. Here the immediate reinforcer is to mark down on a chart a point for having completed the desired piece of behaviour. A contract is formed, often including other members of the family, that if a certain number of points is accrued these can be used to cash in for a larger reinforcer such as an outing. Such systems are particularly useful with children and wall charts can be constructed to show them at a glance how near they are to getting their major reinforcer. Plastic counters can also be used and cashed in later for the reward. The counters have no intrinsic value of course, and in themselves, neither counters nor points are reinforcers. Their value comes solely from the acceptance that they can be used to 'buy' primary reinforcers and in this way are almost identical to bank notes. Just as with bank notes, it is important that confidence is maintained in the token currency and this can only be done by sticking rigidly to any contractual arrangement which might have been made. It is of no value at all if a lethargic child has worked hard all week and gained a lot of points if an equally lethargic parent wriggles out of the much looked forward to weekend outing, to be bought with the points, on some flimsy pretext. To make the system work the contract must always be honoured. If there is a strong probability of anything going wrong, it must not be made in the first place.

2. Shaping Stress Strategies

Our main object so far has been to draw your attention to the fact that if you are exhibiting Low Level Negative Physical Responses you are stress starved. This awareness alone may be sufficient for you to see how you can increase your stress level, perhaps by accepting new challenges in the working environment or, if this is not possible, by adopting much more taxing leisure or family pursuits. The key point to remember is that you must operate at your OSL if you are to be happy, healthy and fulfilled. What all too often happens is that somebody with an unstimulating work schedule leaves that environment for one which is equally lacking in stress. Because they have been taught to regard any form of stress as harmful they believe that they are helping themselves by keeping the stimulation offered by their lifestyle to a minimum level. At a training workshop we were told by one participant that his major problem was a difficulty in making relationships. He was clearly very depressed and it soon became obvious that this was due to his leaving a dull routine job in a computer department and going straight home to a bland environment where he ate alone and watched television. Because there were insufficient reinforcers to motivate him to do more, he would think sadly about going out and just moon around for the rest of the evening without making any effort to do so. As well as presenting him with an RCP Programme for social behaviour we also insisted that he increased the general level of stress activity going on at work and at home. He developed an office 'think tank' which he ran every week as a lunchtime seminar. He also enlisted the aid of a friend who had a flair for interior design and began to make radical changes in his apartment. As he became engrossed in these activities he found his general level of energy rising. Soon he took up new activities, such as going out to clubs and on blind dates and joining a sports society, which opened up his lifestyle to fruitful social intercourse.

In implementing such a Programme it is important to remember to break down the additional stressers into manageable stages. If this is not done, the new behaviours could prove to be overwhelming at first. In our case history above the man started first by considering a change of decor in his living-room. When he had been working at this for a few days he gradually turned his attention towards planning the decor of the whole apartment. He chose this area to start off in because he felt he had more aptitude there than anywhere else but, as he became more confident, he then included the 'think tank' at work and gradually broadened his social outings. This, in behavioural terms, is called a Shaping Programme. In practice what happens is that the reinforcers available for establishing new behaviours are first used for a small increase in stressful activity. When this increase has been established the same reinforcers can then be used to build up to a new level of stress and so on. Further practical help in shaping behaviour can be found in Stage Five.

Let us now look at the only two Lifestyle Stressers which can appropriately be introduced to increase the level of stress in your life. These are *Performance Stressers* and *Threat Stressers*.

3. Performance Stressers

When any piece of behaviour has become so well established that it is a matter of routine then the associated stress levels will become progressively lower and lower. For example, an athlete who has trained correctly should reach an event well prepared but still having in front of him a final challenge which will spur him to a great performance. If he has overtrained, and can see little challenge left in the actual competitive event, he may suffer Low Level Negative Physical Responses and not perform to the best of his ability. At a more general level anyone who has repeated a task for long enough will internalise the skill and find it unchallenging and consequently lacking in stress.

So far as business routine and industrial production line working are concerned, there are certain valuable changes in procedures which management could, and in a few cases have, introduced to help remedy this difficulty and these will be discussed in Stage Six. But even without such managerial interventions it is often possible for the individual to introduce sufficient variation into the most routine behaviour to raise the level of Performance stress. With thought you will probably be able to devise specific strategies for achieving this increase in Performance stress but here are some general strategies which have proved useful.

Varying Performance

Many people think that it is advisable to stick at specific jobs to the bitter end even though they are becoming drowsy and making errors because they have habituated to the task and their stress level has dropped well below the optimum. In fact most people work more effectively if they engage in shorter periods of routine work and mix them with short periods of other different kinds of routine work. For example in an office there might be the following tasks to complete:

Checking routine accounts. Making calls to clients. Visiting clients. Filing reports. Planning progress schedules. Holding meetings or attending them.

Now clearly some of these items will be inflexible. Certain clients may only be available at particular times. The organisation of meetings will depend on the availability of others. Calls may have to be made at specified times. But in almost every routine there is some flexibility and, when planning your week, you should try and build in variety around these invariables. Do not decide to spend all Monday, for instance, with clients and all Tuesday in the office filing papers even though logistically this may seem the most appropriate way of organising your time. In terms of maintaining the stress at an optimum level it might be far better to spend part of Monday seeing clients and the rest of the day on less stimulating routine work. You would then be able to enjoy both. Remember that most of the things which we enjoy in life we enjoy because we compare them with other activities. If we carry on too long with one activity it begins to pall and we need to carry out other behaviours to re-establish the comparative interest.

Change in Methods

Because you have always carried out a certain task in a specific way, this does not necessarily mean that it is the best or only way of achieving the required results. It may be possible to introduce

F

variation in your methods. Often this can be achieved by simply rearranging your environment, moving your desk, shifting your filing cabinets, altering the layout of your lounge or bedroom. In reconstituting your environment in this way new ideas for new behaviours may become obvious. These can range from a more interesting communication network in your office to a more sexually erotic position during love play.

The effect which an environment has on any piece of behaviour is called *stimulus control* and can be affected very greatly by even a small change in the environmental conditions. A couple whose sexual life is routine and boring at home may well find themselves engaging very actively in sex during an overnight stay in an hotel for example. We are not saying that large amounts of money should therefore be spent on staying in hotels, although an occasional visit may be an excellent strategy. Simply repositioning the bed or the room mirrors may provide sufficient change in stimulus control to produce a more enjoyable sex life.

In RCP Programme Three we discuss the use of ideograms for shuffling around thoughts and data on a sheet of paper in order to produce fresh insights and ideas. In exactly the same way you can shuffle around the components of your living or working Areas to introduce variety, generate new approaches and generally increase the scope for Performance Stressers.

Stretch Yourself

Once we have developed a series of methods by which we can 'get through' in life, we tend to cut off any choices which are open to us where we might tax ourselves beyond our limits. However, if there is no challenge left in the physical performance side of life, it may well become essential that physically taxing behaviours are attempted. For the person who has mastered, to a large extent, his chosen sport it may be that opponents have to be found who are so advanced that they will reproduce the same comparative state of stress as when the person was just acquiring the rudiments of the sport in the early stages. If you have avoided some sexual behaviour because you were content to perform in the old, routine way without any bother, then it may be useful to attempt sexual expression by different means. If you have convinced yourself that certain contracts at work are beyond your capabilities then a progressively duller office life may mean that you have to go out on a limb and take on a project where you will really have to struggle. If you have left work to run a home and look after a family, or if you have retired and been away from an active routine for some time, then you may have lost confidence in your physical ability to cope with certain types of stress. But this stress could be the very thing which reintroduces reinforcers into your life and restores your stress level to the optimum.

4. Threat Stressers

There are many people who, far from disliking stress and the associated anxiety responses which it sometimes brings, actually seek out situations which produce this form of stress. Men and women who take part in such sports as skydiving and parachuting, motor racing and mountaineering, aerobatics and motorbike scrambling, ski-ing and skin-diving are sometimes called 'sensation seekers'. We prefer the expression *adrenophiles*, a term we have coined for this type of stimulus seeker. Stress-producing pursuits need not be so obviously threatening however. People who go on safari holidays to remote parts of the world or join singles clubs to meet others and make new friends are also engaging in activities which can produce Threat Stressers. Remember that *anything* in your environment which is perceived and assessed by you as a threat produces this type of stress. Spider phobics, for example, would be able to introduce Threat stresses into their lives simply by reading a book about spiders, observing them in nature or holding them in their hands. If there are some situations or objects about which you are phobic you might use these as Threat Stresser inducers.

You must be careful, of course, not to attempt anything which produces Threat stress without first taking the correct steps to acquire any necessary skills involved. If you want to take up a sport which will raise your stress level then you should only do so after appropriate training and practice. Nor should you make use of Threat Stressers which put other members of the public at risk. The driver who overtakes at speed on a dangerous bend or burns away from you at the traffic lights may well be an understressed individual trying to inject some excitement into his or her life. But this is no defence for putting other road users at risk!

All the Threat inducers discussed so far have involved going out into the environment to seek them. But Threat Stressers can also be developed from internal responses. Frequently people suffering from the effects of low level stress lack the opportunities for releasing pent up aggression in a socially acceptable form. Adolescents in under-stimulating environments may develop their own anti-social strategies for increasing the amount of stress present through vandalism, gang skirmishes or petty crimes often involving considerable amounts of damage. The internalised result of such activities is the release of adrenalin and a temporary top up of the stress level. This same phenomenon can be reproduced in a more practical and acceptable way in families where interpersonal relationships have stagnated and politeness has replaced more intimate feelings. RCP Programmes number Seven and Eight will include detailed strategies for achieving such effects. These Programmes will teach you how to be aggressive and assertive in a productive manner which takes off excessive controls and constraints from your interpersonal relationships.

Summary

Low Level Negative Physical Responses are characterised by low behavioural output and a lack of payoffs or reinforcers in the person's lifestyle. Because of these the stress level is well below the optimum.

The method of dealing with this problem is generally to raise the level of stress by increasing behavioural output in a way which produces more demand on the person and, in turn, results in greater reinforcement and payoff. Such an increase in behaviour can be achieved through attempting more complex tasks and taxing performance capabilities (Performance Stressers) or by exposure to threatening situations (Threat Stressers).

Remember that assessing whether or not you are operating at your OSL in any Life Area is a matter of subjective judgement. If you feel lethargic, bored and depressed then it is certain that your environment is not providing sufficient stress to reach the OSL.

PROGRAMME THREE – RCPs FOR – HIGH LEVEL
NEGATIVE MENTAL RESPONSES

In Stage Three we compared the thinking part of the brain, the cerebral cortex, to a vast telephone switchboard which has a large but finite number of inputs and outputs associated with it. Between the inputs and the outputs lie a similarly finite number of 'channels' in which the processing of information and the working out of the next appropriate piece of behaviour are effected.

The obvious consequence of this arrangement is that it can become overloaded and that there may not be a processing channel free when an urgent or important inflow of information occurs. If this happens and the new and vital situation is not coped with effectively then yet more information will flow into the already overcrowded channels, causing a further build up of unprocessed information and ensuing confusion. Typical among the characteristics of overcrowded processing channels are:

A feeling of the mind 'going blank' on the particular topic which has not been allowed any channel capacity.
A feeling of the room or the head 'spinning around'.
A super speeded-up sensation where thoughts chase themselves unproductively in circles.
An inability to recall previously well-known information.
Rapidly jumping from one train of thought to another completely unrelated to it.
The thought processes becoming fixated on one idea.

Some of these symptoms may seem a little contradictory and this is because different people will experience different types of High Level Negative Mental Response. But practically everybody who has suffered from an overflowing of information into the processing channels will recognise at least one of the above responses.

If we compare this breakdown of the processing mechanism

with the disciplined and controlled characteristics of a well programmed set of mental responses we can extract from the latter several important principles. An analysis of constructive and effective mental Programmes shows that a critical path of cognitive behaviour is followed which involves the mastery of eight major mental skills.

1. Determining Priority

Frequently in a busy person's life there will be a number of items for consideration which compete with one another for the processing channels in the thinking part of the brain. When a breakdown in the processing channels occurs, one of the major reasons is often found to be an inability to determine which are the important or urgent items requiring 'channel time' and which ones can be held back for a less congested period. In order to use available channel capacity in the most effective way it is necessary to determine a clear order of priorities.

If you frequently feel that you do not know which way to turn or which of the several large problems confronting you to attempt first and then spend fruitless periods of time unable to choose between different courses of action, this important skill of determining priorities is almost certainly missing from your repertoire. Behaviourally there are a number of simple steps which you can put into operation to learn the skills but it is important to remember that you will not acquire them immediately. Indeed it may well take you several days of consistent practice before you get into the habit of determining priorities.

The first thing to understand is that any mental process which seems to be performed quite easily in the head almost always began as a piece of external behaviour. For example the simple mental calculations which you carry out in a few seconds when shopping or working out personal finances will have been learned by using counters in infancy and by laboriously writing them out in primary school. In just the same way the mental skill of determining priorities may first have to be done by listing, on paper, all those tasks which, at that particular moment, require your attention. At first such lists will usually have to be compiled at times when you already are under mental pressure and will only add to the demands on channel capacity at a time when you can, apparently, least afford any further pressures. There is no way around this problem. You must just accept the fact that, for an initial period, you will have to divert some time and effort to priority list making at moments when you probably feel you have no surplus of either. The list writing should have priority over all other activities, however urgent and demanding they may appear.

You should practise priority list making, for the first few days, by noting every occasion when there is pressure on your mental processes and writing down an exhaustive list of attention demanding thoughts. For example a list compiled at 2 p.m. by one busy office worker read as follows:

'Answer five letters of complaints about goods. Make three phone calls concerning arrangements for office party in six weeks time. Check secretary has booked train sleeper for tomorrow night. See Mr Brent about quality control. Spend a little time thinking about theatre this evening with wife. Find lost file on Baxter account. Phone garage about car service. Arrange passport renewal.'

A similar list compiled by a woman doctor at 10.30 a.m. on a working day included the following:

'Arrange emergency admission into hospital. Discuss house calls with partner. Fill gap in duty roster. Sort out appointments confusion with receptionist. Ring husband at work to check a bill. Collect notes for First Aid lecture this evening. Return three calls and make five more. Make shopping list. Write prescription for own contraceptive pills.'

By externalising your thoughts in this way you will find it easier both to determine priorities and to leave unattended those less important items which can wait until time is at less of a premium. You can either do this by rewriting the list in order of priority or by numbering the items on the original list. The two primary objects of list making are to give you an awareness of those times when congestion is at its peak and also to provide you with a practical strategy for coping with the situation. When you are confident that you can stop congestion as it arises, through this type of externalising, and deal with priority situations to the exclusion of less important issues, you should start trying to compile the list internally. You may well still wish to keep a written list of major activities to be undertaken during the day but try, at crisis points, to make yourself choose priority items mentally.

2. Anticipation of Congestion

This involves an awareness, gained in many cases through the list making procedure described above, of those times when we are liable to experience congestion problems. Although it may not be possible to remove them completely, an awareness of when they are likely to arise should enable you to spread the incoming demands over a long period of time.

While the list keeping provides a great deal of information about the congestion times we shall also deal with self-recording techniques in Stage Five. These will help you to pinpoint crisis periods.

The purpose of anticipating a congestion point is that when it occurs you are completely prepared for the possibility of mental pressure. Often High Level Negative Mental Responses are caused by the victim being taken unawares and losing control in the ensuing confusion. If you are aware of when such periods occur in your working week then you can be ready to sit down calmly for a few seconds, make your priority lists and

F*

carry out some of the other skills, which we shall describe, in a well planned way.

3. Allocation of Time

After a few days of list making, it should be possible to pinpoint clearly those times of the day, or week, when you meet peaks of channel congestion. In addition the records should help to locate those periods when the pressure is less intense. Armed with this information it is possible to start allocating working time to the different projects and items demanding your attention. To do this you must divide your available working hours into congestion times and slack periods. Write out a timetable based on the total number of hours each week which you can realistically spend on your ongoing work projects and congestion points. For example on the basis of an eight hour day the break down might be as follows:

Eight hour day – After deducting time spent on meals and breaks, unexpected minor interruptions, periods of distractions etc. – comes down to six hour day. Of this, four hours are set aside for ongoing projects. One hour is set aside for congestion periods when there is competition for channel time. The remaining hour is spent tidying up and starting preliminary work on new projects.

Let us suppose your record keeping shows that it is the first hour of the day on a Monday, Tuesday and Wednesday which is the most pressured. On the Thursday and Friday it is the last hour which produces the greatest congestion. Use a priority numbering system to list those tasks which have to be accomplished during the peak period and rigorously exclude non-essentials from this time. These items can be reallocated to a slack period of the day or week.

This type of procedure is not confined to offices. It can be used just as effectively to cope with congestion periods in the home or on the sports field. You should try and reach agreement with friends, work colleagues, children or spouses that you will not be disturbed during the congestion periods. In this way you can get through the peak of the channel demand without being further burdened. It is not unreasonable to ask that you receive no calls, see no visitors or that the children remain quiet and play on their own for a period of sixty minutes, say, each day.

This making of lists, record keeping and timetable planning of your life may strike you as a rather mechanical way to go about things, a system which denies that spontaneity of actions which gives variety to life. But it only appears formal and rather inflexible in the early days while you are having to *think* about it. Soon the procedure becomes so well integrated with your other activities that it begins to come naturally and leaves you much freer to make decisions which are both productive and spontaneous.

4. Allocation of Channel Capacity

For about five days you should notice those many small items on which you expend channel capacity and decide whether they are worth while or whether the same mental processing space could not be put to better use. For example you may spend a lot of time trying to memorise facts and figures which could more effectively be looked up as and when you need them. On the other hand you may use up a lot of time looking up numbers when a little effort spent in memorising key ones could speed up your communications considerably. There are no pat formulae for discovering which information you should devote your channel capacity to. List various mental activities and be quite ruthless in deciding to throw out any which absorb processing space without paying an adequate return.

5. Pacing Yourself

Some people appear to have an almost inexhaustible supply of energy. They seem to take on vast amounts of work and commitments and manage to honour them. But there is usually nothing mysterious about the way such people achieve these high outputs. It is done mostly through adequate *pacing*.

The experienced hard worker knows that there are some days or parts of days which will be extremely busy while others will have periods of dead time and be more relaxed. Although it has to be done in a fairly rough and ready way, the experienced mental manager will look at his week ahead and create an overall strategy for deploying effort in such a way that by the very end of the week they have just used up their quota of available energy, time and channel space before recuperating over the weekend. It is as though the energy available consists of a certain number of quanta, to borrow a phrase from physics. Let us suppose that there are one hundred quanta available for the five day week. It is by no means necessarily the case that twenty quanta will be allocated to each day. Our experienced pacer may look at Monday and see that, although there are two important meetings in the afternoon, the morning is relatively quiet and can be used to deal with the correspondence so Monday may only use up 11 or 12 quanta while Tuesday, with two staff meetings, three interviews and a trip to an outlying factory might necessitate 30 to 35 quanta. So through the whole week the experienced eye of the pacer can apportion approximate quanta to each day leaving something in reserve for emergencies. Even then the process can be more refined. At the start of his 35 quanta Tuesday it would be unwise for our business person to burn away 30 of them in the first half an hour. The quanta should be used up evenly through the day.

This conservation of energy is usually facilitated by the person's using other RCPs to control the effects of the Lifestyle Stressers. An RCP of major importance here is the one used to control High Level Negative Physical Responses which is taught in RCP Programme One.

In order to learn how to develop this facility of pacing you should look at your work schedule or diary for the coming week and roughly assign the percentage of quanta which you think you will need for each day. Use 100 quanta as your weekly allocation and divide these up between the days by comparing the demands of each day with another. Having done this it is then extremely important to match your behaviour and mental energy to the values which you have assigned each day. If Monday and Wednesday are going to be low activity days then make sure you keep them that way so as to save yourself for the three other days of high activity. There is no particular merit in rushing around *looking* for things to fill up the more relaxed moments of your day simply because you feel guilty about taking life more easily. You may have to work on this for two or three weeks to get the idea and convince yourself that the moments of low energy burning are as essential to effective performance as those times when you are running flat out to complete urgent complex tasks.

As an example of this necessity for pacing, taken from home life rather than the perhaps more obvious Area of Work and Study, to which it is also appropriate, let us consider the case of a lady who came to us complaining that she could never sit down and relax or do nothing at home. She always had to be moving around, keeping herself occupied. At any time when she could not do so she quickly became depressed and anxious. In looking at how her problem had developed it quickly became apparent that this was a lady who had always been used to working very hard during the early part of life and now, at the age of sixty-one and retired, no longer had much physical behaviour on which to expend her quanta of energy. Instead she had begun to build up 'problems' which she had to worry about. Previously she would never have bothered about not having dusted the house for a few days or what the evening meals in the coming week would be but now these became almost obsessional considerations in her life.

We taught her to recognise that while she certainly needed to expend her weekly quanta of energy she was doing so in an unproductive way. She learned to use RCP Programmes One (High Level Negative Physical Responses) and Nine (which showed her how to deal with Bereavement Stressers – in her case the bereavement of having lost a job which absorbed her energies). A few months later her obsession with inessential considerations had been replaced by productive and rewarding interests.

It is as essential for us to expend our quanta of energy as it is for a cow to be milked. But it is equally important for this energy to be used in ways which we find constructive and fulfilling rather than squandered.

6. Dealing with Temptation

Very often when we are settling down to or dealing with an important piece of work some minor irritation will suddenly present itself. While trying to use maximum channel capacity to perform efficiently we have an urgent desire to do something which is quite unimportant. We know one businessman who has an overwhelming desire to walk over to the window of his high rise office and view the passing scene just as he starts to dictate his letters. 'Of course I usually resist the temptation,' he commented. A woman confided that she was always irritated when settling down to her day's chores unless she had checked to see that all her house plants were watered, even though she knew that this job had been taken care of. Clearly such minor activities *ought* to have no demands to make on precious channel time. They should be relegated to those activities which, at congestion periods, we can well do without. Yet in practice this is rarely feasible. It may be possible to banish 99 per cent of the trivial, channel wasting activities from our schedules at peak periods but some minor activities may still have to be programmed in simply to prevent a rise in High Level Negative Mental Stress Responses being created by irritation. The best way to deal with such temptations is to give into them on *your* terms. If there are behaviours which you carry out and which interfere with your everyday routine of more important jobs then, if you cannot completely eradicate the behaviour, or do not wish to do so, decide that you will carry out a certain amount of it quite deliberately rather than suddenly find yourself carrying it out and feel guilty. This puts the piece of behaviour in your control and allows you to be able to say that you had *decided* to do it rather than have it happen unexpectedly. Very often such pieces of activity can be used as reinforcers and are helpful in establishing new, desired pieces of behaviour. How they can be used in this way will be explained in RCP Programme Three and in Stage Five.

7. Using Coping Statements

Where the mental confusion arises in the context of an anxiety response it often presents itself as negative statements about the circumstances and likely break down in performance. Such negative statements might range from 'I'll never be able to go to dinner tomorrow night at the Harris's because of that dog of theirs. I am absolutely terrified of him', to 'What an awful shot – it's landed in the rough. I'm bound to make a mess of my next iron shot – I always do on this fairway'.

If you have observed this kind of negative thinking on your part it is important, even if you are using RCP Programme One for physical anxiety reduction, to ensure that you stop the negative spiral effects of such damaging self talk. Remember that, in general, we tend to do what we expect to do. If you expected to fail again – you probably will! On the other hand if you expect to be able to cope then, equally, you probably will.

The coping statement's value is based on that premise. But for the statement to have maximum effect it must be phrased realistically. It is no use replacing your negative self statement with one such as: 'I am going to perform fantastically well and encounter no problems whatsoever.' If you do this any small hitch will undermine the truth of the statement and your own self-confidence. The statement must be of the type: 'This may be a little difficult but I can probably overcome the tricky part by . . .'. In order to fill in where we have put a row of dots it is necessary to appraise the piece of behaviour with which you are dealing carefully. Try and work out how you might cope a little more easily next time you make an attempt. Work this out in a cool way beforehand so that you have already prepared your coping statement, to some extent, before you tackle the problem. Run through the coping statement and the way you might put it into action in your mind's eye before you actually have to do it. Then, when you have attempted the situation and used the coping statement, debrief on how you managed. Never just leave a situation saying: 'That was awful' or 'I did fantastically'. Instead ask yourself, however briefly, *what* you did which made the situation go well or badly. Any little clue which you can find should then be built back into your coping statement so that you will be in a position next time you try to say: 'I may run into one or two difficulties but I will try to overcome them by doing what I did on the last occasion which was . . .'.

In other words remember that nothing happens by chance. You can learn from any experience, good or bad. This is an important point which is developed in greater detail in RCP Programmes Five and Nine.

8. Ideas in Action

There will always be situations which we cannot anticipate or plan for in the ways suggested so far. An examination, which requires quick thinking and the manipulation of ideas, an interview where questions may be thrown at you from all directions or an urgent problem at work where all the data has come in at once and requires sorting out.

You can practise coping with this sort of situation by using a technique called the *ideogram*. For the first few days practise written ideograms by setting yourself topics to explore and discuss in a short time period. If you are practising for examinations you can do this by looking at old examination papers. If you are doing a project at work you can practise by joining one or two of your colleagues' projects temporarily. Take a sheet of paper and begin to pour out any ideas or thoughts you have on the subject quite haphazardly. Write down anything, since if you do not write it down you may forget it, and if it turns out to be irrelevant, you can always cross it out again. When you have exhausted your supply of thoughts begin to look at them in relationship to one another. If you have spaced them out on the paper you will be able to draw arrows between them to link them up into logical trains of thought. From these trains of thought will probably flow yet more ideas, until the answer to a question or the interpretation of the data becomes increasingly clear.

You should practise the general principle of ideograms as often as you can. It is an amusing way to fill up a boring train journey as well as a useful way of spending the time when in the waiting room before an interview. You can jot down items which you want to remember to talk about during the interview as a flexible arrangement on the paper. Play around with connecting them up in different ways before going into the interview room. As you go in, put the ideogram away and the flexible array of ideas will still be fresh in your memory ready to be used when the appropriate questions are asked.

Summary

The procedures discussed in this Programme fall into four major categories which we have called the Four A's.

Analysis.
Anticipation.
Allocation.
Application.

First of all you *Analyse* your day to find those periods when you have the most and the least demands on your channel capacity. Then you *Anticipate* peaks and troughs of energy output and channel usage *Allocating* varying quanta as appropriate. Finally you *Apply* yourself to the structured work load using the strategies we have described above.

PROGRAMME FOUR – RCPs FOR – LOW LEVEL NEGATIVE MENTAL RESPONSES

These responses are frequently, but not inevitably, associated with Low Level Negative Physical Responses. In many cases the strategies for this Programme will be very similar to those described in RCP Programme Two.

Low Level Negative Mental Responses occur when the environment provides levels of mental stress or makes demands on mental capabilities which are insufficient to reach the OSL in the Life Area or activity concerned.

Typical situations in which Low Level Negative Mental Responses are found include:

After retirement from a job which was intellectually taxing.
When working at a job which does not provide sufficient mental interest and challenge.
When working or living with people whose conversation and interactions are lacking in stimulation.
When studying a subject at a level below one's intellectual capabilities.
In a new or unfriendly living environment where the chances of social interactions are limited.
When isolated from intellectual stimulation.

The usual symptoms of this lack of mental challenge are:

Depression.
Boredom.
Lack of inclination to think quickly or deeply.
A feeling that anything which challenges the intellect is too much trouble to bother with.
A loss of confidence in one's ability to reason effectively, memorise facts and figures reliably or respond adequately to an intellectual challenge.

In situations of underuse of mental capacity, the strategies which can be adopted fall into two categories. The first involves augmenting the existing mental stress in the Area of concern by directly adding to the stress level in the particular Life Area. The second group of strategies are to be used either together with this first approach or in place of them in those situations where it is impossible to add stresses directly to the Area under consideration. They involve increasing stress levels in alternative Life Areas while leaving the stress level in the Life Area concerned still at a low level. This increase in the overall, general, level of stress will enable the OSL to be reached.

For example, a student working on a course of study which, because of an extremely high aptitude she finds untaxing and where she has no difficulty in keeping up with the syllabus, may first try to increase her level of stress, and with it her level of enjoyment of the subject, by seeking out tutors and lecturers to ask if they can give her extra supervision and guidance into more advanced areas than the course is currently offering. This would be an ideal state of affairs for most students of this type but pressures on teaching staff make it impractical. In this case she may have to increase her mental stress load by attending lectures and courses *in addition* to her main course and also, possibly, by becoming active in an intellectual leisure pursuit such as chess or bridge or by developing an interest in literary or artistic pursuits. She might also decide to increase the mental stress level in emotional relationships. Quite often this type of individual becomes involved in an affair which provides emotional obstacles which have to be surmounted regularly in order for it to continue. It does seem from our clinical experience that it is among the more gifted and intelligent people that the most difficult romantic entanglements occur – usually because life might otherwise not provide sufficient difficulties and mental stresses.

Another example is that of a young mother with pre-school children who has given up a job outside the home to look after her family. In this case, while the physical demands of running the home may be very high, this young woman might well find that there is very little mental taxing of her capabilities. The first category of strategies, involving an augmenting of the mental stress level at home, might well be very difficult to implement in such a situation. She may have to look at other possibilities for increasing mental stress, such as taking up a course of evening study, when her husband can look after the children, and using this to provide her with periods of stimulation during the day when she is carrying out projects for the class. In time she may then be able to develop the skill of thinking about and planning for her course of study while carrying out physical chores around the house.

Many people, once they are aware of a lack of mental stress in certain Areas, and have acquired an understanding of the symptoms produced by the resulting Low Level Negative Mental Stress Responses, are able to devise specific strategies for themselves. The task of conceiving and putting into effect such strategies, possibly along the structured lines which will be described in Stage Five, could be the first such mental exercise designed to increase stress.

As in our RCP Programme Two, for Low Level Negative Physical Responses, we shall concentrate on the general principles of establishing the extra mental stresses necessary.

1. The Positive Payoff

As this part of the procedure is so similar to that described in Programme Two we advise you, at this point, to read the section on the Positive Payoff on pages 154–158.

However, it is important to make some additional statements for this RCP since often, when mental stress is well below the OSL, there is considerable lowering of personal self-image or confidence in one's abilities. We are including procedures for dealing with such a loss of confidence in this RCP Programme but we would remind you that it may well also occur with Low Level Negative Physical Responses.

To summarise briefly the Positive Payoff Principles as detailed in Programme Two remember the following key points:

Depression and feelings of uselessness are a direct product of your receiving insufficient rewards from your environment for your efforts.
Because you have received too few rewards for your efforts, they, in turn, decrease so, of course, the chances of receiving rewards also decreases.

It is this downward spiral of lack of effort chasing lack of reward which results in the Low Level Negative Mental Responses.

In order to increase the rewards or payoffs and so lift the depression it is necessary first to structure a significant but manageable increase in mental behaviour and then, having carried it out, to reinforce it using the type of payoffs which we noted in Programme Two and which we will tell you how to gather in more detail in Stage Five. For example, the young mother at home all day might begin by writing short stories for her and her neighbours' children and each time she completes a story, perhaps taking her two hours, she would give herself an anticipated reward such as soaking luxuriantly in a hot bath or going straight out to buy herself a new magazine.

Let us turn now to the problem of self-image. It is important to understand that if you frequently tell yourself that you are unable to do something or that it is not worth the effort to try to do something then you are almost certainly making a prophesy which will be fulfilled. In general we *are* what we expect to be and *do* what we expect to do. If you are constantly telling yourself, and others, that you are 'hopeless at sums', can 'never remember facts and figures for more than a few moments', are 'too unintelligent to attempt something new' or just plain 'impatient', then you will be setting yourself up to fail or not even try. Because of this it is of utmost importance that whenever you attempt a new piece of mental behaviour, whether you succeed or not, you should think about it afterwards and tell yourself all the positive and useful aspects of what you did. Consider the negative aspects only in terms of how you can work on them and get rid of them the next time. Do not dwell on them in a self-recriminatory way. When you succeed, spend time considering the positive features of your success and lavish praise upon yourself telling yourself that you *are* a competent person because you have *demonstrated* that you can perform a piece of behaviour effectively. Do not pass it off lightly as luck but spend several minutes in this self-congratulatory way.

2. The Psychological Value of Forward Planning

If you have reached the position that doing anything of a mental nature seems pointless because it will not interest you, a related problem will almost certainly be that you have lost sight of long-term goals. In *The Success Factor* we discussed at some length the importance of having both long-term goals and short-term strategies occurring at the same time since each gives a rationale for the other.

Let us look at how a large corporation keeps itself functioning and motivated and see how a directly similar procedure can be adopted by an individual. To understand how a company uses forward planning it is first necessary to understand the difference between strategies and tactics.

A *strategy* refers to an overall goal or aim within a specified period of time. For example, one company's strategy may be to develop a completely new product by the end of the next two years and to acquire, by take-overs, three new subsidiary companies to assist in the production of this new product so that they effectively control an entirely self-sufficient production plant.

A *tactic* is one of the means of reaching this overall strategic position. The tactics used will be determined by the immediate needs of the moment on the way to the overall strategy. They will be developed according to changes in the economic climate, changes in managerial staff, changes in availability in materials for the product and the results of research and development. In other words a tactic deals with those situations which cannot be predicted with any great accuracy.

Let us suppose that in a large corporation a five-year forward planning strategy is established in year one. The object of that strategy is that by the end of year five a product will have been researched, developed, in production and completely controlled by the parent organisation. In year one, however, certain tactical decisions will have to be taken in order to reach the first stages of this overall strategy. The results of early research will have to be assessed, the viability of different companies under investigation appraised and so on. By the end of the first year a very different 'state of the arts' may have emerged.

At this point, one year after beginning, the organisation planners look at the results of the efforts to date and, on this basis, create a new five-year strategy which may be identical with the first one or modified in the light of experience. Whatever the case they have now decided on a fresh five-year strategy to end at the end of year six. Exactly the same tactical and assessment procedures are carried on for the second year and at the end of that year a new overall strategy is developed for the coming five years.

It may seem, at first, as though the planners could be changing their minds drastically every year and so never get anywhere with their products. But, in fact, this mixture of the tactics with the strategies forms the best sort of security against making disastrous decisions and becoming irrevocably committed, while ensuring that even better decisions are not overlooked. For example if, in the early stages of development, it is obvious that a project is going to be less profitable and tie up more capital than was at first anticipated it can be dropped after only one year of effort on the firm's part. Even more useful, however, are the frequent off-shoot projects which evolve out of some of the tactics which have been employed in the first year or two. Very often, when trying to reach one overall goal, it becomes clear along the way that another goal is possible and even more viable than the first. In that case the planners will examine this sort of tactical outcome and may then adjust the overall strategy towards this newer and more viable goal. A good illustration of these procedures in action is the development of the drug Nootropil (2-oxo-pyrrolidine acetamide) by the Belgian pharmaceutical company Union Cepha Belgique. In 1963 this firm synthesised a compound, named Piracetam, which they thought might be effective as a sedative. However, tests proved disappointing. They then changed tactics and tested the drug as an antidote to motion sickness. Once again results were disappointing. Then it was thought that Piracetam might be useful in the treatment of Nystagmus, a disease which causes eye flicker. Again they encountered failure. So a fresh tactic was adopted, based on the finding that during trials with patients many of those treated had reported an improvement of memory. Later tests with animals, based on these reports, proved that Piracetam was able to increase the transfer of information from one side of the brain to the other. It was renamed Nootropil (it means 'towards mind') and further tested as a memory improvement drug. Today it is widely used in Europe for this purpose.

This example shows clearly the major values to be gained from the correct use of tactics and strategies. UCB's overall strategy was to develop a new drug which could be used as a sedative. But they found, by careful appraisal of chance factors in their research programme, that much more interesting properties could be attributed to the drug and decided, on the basis of these tactical findings, to create a new overall strategy. But this change was made on well-defined grounds and research findings. It was not a haphazard shift in direction.

The same procedures can be used to control low levels of mental stress in everyday life. Just as a large organisation must operate with a flexible mixture of long-term strategies and practical, short-term tactics, so too do we need such a combination of goals and tactics in order to carve a pathway through the jungle of ideas and possibilities which confront us in life.

Take the case of an adolescent in his last years at school who has the ambition of becoming a doctor. This is a long-term goal which he knows he will not be able to achieve for at least ten years. In order to reach this goal he is advised to use certain tactics. These involve following the right courses of study in order to gain the correct educational qualifications for him to enter medical college. As a result of using these tactics successfully he is able to start his medical studies. But, during the first year of the course, he finds that he is less interested in medicine than in the subsidiary course of sociology. At the end of that year he makes the decision, on the basis of information only now available to him, to change to the sociology course and he obtains a degree in that subject through using the necessary tactics of study and practical work. On leaving university he starts work. His long-term goal now is to head the social services department of which he is a junior member. Accordingly he uses tactics to attain promotion and develop his skills. Later, by chance, he meets a fiction writer and they collaborate on a novel dealing with the society of the future and its dependency on drugs and medicine. The book is a best seller and causes yet another change of direction in his life. He decides to become a fiction writer working in a specialised field. None of these changes has been rushed into. All have depended on the outcome of tactical decisions and a careful appraisal of the twists of circumstances.

Clearly not all such changes of strategy and tactics are as glamorous or successful as those in our example. Most of the long-term strategies with which we deal in our lives involve such decisions as where to live, what careers to follow, how to bring up our children, how to achieve recognition in society, how to fill our leisure time and where to go on holidays. Without these major overall goals there would be little point in the day-to-day tactical behaviour of a working routine, deciding on which schools offer the best education, looking through travel brochures, and so on.

In order to remain mentally stimulated you must do two

things. First plan, in definite terms, goals in all of your Life Areas to be reached in the medium term – say between one and five years ahead. For example:

Life Area	Medium Term Goals
'A': Work and Study	Obtaining a degree. Becoming managing director of a subsidiary company. Returning to work career after children have left home.
'B': Family, Marriage, Sex and Intimacy	Getting married. Completing children's education. Learning to satisfy partner's sexual needs.
'C': Social and Interpersonal Relationships	Becoming popular as an after-dinner speaker. Spending time regularly with an intimate. Losing weight and maintaining the loss. Stopping smoking.
'D': Leisure and Sport	Playing a game of golf off scratch. Becoming a regular member of competition team. Deciding on holiday location.

Secondly, develop and follow a series of structured tactics which will lead you towards those overall goals. This is probably best done in the following manner.

The Method Maze

Having written out all the major goals you would like to achieve in the four Life Areas, select one goal on which to make a start. Write this goal at the bottom right hand corner of a large sheet of paper. On the top left hand corner write your starting point, where you stand at this moment in terms of the overall goal.

For example, in the case of our first goal in Life Area A 'Obtaining a degree', the starting point would clearly be your educational qualifications and current interests. Now write down, at random and as they come into your mind, all the steps which would be needed to achieve the overall goal. These might include: preparing a letter of application to a suitable college, listing your qualification for a place on a desired course, sending away for details of degree courses available, preparing a short list of convenient colleges, finding out about grants and scholarships, planning to gain additional qualifications if necessary to reach required standard and so on. Jot all these ideas down in the space between current attainment and desired goal. Once you have emptied all the thoughts on the subject from your mind you should start to join up the ideas with arrows in a logical sequence of priority. Frequently while doing this new ideas and the need for further intermediate tactics will occur to you and can be written in. Once the 'Method Maze' has been completed copy out the information, listing all the tactical steps in numerical order. To achieve the overall goal you must now work through this list from tactic to tactic. Of course, as we made clear in our general examples, situations can change and some tactics may become redundant. Alternatively you may find that changes in your own attitudes or ambitions cause switches in tactics and, perhaps, shifts in the overall goal. But these changes can be made on the basis of an *objective* decision arrived at from an appraisal of the available information, not on a whim or simply for the sake of changing. This system is very effective in stimulating the mind and helping you to overcome low level stress.

3. Mental Massage and the Thought Tank

The second general procedure which is helpful in this area of Low Level Negative Mental Responses we have termed 'Mental Massage'. Its aim is to raise the overall taxing of mental capacities. In Programme Three we drew an analogy to a telephone switchboard and said that as with a switchboard, mental channel capacity could suffer from overflow problems. If a complex piece of electronic equipment like a switchboard is left unused or is underused for an extended period, it may develop faults through neglect. So too can your mental functioning atrophy. The object of Mental Massage is to ensure that the brain's circuitry gets a regular 'flow through' of stimulation even during periods of life which are not very taxing. The main procedure for Mental Massage is the Thought Tank.

Preparing a Thought Tank

Each day, set aside around thirty minutes and settle down with a pen or pencil and some large sheets of paper. Write down every thought which you have on a particular subject. You can draw inspiration from any source you like, gossip and chance remarks, TV or radio programmes, books or newspaper articles. The subject chosen can be unrelated to anything currently happening in your life, or it can involve some project or problem you are confronting at the moment. The bored office worker may find it more interesting to pick a general topic on which to exercise the mind. A student busy with revision might find it more helpful to relate the Thought Tank to an area of study.

Once you have filled as much of the sheet as possible with the first outpourings of ideas start to juggle them around by using arrows to link one concept to the next, one thought to another. You must form the connections in a logical manner, if necessary writing down additional phrases to make such join ups possible. Thought Tanks not only use the mind in a creative and interesting way, they can produce valuable spin-offs. The student may find a fresh way of looking at well-known material, the businessman discover a new approach to a nagging problem, the housewife uncover valuable insights about a troubling relationship.

You will find that there is a direct connection between the number of apparently unconnected thoughts that you can write down and the number of interesting conclusions which can be drawn from the Thought Tank. When you have become proficient in creating individual Tanks you should start joining the sheets up to form Hyper-Thought Tanks. We often advise students who are revising to create Thought Tanks for each of their subject areas and then to stick these up on a wall to make one large Thought Tank for the entire field to be revised. This is when the Thought Tanks become most fascinating and valuable, as different areas of thought begin to connect up and produce hybrid thoughts and ideas. Such a technique is not limited to students' revision programmes. The Critical Path Analysis chart has long been popular in business and the Hyper-Thought Tank can be seen as the qualitative complement of the more quantitative and time-based Critical Path Analysis. In the home Hyper-Thought Tanks can give a whole family ideas about holiday arrangements, leisure pursuits, and, most important of all, topics of conversation and discussion as each member of the family can begin to add ideas and connections to the Hyper-Thought Tank which includes separate contributions from everybody. It is rather like a wall full of graffiti but serves a much more valuable and practical function. Try it and see how compelling it can be to add your next thought on a subject. The chart can be pinned up on the wall of any suitable room but one in which we have found it to be the most fruitful for ideas is the bathroom!

Summary

To overcome depression and lack of drive resulting from Low Level Negative Mental Responses you must raise the level of mental stress to the OSL.

This can be achieved by augmenting the amount of stress in the Life Area or activity directly concerned, by raising the stress levels in other Areas so as to bring up the overall level, or through a combination of both approaches.

Your current mental self-image is largely determined by the

view you hold of yourself in relation to the world around you. Negative comments about your thoughts and abilities are harmful and increase Negative Mental Responses. Always be positive about yourself and your capabilities.

After any situation which you have found mentally stimulating or pleasing, debrief yourself to find out exactly what you said, or did, which was so satisfying. Develop and use these items in the future.

In order to exercise the mind and prevent atrophy through neglect, use Mental Massage and Thought Tanks. Use reinforcement procedures to build up confidence, achieving a good self-image and establish new pieces of mental behaviour.

PROGRAMME FIVE – RCPs FOR – PERFORMANCE LIFESTYLE STRESSERS

Performance Stressers arise when the degree of complexity of any piece of behaviour which you are attempting increases to a point where your existing skill level is exceeded.

Under these circumstances new skills have to be generated to cope with the additional demands on Performance. These skills, like any others which have been used to deal with previous tasks, have to be learned in a methodical way and it is important to understand that the mastering of any new skill goes through three major stages.

The first is called **Acquisition**. In this stage you learn to deal with progressively more and more complex aspects of the behaviour which you are trying to perfect. It is during this phase that you will go through periods of change in the rate of progress at which you master the skill because you are constantly being met with new tasks to which you have to give a lot of thought and work out how to cope with them. Good examples of this are learning to drive a car, play a sport or musical instrument, speak another language or use a typewriter.

After this **Acquisition** comes the **Plateau or Internalisation** phase where, because of a lot of practice at the skill, you begin to carry it out without having to think about it. Your responses to a particular task become automatic and quite often you can think of other things while carrying it out.

The third stage is **Generalisation**. This refers to the ability to carry out a similar skill but under different conditions – such as driving different makes of car, typing on a variety of machines, switching from one sport to another slightly different one or acquiring a third language more easily than the second because the principles of language learning in general have been acquired.

If you are faced with a challenging situation which requires new Performance skills and produces a Performance Stresser, you must work towards controlling this Stresser by acquiring the skill to a degree where it becomes *Internalised*. If you always have to stop and think laboriously how to do it the Performance stress will remain quite high.

Clearly if the problems confronting you arise as a result of Low Level Negative Responses, then one way of raising your stress level towards the OSL is to make a habit of acquiring new skills every so often so there is always a Performance Stresser of *Acquisition* somewhere in your lifestyle. But more often than not you will wish to reduce the stress because you are suffering from High Level Negative Stress Responses. This can be achieved using the strategies described in general in RCP Programmes One and Three and the more specific procedures which now follow.

Possible Sources of Performance Stress in the Four Life Areas

The following types of behaviours, some of which you may not have previously considered as Stressers, can give rise to Performance Stress if they have been insufficiently practised to become *Internalised*.

Life Area — Work and Study

Dealing with employees' mistakes; approaching employer to ask for a pay rise; holding office meetings; attending interviews; taking examinations; revising; note taking; finishing projects on schedule; answering correspondence; planning weekly office routine; answering telephone calls; interviewing potential employees; operating new machinery; dealing with enquiries and complaints; adapting to new work schedule or conditions.

Life Area B — Family, Marriage, Sex and Intimacy

Conversing with partner in family; talking to children; accepting partner's individual needs; asserting your own requirements; having a productive row; showing affection; giving compliments and credit; making love; compromising; disclosing intimate thoughts and needs.

Life Area C – Social and Interpersonal Relationships

Making new friends; approaching groups for conversation; telling an anecdote; speaking in public; saying 'no' without embarrassment; giving and receiving deserved compliments; dating somebody you are interested in; giving a party; conversing with strangers.

Life Area D – Leisure and Sport

Playing a better game of golf or other favourite sport; travelling on holiday; starting a new hobby; approaching retirement; learning a new sport or joining a new club.

Diverse as all these pieces of behaviour may seem, there are fundamental rules which can be applied in order to make their Performance easier and less stressful.

1. Specifying the Goal

Before you can increase your Performance effectively, the first requirement is that you specify the skill which you are trying to acquire or the goal you are trying to obtain. This must be done quite specifically and rather than vaguely stated such as: 'I wish my wife and I had enjoyable conversations' or 'I wish my golf was better'. You should state your goals in the following way: 'My wife and I will aim towards a half hour period each evening free of interruptions when we can each present our points of view on items of personal interest and discuss our day', or 'I must concentrate on my strokes on the greens and develop tactics for the short game'.

In stating any goal it is necessary to include three main components.

(1) You must make the goal specific and refer to particular times and places relevant to the behaviour. For example: 'At work when discussing a problem with colleagues I would like to present myself more forcefully', rather than: 'I wish I were better at meetings.'

(2) You must make the goal positive: 'I would like to be able

G

to . . .' rather than 'I wish I did not . . .'. For example:
'I would like to be able to make love more enjoyably with
my partner' rather than: 'I wish I did not become so tense
and inhibited when making love.'

(3) You must make the goal realistic, since if you are aiming
for an unattainable goal you will inevitably be subjected
to failure and depression.

2. Structuring a Pathway

Having specified a goal in the correct way, the next step is to
create a pathway of sub-goals which will allow you to reach it
in the most rapid and effective way. It is important when
selecting sub-goals to ensure that they do not represent too
great a jump in behaviour acquisition. If they do then you run
the risk of failing when you attempt the next sub-goal and so
lowering your motivation towards obtaining the main goal. On
the other hand the steps must not be too small or you may make
such slow progress that you become bored and lose motivation
this way. You should try to use the method, described in
Programme Four, of writing down the desired goal at the bottom
right hand side of a large piece of paper and the current
situation, in relation to that goal, in the top left hand corner.
The sheet can then be filled with possible sub-goals taken at
random from your knowledge of what must be done in order to
acquire the final skill. These ideas should be linked with arrows
so that a separate list of sub-goal skills can be drawn up with
each successive sub-goal following on logically from the last.

The best way of illustrating this procedure is to take examples
of goals and sub-goals from typical ambitions in the four Life
Areas. It should however be noted that this RCP is designed to
provide an *overall* strategy for learning the relevant sub-goal
skills which will eliminate Performance Stressers. To acquire the
specific skills contained in many of the sub-goals which we
detail below it may be necessary to refer to a specialist reference
work, for example a sex education manual, a book on

accountancy or business management or a practical guide to performing a particular sport. Alternatively you may care to read our earlier book *The Success Factor* which deals with a large number of commonly expressed goals in the four Life Areas and gives specific, practical strategies.

Life Area A – Work and Study

Major Goal: 'I would like to be able to present material more effectively to groups of colleagues at work.' Note that this goal is correctly stated since it is:

(1) Specific and refers to particular times and places in which the new skill is to be performed.
(2) Positive.
(3) Realistic.

Current Situation: 'Feel my current presentations are dull and do not bring out the best points. Hard to hold attention of colleagues. Feel tense and uncomfortable. Resent criticism and unable to deal with it effectively.'

Random Jottings of Possible Sub-Goal Skills: Learn to speak more slowly. Speak more forcefully. Increase voice volume. Make better notes from which to work. Prepare major points for any argument or discussion. Learn to relax quickly to combat anxiety. Learn to steer discussion back to major topic when it has strayed from point. Be more assertive. Prepare for criticisms. Be able to dismiss trivial interventions. Be more confident about my ability. Be less in awe of some colleagues.

Random Jottings Rewritten as Ordered Sub-Goal Skills

(1) Learn relaxation from RCP Programme One.
(2) Learn principles of structuring information quickly from RCP Programme Three. (If the analysis programme in Stage Three had been carried out correctly a person suffering from this Stresser would have been directed to these Programmes automatically.)
(3) Take elocution lessons or practise at home with tape recorder to get pace and volume of speech correct.

(4) Practise speaking at home with small group of friends to gain confidence.

(5) Learn to make good notes which quite clearly state the major points.

(6) Learn to stick to main points even though there is considerable pressure to change course. Use friends to play 'devil's advocates' in mock presentation situations.

Once these skills have been *Internalised* the inevitable increase in confidence will enable this man to assert his position and ability firmly, to deal with trivial criticisms firmly and to relate to his colleagues as an equal.

Life Area B – Family, Marriage, Sex and Intimacy

Major Goal: 'I would like to be able to control my rapid ejaculation when having sex with my wife.'

Current Situation: 'Feel anxious when about to make love. Thought keeps going through my mind I will ejaculate prematurely. Worried wife will be unsatisfied.'

Random Jottings of Possible Sub-Goal Skills: 'Must learn to relax. Must learn to think more positively about sex. Must make sex more fun. Discuss situation with wife. Must learn to notice moment when I lose control. Attempt different positions to see if that helps. Try to control ejaculation while stimulating penis by hand.'

Random Jottings Rewritten as Ordered Sub-Goal Skills

(1) Discuss building up programme with wife.

(2) Learn positive coping statements from RCP Programme Three. (Once again correct analysis of the situation in Stage Three will have directed a man with this type of Negative Stress Response towards this Programme.)

(3) Learn relaxation from RCP Programme One.

(4) While relaxed get wife to stimulate penis manually stopping her when I get close to orgasm.

(5) While relaxing on my back have wife insert my penis into her vagina staying still so that I can control the situation.

(6) Ask wife to move up and down on my penis while I am lying on my back.

(7) Insert my penis into wife's vagina in other positions.

(8) Insert my penis and increase the amount of thrusting and resting each time I feel ejaculation imminent.

Life Area C — Social and Interpersonal Relationships

Major Goal: 'I would like to be able to make new friends.'

Current Situation: 'Feel lonely and isolated in new neighbourhood. Shy and do not like making the first move to start conversation. Worried about appearance. Lack confidence.'

Random Jottings of Possible Sub-Goal Skills: 'Go to local clubs. Try evening classes. Arrange party. Invite neighbours for coffee morning. Dinner party. Local sports club. Learn to approach groups and join conversations. Increase confidence. Control tension when talking to people. Learn to listen to what people are saying. Learn how to tell anecdotes.'

Random Jottings Rewritten as Ordered Sub-Goal Skills

(1) Learn Quick and Differential relaxation skills from RCP Programme One.

(2) Find out where local clubs meet and evening classes are held.

(3) Set up role-playing situation at home, possibly with members of the family, to practise approaching and joining a group for conversation.

(4) Practising listening skills and picking up other people's interests.

(5) Learning how to tell an anecdote well so as to avoid boring people, again through practice with someone who could provide constructive criticism about pace, volume and timing etc.

(6) Start going to clubs and classes.

(7) Approach people for conversation at such meetings.

(8) Offer invitations and accept those offered to you by others.

Life Area D — Leisure and Sport

Major Goal: 'I would like to be able to develop an interest in dancing.'

Current Situation: 'Very little experience of dancing. Afraid I will be no good at it and may make a fool of myself.'

Random Jottings of Possible Sub-Goal Skills: 'Join dancing class. Ask friends who dance to recommend private teacher. Go to dances to watch how others perform. Read book on dancing. Learn to move easily and without tension. Become more confident. Practise steps in privacy of home. Find partner who will be helpful and not critical in early stages. Experiment with different types of dancing to find one I like best. Go to dances. Say "Yes" when asked to dance.'

Random Jottings Rewritten as Ordered Sub-Goal Skills

(1) Find out details of suitable class to join.

(2) Learn Differential relaxation, to be used when dancing, from Programme One.

(3) Go to first two or three classes with a friend who is at my level of competence.

(4) Practise at home.

(5) Go to smaller dances and practise further.

(6) Accept dance invitations and practise with partner.

In the above situations it should be noticed that not all the random jottings were used as not all of them were very meaningful. 'Increase confidence' stated as a possible sub-goal skill in the last example is not much use on its own and would come as a natural consequence of more practice at the activity.

3. Self-Reinforcement

As we described in RCP Programmes Two and Four the important principle of reinforcement can be used to help establish the desired behaviours. After each practice period you should try to spend a few minutes doing two very important things and in this order:

(1) Carry out some pleasant activity or enjoy some pleasurable reward for having attempted and practised the behaviour.

(2) Debrief on your practice period by going over what you have done and seeing why things went well, when they did, and how you can improve on the patches which were not so good.

4. Constant Practice

The development of any skill is directly related to the consistency with which it is practised. It is much better to practise little and often than to go for days without doing anything and then guiltily engage in a long period of practice as you will then 'habituate' much too quickly. That is you will stop analysing your progress and carry on making the same unnecessary mistakes. If you practise little and often you will be able to carry on the debriefing regularly after each practice session and ultimately to learn much more quickly.

Summary

Performance Stress occurs when a skill is insufficiently developed to meet current demands, which can be physical, mental or a mixture of both, on the individual.

A skill is only properly learned if it is *Internalised* and can be carried out without having to think about it.

Skills can only be learned if they are accurately specified and if the sub-skills are learned in a logical and analytical series of steps. This will require consistent practice and debriefing together with self-reinforcement for each attempt at a practical session.

Remember that putting this Programme or any other part of this book into effect is a learned piece of behaviour so that the principles which we have discussed here apply to the ways in which you gradually acquire RCPs. At first you may find the procedures rather mechanical and demanding of your time. This is inevitable in the *Acquisition* stage. Once you have *Internalised* any RCP Programme, however, it becomes a natural and easily implemented part of your behavioural repertoire.

PROGRAMME SIX – RCPs FOR – THREAT
LIFESTYLE STRESSERS

Threat Stressers arise when elements in an individual's environment are assessed as threatening to survival. Typical situations in which Threat Stressers are found include:

Occupations or sports involving actual danger. For example, working in a hazardous environment, in some sections of heavy industry, in many construction jobs, as a demolition or mining engineer, as a test pilot or deep sea diver; in such sports as parachuting, sky-diving, climbing and mountaineering, racing, pot-holing, hang-gliding, aerobatics and motorcycle scrambling.

Being in a supervisory capacity which involves placing others at risk.

In areas of war, riot, violent demonstrations, civil disorder or high crime risk.

Reports of any of these situations occurring can also give rise to Threat Stressers. Many people live in a state of underlying tension at the thought of international conflicts even though their own country is not primarily concerned. Threat Stressers also exist in situations where a person *believes* that some physical danger exists even though it objectively does not. These responses constitute what are commonly called phobias.

The effects of exposure to this form of stress vary according to the type and duration of the Stresser but generally speaking it is convenient to break these effects down into three major components.

Initial Anxiety Surge

At the moment of being confronted by the Threat Stresser, which may be an actual danger or a phobic situation, there is an initial surge of anxiety which can be either physical or mental in nature or a mixture of both responses.

Physical responses vary from one person to the next but will generally be experienced as one or more of the following:

Stomach turning over, nausea, feeling faint, rapid heart rate, increased perspiration, irregular or rapid breathing, muscle tension, dry throat, dizziness.

Mental responses usually take the form of one of two types of statements in the face of the Threat:

'I am going to panic and lose control very quickly', or:
'I must get away from here. I can't carry on in this situation any longer.'

In the majority of cases both a mental and physical anxiety surge will be felt more or less at the same time. It is at this stage that the person may become afraid or anxious about the initial surge of fear *itself*. When this happens there is not only anxiety about the threatening situation but stress from inside the body to add to that environmental stress. After this initial anxiety surge the stressed person is frequently poised to become anxious about the anxiety.

Panic and the Anxiety Spiral

After the initial anxiety surge the situation has changed considerably. The stressed person is now no longer faced with an objective situation but by a mixture of an objectively stressful environment plus a subjective strain level. The total of these two produces an overall environmental stress *greater* than that which produced the initial anxiety surge. As we explained in Stage Two, this heightened environmental stress produces another anxiety surge greater than the initial one. This is even more frightening for the person experiencing it and, again, this second anxiety surge adds itself to the first one and the environmental stress to produce a third overall stress level which is greater still. The whole cycle continues to spiral until the person is totally panic

G*

stricken with uncontrolled anxiety. At this point the usual experience is one of complete mental confusion with the only thought being a wish to escape completely, together with extremes of physical tension, racing heart, excessive perspiration and possibly even total faint. The condition will continue at this level for a variable period of time. The anxiety having reached panic proportions stops at a plateau beyond which the body is actually incapable of increasing the fear response. This is known as the '*Panic Plateau*'.

Habituation and Recuperation

In the majority of cases a person suffering from an anxiety spiral makes a strenuous, and frequently successful, attempt to escape from the environmental Stresser. If this is achieved then the anxiety level will drop, heart beat and respiration return to normal and the mind start functioning clearly again. If the Threat is produced by an objective danger then such an escape may be the most sensible and safest method of dealing with the Stresser. But there are many situations where flight is either impossible or will produce very undesirable consequences.

If a person remains in the presence of a Threat Stresser the level of anxiety may rise quickly to the Panic Plateau above which it is impossible for the body to experience further anxiety. After a while the body will apply its own braking mechanism and the anxiety level will start to decrease and even disappear as the condition of stress is habituated (see Diagram Five). As the anxiety level drops, thinking becomes more rational and the body starts to relax. Finally the person becomes free of anxiety and is able to carry out normal behaviour once again while still in the presence of the anxiety producing Stresser. Habituation occurs because the individual has learned, by experience, that there is no need for the extremes of anxiety. The environment, although apparently threatening, has not harmed them.

Take, for example, the plight of a motorist stranded at night while driving through African bush land. At first he is terrified

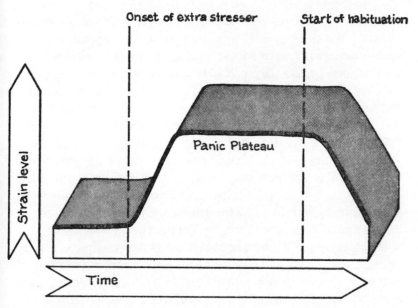

Diagram Five: Showing habituation to a constant source of stress in the presence of which there is no actual need for high levels of sympathetic arousal (e.g. in the presence of a phobic stimulus).

by the intense darkness, the unfamiliar sounds and the occasional gleam of eyes from the blackness. If he is without experience of such an environment, panic may well set in. But, after a time, as nothing terrible happens to him, his level of anxiety will fall away and he will be able to function in a normal manner. The same situation can arise when a person from a small country town moves into a big city with a reputation for violent crime. The first time he or she goes out alone on the streets a high level of anxiety may occur, perhaps amounting to panic. But, provided nothing actually happens to them – and statistically it probably will not, even in the most ill-reputed city – they become increasingly confident about their ability to survive. After a time they probably feel no anxiety at all.

In both these examples there were good reasons for assessing the environment as dangerous and threatening. But in a phobic situation the sufferer may perceive danger in some object or situation which does not, in reality, pose any Threat at all. If such a person is forced to confront that object or situation for an extended period they will habituate to it and no longer feel anxious. This fact is the basis of a form of treatment for phobias known as *'flooding'*. In *flooding* the phobic is confronted with the Threat Stresser in a situation where escape is impossible. Spider phobics, for instance, might be locked in a room filled with large hairy spiders. Unable to get away they will experience extremes of terror and their anxiety will rapidly reach panic proportions. But as their pleas to be released go unanswered they gradually habituate to the animals. Eventually they will no longer feel any anxiety even if spiders crawl all over them.

If you experience all three components of a complete anxiety or panic spiral you will emerge at the end of the cycle in one of two main ways. Either you will have habituated to the situation and no longer feel any of the discomforting effects of anxiety or you will have reduced anxiety slightly from the Panic Plateau but still be functioning at an excessively high level of strain. Whether you have habituated to the situation or simply adapted to the high level of strain should be apparent from a subjective appraisal of how you feel. If you are performing quite competently, comfortably and under control after the cycle of anxiety then you have probably habituated. The next time you go into that situation it will be much less likely to throw you into an anxiety spiral. Even if it does you will know that you can habituate to the situation as you did on the previous occasion. If, after the stress spiral, you are able to carry on but you still experience exhaustingly high levels of physical anxiety then you are probably only adapting to the strain level and simply putting up with the fact that you are still highly aroused.

It is clearly possible, if very unpleasant, to use habituation as a means of controlling anxiety. Fortunately there is an RCP for use with Threat Stressers which entirely removes the second and third components of the anxiety spiral. Before we explain how this RCP works, however, it will be as well to look at the damaging consequences of the two most commonly chosen strategies for dealing with Threat Stressers, those of *Avoidance* and *Adaptation*.

Avoidance

As the anxiety spiral begins to accelerate or when the Panic Plateau has been reached one tactic which the sufferer will often use is that of escape. Clearly this is a very effective way of reducing the Threat Stresser. But it has highly undesirable side effects, the most obvious one being that it limits your lifestyle and reduces your potential. You may be unable to visit certain places, talk to certain people, do certain jobs of work, travel by a particular means of transport, stay in desired locations or perform pieces of behaviour which others take for granted. This is incapacitating enough each time the situation arises but the less obvious undesirable effect can be even more damaging because it is much more insidious. To understand this we must explain about *Negative Reinforcement*.

We have already said that behaviour which is followed by a positive reward (that is something which you enjoy happening to you) rapidly becomes established and is likely to occur frequently. However, the same is true if a piece of behaviour is immediately followed by the *removal* of a very *unpleasant* or punishing occurence. There are two ways in which a piece of behaviour can become a rigid part of your repertoire; either by following it with a positive reward or by following it with the removal of something punishing.

Now we can see the undesirable consequence of fleeing from a situation which is providing stress and anxiety. As soon as you successfully escape from it the escape behaviour is followed by an immediate removal of something punishing – that is, anxiety feelings. As a result, the behaviour of escaping becomes reinforced and therefore more likely to be repeated in future. This is just what happens. Each time a person is faced with a situation providing anxiety spirals the escape response is chosen because it has been reinforced in the past. Eventually the escape is carried out *even* when the situation is only *anticipated as possibly arising*. This is called avoidance responding. You avoid going into any situation where you may become anxious because of anticipatory anxiety. This anxiety is then removed and the negative reinforcement such avoidance produced helps to establish up a whole repertoire of avoidance behaviour. It is in this way that a phobic response is established. The potential air phobic, for example, anticipates the anxiety of a journey by plane and instead travels by boat and train in order to avoid the anxiety producing situation. If this behaviour is repeated, and the presence of negative reinforcers – relief at not having to fly – make it very likely that it will be, then that person becomes phobic about flying. Similarly an employee who avoids a direct confrontation with his or her boss, perhaps over pay and conditions, may build up a repertoire of escaping strategies. By writing memos, leaving messages with secretaries or attempting to negotiate through a third party, they rapidly reach a stage where they have become phobic about their boss. In the same way a wife who refuses to discuss certain subjects with her husband or children, perhaps through a feeling of inhibition, may develop avoidance strategies such as changing the subject, refusing to talk about that particular topic or even leaving the room each time the subject is brought up. Avoidance brings relief, relief provides negative reinforcement which establishes the behaviour. Avoidance patterns gradually generalise until whole areas of living have become completely obstructed. This is particularly obvious in the case of most agoraphobics, who are usually not only entirely housebound but also have other phobias and difficulties, often of a sexual or interpersonal nature all of which operate within an avoidance system.

Clearly in times of real physical danger – for instance under battle conditions, or if about to be subjected to a criminal attack – avoidance may be the only logical and effective step to take. But in all normal circumstances there is only one safe way of dealing with avoidance – avoid it!

Adaptation

If, no matter how desirable it may seem at the time, avoidance is not possible, then the only alternative – once an anxiety spiral is in full operation – is to accept the fact that high levels of stress and strain are going to be a part of life.

A distinction must be drawn here between habituation to a Threat Stresser and adaptation to it. In habituation the person eventually loses any trace of anxiety connected with the Stresser. Stress which will have soared above the OSL during the early stages, will have gradually returned to its old level. In adaptation the individual lives with anxiety which is never habituated because it stems from a constant stream of slightly different environmental Stressers. For example, a front line soldier will habituate to a certain amount of Threat posed by the dangers of battle. After extended exposure to the sights and sounds of war, his initial high anxiety level will diminish. Things which were earlier perceived as being extremely dangerous, perhaps the distant rumble of guns or the sounds of machine-gun fire, will no longer produce anxiety. But there will also be a high level of anxiety from hour by hour and day by day Threat Stressers. The shell which bursts just above the trench, the man who is shot by sniper fire in the immediate vicinity, the explosion that destroys a nearby building. These will be coped with through adaptation to an excessively high level of stress. In the same way a businessman working under great pressure, threatened by redundancy, by competitors, by inefficiency on the shop floor, will habituate to many of the Threat Stressers. But at the same time the unpredictable nature of other Stressers in his environment will prevent them from being habituated. He will simply learn to live, as effectively as he can, under great strain. Such adaptation can only be bought at a cost of physical and mental health and the price is often paid in heart disease, high blood pressure, ulcers or a nervous breakdown.

Furthermore, while trying to live under excessive stress the individual will not be able to perform at full potential because, as should now be clear, this can only be achieved at the OSL.

The RCP Programme detailed here is free of the negative consequences of **Avoidance** and **Adaptation** and concentrates on the beneficial and easily implemented procedure of **Anxiety Management**.

This Programme has also been recorded by one of the authors of this book (Dr Robert Sharpe) as an audio home training programme and is available through *Stresswatch*. It contains detailed instructions in the methods we now describe.

Anxiety Management

1. The Relaxation Response

The first step in your Anxiety Management RCP is to follow the instructions given in Programme One on Relaxation training. You should first become confident in your ability to relax at will in non-stressful situations as described in that Programme. If you practise the RCP twice each day you should find that you can relax within a few seconds whether you are stationary or moving around.

2. Developing Positive Self-Talk

The second step is to learn how to prepare and use Coping Statements and Positive Self-Talk as described in Programme Three. Devise a list of strategies which you can repeat to yourself very quickly. Here again you should first practise in non-stressful environments. Remember that the mental strategies or positive self-talk statements should always be realistic and accept that difficulties will arise but also provide some way of coping with the situation other than avoiding it. For example if dealing with a superior about whom you are anxious you might use a coping statement along the lines: 'He is bound to attack me on points of detail but if I can remember the main parts of my argument and stick to them I will be able to face up to the interview and deal with him more effectively.' Or, in a situation where a wife wants to ask her unco-operative husband for something: 'I know that he will try to argue his way out of it but no matter how guilty he tries to make me feel I will stick to my request.'

Obviously, when you later use these positive self-talk statements in the real situation you may still not get what you want completely or may still find difficulties. But now *you* will be in control of the situation and gradually able to improve on how you handle it rather than the situation completely controlling you.

3. Tension Control

In step three you must learn how to use the Relaxation Response actively to regulate the spiralling of anxiety feelings. Two essential skills have to be mastered. First you must learn to notice very quickly the initial surge of anxiety and the internal feelings which it generates. Second, having learned to recognise the effects of the initial surge of anxiety you must learn how to use this as a trigger to relax very quickly as soon as the feelings begin.

In order to learn the first skill you should enlist the aid of a member of the family or a friend. Select a quiet room, settle down in a comfortable chair and relax yourself for a few seconds. Without any warning of exactly when it will happen, your helper should then make a loud noise close to your head, either by clapping their hands sharply, or bursting a paper bag or balloon. The noise must be loud enough to produce a quite automatic response called the *Startle Reflex*. This sudden noise will have the effect of making you jump and experiencing the internal feelings of anxiety, which are extremely close in effect to those which you experience in the presence of your Threat Stressers. In other words your helper is artificially producing the same internal strain conditions that you experience when you become anxious in a real situation. You may feel your stomach turn over, muscles tense, heart beat rapidly, perspiration increase or a sharp intake of breath. After you have settled down again for a few minutes your friend should then repeat the procedure, using a different means to startle you, so that you again experience the Startle Reflex. After one or two sessions like this you will easily be able to recognise the component parts of your physical anxiety response and be ready to move on to the second skill.

Having come to recognise the effects of startle or initial surge of anxiety, you must now learn to relax very quickly as soon as these feelings begin. Again your friend can help you by following the same procedure as before but this time, having been startled, you must spend a few minutes implementing your Quick Relaxation skills. What you are doing at this point is teaching your body's ANS (which we described in Stage Two) to respond with relaxation feelings rather than with an anxiety spiral to the trigger or signal of small anxiety surges. It is very important to catch the initial surge of anxiety in the early stages and put the Relaxation Response into action as quickly and strongly as possible so that it swamps out the anxiety spiral which might otherwise ensue.

This skill should be practised as often as possible – but at least six times each day for about five minutes each. Over about five days you will find that the Relaxation Response comes automatically and quickly whenever the Startle Response is felt. As you master the procedure try and use other more unusual types of startle trigger, such as somebody suddenly shouting close to you, a tray being dropped or anything else which you or your friend can devise. During this period of Anxiety Management training you should be perfecting Differential Relaxation. If you are following the training schedule laid down in Stage Five you will reach this skill on the sixth day of the Programme. Once you have become proficient at implementing Differential Relaxation you should practise triggering the Startle Response while standing up and walking around.

4. Imagery Training

Having mastered the skill of Tension Control you are now equipped with a procedure for combating anxiety spirals in any situation. However, you will need extra training in order to extend or generalise the ability to control anxiety caused by the

Startle Reflex, into areas which give rise to your own particular stresses.

First it is necessary for you to construct a hierarchy, or graded list, of situations which all have a bearing on your particular Threat stress area. If you have more than one area of Threat stress you should construct a hierarchy for each and deal with each in a similar way. In constructing your hierarchy, it is important to have an accurate description of each scene in terms of the time and place; people present; objects, inanimate or animate, present; mood and general thoughts usually present in the situation; and any other relevant details which make the description true to life. If you find any difficulty in doing this accurately then you will find it helpful to follow the Programme in Stage Five.

As examples of hierarchies, a travel phobic may have scenes depicting:

a. Travel over short distances while driving a car.
b. Travel in a crowded bus.
c. Travel in an empty underground train.
d. Travel over long distances in the back of a car.

. . . and so on.

A golfer suffering from match play anxiety may include scenes such as:

a. Addressing a three-foot putt.
b. Driving with a particular wood.
c. Approaching a ball lying badly in the rough.
d. Addressing the ball after a previous miss hit.

. . . and so on.

The executive may devise a list involving:

a. Heated exchanges with a superior.
b. Boardroom negotiations.

    c. Disciplining a subordinate.

    d. Dealing with an aggressive client.

. . . and so on.

It will take a little imagination and concentration in order to develop your own list and you may have to keep records over a few days to build up a variety of situations to use in this list or lists. Stage Five will help you to do this correctly.

When the situations have been collected order them in degrees of stress they produce – from very high at the top to very low at the bottom. Try not to have too wide a gap between any two items – but have them fairly evenly spaced in stress content.

Now it will be possible to use items from this hierarchy to learn how to control the anxiety or tension they produce in imagination. Take one of the low stress items and, while relaxed, imagine it very vividly. Then use the Relaxation Response, as you did with the startle exercises, to control the anxiety from spiralling in relation to the image. When you are confident of controlling anxiety with this image go on to the next and so on.

While you are practising this it is important to notice any negative thoughts which may enter your mind when considering the situation. This is a good opportunity to add to your list of Positive Self-Talk Statements by reversing any negative thoughts you may have particularly noted, for example: 'I cannot cope . . .', 'Everything will go wrong, I know it . . .', 'I am losing control . . .', 'I've got to get away from it . . .' and so on. You will find it increasingly easy to add Positive Self-Talk Statements as you continue to practise and new ideas suggest themselves to you. After every practice session you should note any negative thoughts and devise coping statements to deal with them. Practise making your coping statements more and more flexible to include more and more different situations.

Finally, in Imagery Training, you should, when you have completed the hierarchy, go through the situations again for a few sessions, and practise imagining yourself in the situation using Positive Self-Talk and also picturing yourself carrying out all the activities in a calm, unhurried and relaxed way. Remember the more slowly and calmly you go about things, the more ideas and strategies you will develop for dealing with the situations.

5. Active Threat Stress Control: Briefing

By now you should have developed the ability to imagine, in detail, several situations which produce stress effects and to have learned to reduce the internal stress effects or anxiety produced by these situations by using Quick and Differential Relaxation and Positive Self-Talk. This will probably have taken you between ten and fifteen days and, if you are confident with your ability, you can now begin to put these RCPs into practical operation in real life.

You should first carry out Differential Relaxation exercises for a few minutes so that you are relaxed in a standing position ready to move around. Next you should try to imagine yourself actually in the stressful situation, choosing objects (or even people if you can get friends to help) as mock representations of the real environmental circumstances. For example two or three friends might act as an audience for a public speaking phobic; a china ornament could represent an animal to an animal phobic; a spare bedroom can become the office of a stressed executive; a desk may stand in for a group of people at a party for the person with social stresses.

Using these artificial representations you should now begin to behave as you would like to in the real situation. Talk to, look at, touch, smell and generally interact with the mock environment as though it were real. Again, notice any negative thoughts of anxiety and intervene quickly with the Relaxation Response and Positive Self-Talk. Address yourself each time to only *one* of the situations on your graded list. Start with an easy one so that it is not difficult to control anxiety. When you feel confident that you are in control of the anxiety in a mock situation you should then go on and practise in real life using the actual stress situation.

6. The RCP in Action

While practising the RCP in real life remember to keep all actions slow and deliberate. Do not hurry or be afraid to take rest pauses, pauses for thought or to look around and absorb what you are doing.

Use the mnemonic (memory jogger) WASP to help you.
It stands for *W*ait, *A*bsorb and *S*lowly *P*roceed.

By *Wait* we mean rest every so often to get any mounting levels of tension back under control using Relaxation Response and Positive Self-Talk.

By *Absorb* we mean assimilating every possible detail of your environment. Many people who are phobic or highly stressed in certain situations will tend to rush from them and blot out details in an attempt to avoid admitting that they are there. To combat this you *must* absorb every detail and notice it as carefully as you can.

By *Slowly Proceed* we mean continue on your way in an unhurried fashion so that you do not become tense through sheer physical exertion.

If you get stuck at any point while going through the different situations in your hierarchy, or if you have difficulty with any of the practice sessions, do *not* give up. First go back and practise the last situation with which you felt confident. Then try to work out an even more positive Self-Talk Programme for the new situation – or put an intermediate one in before trying it again. Use your Relaxation, increased Positive Self-Talk and WASP to keep trying. Go gradually and slowly and the stress level will reduce as you proceed.

Finally remember that you must practise regularly and consistently. Do not have long periods when you stop practising or the new skill will take very much longer to acquire. A week or two of practising in the real situation should get you to a point where you can manage it without too much difficulty.

7. Active Threat Stress Control: Debriefing

On your return from carrying out all your Threat Stress control methods in the real life stress situations, you should sit down comfortably, relax and go over your performance. In particular you should think about how you managed to keep the anxiety under control. All too often people make the mistake of putting this down to sheer good fortune. In fact it is due to correctly carried out Anxiety Management procedures. Note any extra methods which you used beyond those which you planned on using. Then build up yet more Positive Self-Talk based on how you managed in real life so that you can feed these into your list of anxiety reducing statements. In this way the Positive Self-Talk will become more and more realistic.

Also be pleased with yourself. Congratulate yourself on the positive aspects of your behaviour and even, if you wish, give yourself a reward for doing your best. It is important to make your practice worthwhile in this way and you should not think it wrong to bask in your successes, using them to spur you on to the next situation. Do not criticise yourself if you have not done too well in practice but congratulate yourself for just trying and performing as well as you were able.

Practise debriefing in each situation several times before going to the next. Keep refining your Quick Relaxation and Positive Self-Talk until it comes naturally and easily. When you are confident about your ability to control stress in one situation move on to the next in the hierarchy but remember to keep practising as often as you can all the items in the hierarchy as you master them.

Summary

Threat Lifestyle Stressers produce excessively high levels of strain in situations which are either dangerous or potentially harmful or which produce a phobic or anxiety response without being objectively harmful.

There are three components to an anxiety spiral with this sort of Stresser: Initial Anxiety Surge; Panic and the Anxiety Spiral; and Habituation and Recuperation. When a high level of stress has been habituated the Negative Stress Responses return to normal and you will no longer feel any discomfort in the presence of that Stresser. Habituation to high stress levels is not a very pleasant business since the individual must first experience maximum anxiety from that situation.

There are two ways in which people generally cope with Threat Lifestyle Stressers. The first is through Avoidance, the second by means of Adaptation.

Avoidance, as its name implies, means trying not to encounter the Threat Stresser.

Adaptation involves accepting the discomfort of high stress levels, coping with the impairment in performance which these levels produce and generally trying to put up with it.

Both these popular responses have undesirable consequences. Because it rewards through Negative Reinforcement, Avoidance makes it harder to face the Threat Stresser on a subsequent occasion. After a time persistent Avoidance can lead to the person becoming phobic.

Adaptation to stress levels greater than the OSL can lead to health damage.

The correct RCP to use is Anxiety Management.

Anxiety Management involves learning to recognise the initial surge of anxiety and using this very low level of arousal to trigger the Relaxation Response. In order to use Anxiety Management you must acquire the following seven skills:

(1) Relaxation.
(2) Positive Self-Talk.
(3) Tension Control.
(4) Imagery Training.
(5) Active Threat Stress Control: Briefing.
(6) WASP.
(7) Active Threat Stress Control: Debriefing.

PROGRAMME SEVEN – RCPs FOR – BOREDOM LIFESTYLE STRESSERS

Boredom Stressers occur when there is insufficient stress present in an individual's environment. They are all produced as a result of the stress level never reaching the OSL and cause Low Level Negative Mental or Low Level Negative Physical Responses to arise. Before reading this Programme, therefore, you should carry out the RCPs described in Programmes Two and Four.

Situations in which Boredom Lifestyle Stressers are to be found include:

Occupations which involve repetitive mental or physical activities.

Family situations where there is little communication or mutual interest.

Redundancy or retirement from work.

Moving to live in an isolated or unfriendly location.

Confinement to bed because of illness.

Imprisonment.

Lack of opportunity or inclination to develop a leisure pursuit.

A sex life which offers insufficient stimulation or variety.

A game or sport played against opponents who provide too little competition.

A repetitive and unstimulating social life.

The symptoms, in terms of the internal strain response to this type of Stresser, are typically:

Depression.

Inability to concentrate.

Disinclination to participate in the activities.

Lowering of physical and mental performance.

Lethargy.

Fatigue.

Day dreaming.

Inability to make a start on fresh projects.

Outbursts of aggression.

Thrill seeking, often taking an antisocial or self-destructive form.

Boredom and Reinforcers

In Programme Four we talked about the need for reinforcers, or positive payoffs, in order to counter the Low Level Negative Mental Stress Responses. In general boredom can be said to arise when there are insufficient reinforcers in an individual's lifestyle. To explain why this happens we should start by describing how boredom is viewed in behavioural psychology. The popular view of boredom is that it is an unnatural state into which people sink at a time when they are understimulated by work, family interactions or leisure pursuits. In fact boredom is the *natural* state of man and woman and the condition of 'not being bored' one which we create for ourselves by carrying out interesting and challenging activities. A good way of looking at this behavioural concept of boredom is to imagine it as a backdrop onto which we paint, through our own efforts, an interesting picture consisting of reinforcers. These reinforcers can be work which stimulates us, a fulfilling social round, exciting leisure pursuits, the pleasure of a quiet home life, the intellectual delights of studying or listening to music. In these different ways and many, many more besides, we may cover up the basic background of boredom for most of the time during our lives. But if any of these reinforcers is removed or obstructed then patches of boredom background start to show through. During life, of course, reinforcers are constantly fading or being taken away as we grow older, develop different interests, lose some of our friends, change jobs and so on. Provided that these losses are made good by new sets of reinforcers no harm is done. But if they are not replaced and only diminish then the individual reverts closer and closer to the natural state of being bored. As an example of this let us look at what may happen to the same man at two points in his life: at middle-age as a successful business executive and the father of a teenage family, and twenty-five years later after retirement from work. In his mid years this individual has a wide range of powerful reinforcers at his disposal. He finds his work stimulating and challenging. It pays him well in terms of income and prestige. He has a wide circle of business friends, eats out regularly in agreeable restaurants and travels comfortably on an expense account. He has the respect of his colleagues and power over subordinates. He enjoys active leisure pursuits, sailing and squash, and takes a regular holiday abroad. At home his wife and teenage family involve him in various activities, many of which he finds interesting.

After retirement his income drops. His work is no longer there to sustain him and his children have moved away from home. He is not active enough to carry on with his favourite sports and is forced into the unwelcome role of a spectator rather than a participator. He seldom sees his business colleagues or friends. Perhaps, like many people on retirement, he has decided to move out of the city to a new life on the coast or in the country. In doing so he may make some positive health gains from cleaner air but he loses important sources of reinforcement from familiar surroundings, local churches, clubs and societies. He is no longer a known and respected member of the community but a stranger.

If he has been prudent, all these changes in his lifestyle will have been anticipated and prepared for. By spending holidays in the neighbourhood to which they intend to move he and his wife will have made new friends in their retirement area. When they move it will not be to live amongst complete strangers. As his strenuous sports became too much for him, he will have cultivated fresh interests. In anticipation of leaving work he will have developed an interesting hobby or planned to take on part-time work of some kind. In this case the reinforcers which were lost on retirement will have been successfully restored from other sources. But if he has failed to take these necessary precautions then the number of reinforcements available from his new lifestyle may be insufficient to cover natural boredom.

Reinforcement and Behaviour

In order to acquire reinforcers it is necessary to carry out behaviours through which they can be experienced. For example it is clearly impossible for us to experience the reinforcers which occur when people are friendly with us, admire or like us, work with us or want to have sexual relations with us, if we live like hermits and shun contact with others. The problem is that a reduction of reinforcers produces boredom and one of the symptoms of boredom, as we have said earlier, is a disinclination to take part in fresh activities. We think: 'What the hell . . . it is all too much effort. I don't want to go out to that party. It is so much easier to sit at home with the television on and do nothing in particular.' This response leads to a further reduction in reinforcers, an increase in the level of Boredom Stressers and even less inclination to break out of the vicious circle!

The chain of events leading to this situation can be summed up as follows:

Loss of reinforcers or lack of them in lifestyle →
Loss of or lack of reinforcers from environment →
Increase in Boredom Stressers → Disinclination to carry out reinforcing behaviours → Reduction in reinforcers present → Further increase in Boredom Stressers . . . and so on. . . .

To break out of this chain we must start painting over the boredom background with positive reinforcers. This will produce a new situation as follows:

Active and appropriate behaviours → Increase in reinforcers → Interest rises above basic boredom level →
Motivation for further appropriate behaviours → Further reinforcement . . . and so on. . . .

But once we have arrived at a position where added interest has been introduced into our lives, it is not safe to rest on our laurels and imagine that the situation will remain stable. There are bound to be changes in our lifestyle which will remove or obstruct many of the reinforcers. Unless the sources of reinforcement are constantly kept fresh, this decrease, as in the case of a man or woman unprepared for the changes caused by retirement, will cause a decrease in the interest level and a re-emergence of the boredom background.

In some cases of lack or loss of reinforcers the answer to the problem of ensuing boredom is to find some other Life Area activity from which to draw alternative types of reinforcer. For example, on retirement it is possible for many people to replace work reinforcers with family or leisure reinforcers quite happily and so keep their general level of reinforcers high above basic boredom. In this Programme we will develop some strategies which are based on this replacement principle. However, in some cases it is not possible to replace a certain type of reinforcer from an alternative source because the type of reinforcer is very specific to a certain kind of activity. The type of reinforcer most commonly encountered which falls into this category is the *Excitement Reinforcer*. It is this kind of reinforcer which often keeps compulsive gamblers, shoplifters, vandals, and some types of sex offenders continuing with their usually maladaptive behaviour. In all of these types of behaviour there is a common element of excitement which stems from the prospect of being caught or in some way running a risk. This need for excitement reinforcement can produce important consequences for society which will be discussed in Stage Six.

The very special nature of Excitement Reinforcers makes it difficult to control the behaviours which they produce with alternative reinforcers from one or other of the four Life Areas. Usually the only effective way of replacing one form of Excitement Reinforcer is with another Excitement Reinforcer. This means, for example, that if a compulsive gambler wants to break his or her self-destructive habit it will be relatively little use for them to try and do so by involving themselves in fairly routine work or to attempt to swop the roulette wheel and playing cards for a non-risk leisure activity such as golf or tennis. In order to terminate the excitement-producing behaviour of gambling it will be necessary to substitute a different type of Excitement Reinforcer. The experience of one of the authors (Dr Robert Sharpe) in such cases has been that damaging Excitement Reinforcers must be replaced by constructive Excitement Reinforcers for the most lasting changes in behaviour to take place. For example, one compulsive gambler who was success-fully treated for his habit was encouraged to take up rock climbing at the same time as he was reducing his gambling behaviour; while a man who had been convicted of exhibition-ism was able to cease these activities after he had been taught to introduce Excitement Reinforcers into his sexual activities with his wife.

The general principle for relieving boredom is, then, to increase the number of reinforcers present in your lifestyle. For most people this can be done by topping up the reinforcers in any of the Life Areas. For example, boredom which arises from an uninteresting work routine can be countered by increasing the stress levels in, say, leisure activities. Excitement Reinforcers which are damaging should be replaced with beneficial Excite-ment Reinforcers, that is ones which will improve rather than injure one's physical or mental health or increase rather than diminish one's financial resources.

It is essential that you are honest with yourself about whether or not you have a need for Excitement Reinforcers in your life. Many people who do are ashamed to admit the fact and try to seek out different types of reinforcers which they think are more socially acceptable. For example, the bored housewife who uses that popular strategy of voluntary social work as a source of extra reinforcements may be doing both herself and the com-munity a favour. But if she does not really enjoy what she is doing and only carries on with the work because it is 'socially laudable' then she may be reducing rather than increasing her reinforcers and thereby adding to her feelings of boredom. Perhaps what she *really* needs is the excitement of a challenging job, a risky leisure pursuit or an illicit love affair!

Let us look now at four major strategies for increasing the level of reinforcers in order to combat the Boredom Stresser.

1. Programmed Performance Pitfalls

A prime reason for many types of boredom is that the person always succeeds in what has been attempted in any of the Life Areas. Either because the tasks themselves are very simple, or because they are particularly gifted and able but never give themselves a chance to be stretched and so fulfil their own potential. For example routine house or office work, always sticking to the same comfortable social round or going to the same place on holiday may put little or no stress on the average person's capabilities. Being at an ordinary school and following a normal college education may equally leave a youngster with an IQ of 165 bored and unstretched.

Pleasant though continued success may be, attainments which are not particularly striven for very quickly begin to pall and lose their reinforcing value. An extreme example of this is the child or young adult who can 'never do anything wrong' at home. Such an individual may often feel bored and apathetic, expressing the attitude: 'What's the point of trying to do anything when I still get all I need if I just do nothing?'

It is just as damaging to give praise when it is not deserved as to withhold it when it is.

The way to overcome this particular boredom barrier is first of all to make a list of every routine piece of behaviour and situation which is currently present in all four of your Life Areas. Note such details as projects at work or in study, means of travel, the people you talk to, and the sports you play, where, although you may feel that you perform successfully, you also feel unfulfilled. Consider how many of these situations or activities have become comfortable habits which simply fill up spaces in your life.

When you have completed this list you should first consider whether any of the behaviours can be replaced by new ones and secondly, if this is not possible, whether fresh goals can be established within the same area of behaviour which will stretch your abilities to a new limit. Try to establish some realistically high goals which will stretch you but at which you are still likely to succeed, as well as others at a level of aspiration beyond that point so that you can experience occasional failures by the side of which your achievements will be all the more enjoyable. For example, suppose you visit the local tennis club each week and generally manage to defeat most of the regular players. After a while inevitable success will lead to boredom. You know all the tactics which will be offered against you and the standard of play of your usual opponents. The first goal might be to visit a different club where the standard of play will be much the same but where you will be exposed to fresh players and different match tactics. In such circumstances you will probably have to work hard to sustain your previous level of success. The second goal could be to play at a much higher standard than you are used to, perhaps by taking part in area competitions and elimination matches. Here you run the risk of failure, but defeat will not be inglorious and it will be coupled with the fulfilment which comes from having striven hard in a series of stimulating games.

In a business situation you might get a first set of goals which involved tackling different jobs in your same general area of expertise. The higher aspiration goals could involve working on projects which require additional skills or offer unusual challenges. Perhaps this will mean competing for a contract against much larger firms, working with a new client in a foreign language or coping with problems presented by a radically different production or marketing operation. Ultimate success in any of these areas will be a pleasant and, hopefully, profitable bonus. But the certain and immediate reward comes from having stretched one's abilities to the full and a little beyond. Of course, as you gain experience the first set of goals may become routine and the second set quite manageable. When this happens you must rethink your goals, again selecting some which are just within your capabilities and others which are just beyond them.

It is not necessary to make complete changes in any Life Area in order to programme in pitfalls. Rather you should identify and break out of existing habits and build up new patterns of behaviour.

In previous Programmes where we have discussed failure, we have warned that it can lead to a decrease in motivation. But the failures which will result from the pitfalls we suggest you programme into your performance are being used in a controlled and anticipated way in order to form a comparison for the successes.

If holidays have become a boring routine of staying in the same kind of hotels and doing the same kind of things, or if life in general has grown tedious, you could try an 'unrest cure'. Rather than trying to decrease stress levels, as you would during a conventional 'rest cure', you should actively plan to disrupt your routine as much as possible. If you habitually travel first class on an expense account, try taking a camping holiday with only the most basic equipment. If your holidays normally consist of staying in air conditioned hotels and visiting tourist traps, sign up for a safari tour which takes you right off the beaten track. A type of holiday which is becoming increasingly popular, especially in America, is the 'learning vacation' where you learn some sport or artistic or academic subject, such as pottery, archaeology, skin-diving, parachuting, horse riding and so on. For a married couple separate holidays may provide a welcome break which will help to revitalise the marriage. Be adventurous. Expand the possibilities for change and excitement in your life. Do not be one of those people who fondly believe that they have had many years' experience of living when all they have actually had is one year's experience repeated many times over!

H

2. Run Some Risks

Another major source of boredom for many people is the certainty of their lives. This is why, in retrospect, most men look back on wars and conflicts almost nostalgically. It is a noble sentiment to espouse the principle of 'make love not war' but it must be remembered that man (and woman) has programmed into his potential behavioural repertoire a capacity for dealing with danger situations. This is often unexercised but it may make its unfulfilled presence known through delinquent or self-endangering behaviours. In order to capitalise on this human function of dealing with dangers we can, however, increase risk in our lives while still remaining relatively safe and without having to use international warfare! If you have daydreamed about being a mercenary, an explorer, a spy or following some other 'exotic' lifestyle and compared these dreams to your real lifestyle with bored disfavour, then probably you should begin to explore the possibilities of adding some risk to your life in terms of putting yourself in situations where you have to use your wits and physical abilities in order to perform effectively.

This can be achieved in two ways. By taking a job, perhaps part-time, which involved elements of danger, for example as a part-time fireman, in the auxiliary police, with a rescue organisation or in one of the armed forces. Alternatively you might take up a risky leisure pursuit such as mountaineering, skin-diving, sky-diving, flying, hang-gliding, horse riding, motor-bike scrambling, auto-cross, stock car racing or power boating. Of particular value are sports where you are matching yourself against the environment. Needless to say, all these sports should be learned in controlled circumstances by joining a club in which you can get professional coaching from skilled instructors.

3. Take a Chance

In modern society there is a greater and greater tendency towards standardisation, concepts of normality, categorisation and the elimination of the chance element. Indeed this is often held to be the prime function of responsible government and even when speaking of Hitler and Mussolini most people acknowledge, with some admiration, that they 'made the trains run on time'. This trend towards total conformity does, of course, result in legislative and social convenience. But it also means that life is growing more and more predictable. As we have seen, reinforcers which become too predictable lose their power to combat boredom. In Stage Six we will consider the social consequences of this and point out that strikes and vandalism, far from being aberrations are the inevitable consequences of a risk starved society.

In order to develop more chance elements in an otherwise largely predictable lifestyle, it is first necessary to train yourself in the, at present, unusual, art of Taking a Chance. One strategy which we have found effective in clinical practice, and which also helps very greatly with people who are unable to make decisions in case they are wrong, is to use a coin or dice to select one of several alternative course of action. The method requires you to choose a number of different goals which you can aim for during the course of a day or week, some of which you may have been avoiding because you might fail at them or because they might tax you considerably. For practice purposes it is often useful to include a few choices which you may not consider particularly suitable. This might mean including a type of food which you have always been prejudiced against, a sexual act which you have avoided or always been embarrassed by, a topic of conversation which you have not felt competent to talk about, or making a request to a friend or a sexual partner which may result in rejection.

It is imperative, if you decide to use a coin or dice in order to learn the art of chance-taking, that you really do follow the course of action which chance dictates. If you back out of the agreement because you really dislike or cannot face the choice selected for you in this random way then the whole exercise becomes pointless. At first you should include in your list of alternatives only those behaviours which you feel you can carry out without undue difficulty. As you grow more used to following activities dictated for you by chance you can gradually introduce one or more anxiety producing options. For example a businessman might initially write the following list of options to be decided on the throw of a dice.

(1) Tackle project which I have been avoiding because of the unusual difficulties involved.
(2) Make phone call to client I know is going to be aggressive and whom I have been avoiding for that reason.
(3) Go and see superior about free time due to me.
(4) Complete present task.
(5) Stop work and talk to colleague for fifteen minutes.
(6) Tackle colleague who has been dilatory and increasing work schedule in consequence.

A later list could include a number of moderately stressful situations plus one or two involving a major task or confrontation. For instance demanding a justified rise from an irritable boss, or applying for another job.

This procedure has been found to be of particular value in sexual and intimacy situations where routine has led to boredom. In this Area the lists will start off with fairly simple additions to the sexual repertoire, such as variations in position and foreplay, and might gradually include such explorations as using vibrators, experimenting with oral stimulation, and making love in different environments. Group sex and wife-swapping, as well as bisexuality are becoming increasingly included in people's sexual repertoire and there is no reason why, if all those concerned are in agreement, you should not include these. We would, however, suggest that it is probably because individual couples are not imaginative or exploratory enough to develop fresh sexual behaviour patterns that group orientated sex acts are becoming more popular. It may well be that for most people there will be no need for such activities but we would emphasise that we do not have any particular argument for or against these behaviours.

4. Blow Your Mind

The object of this procedure is twofold. Firstly it can be used in times of enforced boredom, such as when confined to a sick bed or on a long journey; and secondly it is useful for blowing away the cobwebs of an underused mental capacity and training you up to explore the hitherto unrealised dimensions of material which had always seemed dull and routine.

We have called this procedure the *Mind Bender* because its purpose is to encourage you to twist your mental processes away from conventional ways of looking and thinking about different concepts. In doing so you not only give the mind beneficial exercise of viewing ideas from unusual angles but you can also reach fresh conclusions and come up with novel ways of looking at the familiar which have a practical value in solving current difficulties and problems. The *Mind Bender* can be used at home, in the office or during academic studies. It consists of a pack of fifty square cards which you can make by cutting up post cards or small index cards. Onto these you must write four nouns selected at random from any source you choose. The most obvious reference work for general use is a dictionary. Open this anywhere, close your eyes and run a finger down the list of words. Stop at random and, if the word is a noun, note it down. If it is not a noun find the noun nearest to it and use this. If you want the *Mind Bender* to relate particularly to your area of work or study then select key nouns, which can refer to larger concepts, from text books and manuals. Try to keep each concept to one or at most two nouns which have a particular meaning in your chosen topic. These words should be written, four to a card, as shown in Diagram Six. A complete set of *Mind Bender* concept cards will contain two hundred random nouns, or two hundred nouns representing wider concepts in a specialised area. Now shuffle the pack of cards by placing them word side downwards on a flat surface and mixing them around.

Diagram Six: Mind Bender Concept Card showing how words should be laid out.

Gather them up, give them one final conventional shuffle and deal yourself out any number of cards up to six – more than that will probably bend your mind a little too far! Turn them over and note the word in the top left hand corner of each card. Now begin to juggle the nouns and associated concepts around, possibly still by keeping the cards before you and moving them around or by rewriting them in a list. The idea is to try and produce a logical order, or rational connective link between randomised concepts. The easiest way of doing this, where non-specialist nouns are concerned, is to construct a short story, or fictionalised episode which naturally links the elements contained on the cards. However, this is very much the easy way out and it is far more interesting, and potentially valuable, to try and construct something of practical use, either a new approach to some situation, a new gadget or technique for handling or investigating a problem or a fresh use for some familiar object. It is, of course, essential to adopt this approach when using specialist cards to explore an area of work or study.

At first glance it may seem impossible to discover any association or link between the concepts presented by the cards. Probably you will really have to stretch your mind – and your imagination – in order to do this. As you shift around ideas and juggle with the concepts, whole new vistas may open up for you. Because we normally think in a logical sequence, with one idea following on from the next, our thought processes tend to be strait-jacketed much of the time. *Mind Bending* is a way of breaking out of the strait jacket and expanding one's ability to see routine concepts in a fresh way.

There is no need to play *Mind Bender* on your own. It can provide an interesting and constructive basis for discussion between members of an office team or study group.

Here is an example of how the random nouns can stimulate the thought processes. The words were taken from the *Stress-watch Mind Bender Concept Cards* which have been developed by sampling a cross-section of nouns which appear with varying degrees of statistically analysed frequency.

Graveyard.
Suitcase.
Goldfish.
Light.
Cloud.
Telepathy.

In one *Mind Bender* session these words produced the following line of thought:

'Graveyard, makes me think of death, dying, funerals. How bleak these places look especially in cities where the tomb-stones have become stained with smoke and grime. It might almost be a good idea to have them coated with some kind of plastic layer to keep the stone pure and white. A graveyard for animals. Pets' cemeteries. You could hardly bury goldfish! What about clouds. Heavenly clouds. Heaven. Link between death and heaven. The life hereafter. Telepathic communication with the dead perhaps. Links between this world and the next. Any evidence for this? Great deal of fraud in mediumship and seances. What about goldfish? Communication between pet owners and their pets. Many people claim to be able to communicate in this way with cats and dogs. Why not fish? Could telepathy be a sixth sense which has diminished in humans as we developed the power of speech? Are animals better able to use telepathy than we are? Certainly their normal senses are far more acute than ours, hearing, sight. They seem to be able to anticipate dangers before we are aware of them. Birds often fly out of areas threatened with earthquakes, cats and dogs are anxious for days beforehand. I remember reading sometime back that ornamental fish in a Chinese city were seen swimming very agitatedly before a major earth tremor. Probably able to detect subtle pressure changes through the water. Could they be used to predict natural disasters? Clearly necessary to study behaviour very closely to see swim patterns under normal conditions and in conditions where some natural disaster threatens. Suitcase. This suggests something portable, light and easy to carry around. Some type of instrument perhaps for predicting natural disasters. Equipment which uses animals or fish as the detector? Like canaries were used to detect dangerous gas in the mines? Perhaps changes in rate of swim patterns could be monitored by using some kind of photo-electric equipment. The more frequently a beam of light was broken the more rapidly the fish was swimming. Could such a device provide a low cost early warning system for remote coastal villages in earthquake belt regions? A way of saving life by predicting tidal waves resulting from undersea eruptions and quakes. Areas where communications are bad might not get any warning otherwise. Certainly this is a problem which causes great danger and occasional high loss of life. Fish could be caught locally. . . .'

So from this completely random collection of nouns emerged an idea for a potentially practical and lifesaving gadget. As a result of this train of thought a research project along these lines has, in fact, been instigated.

Try the *Mind Bender* for yourself and see how effective it can be for blowing away the cobwebs caused by mental boredom.

Summary

Boredom results from an insufficient supply of reinforcers. It is a natural state which we overcome by performing behaviours which result in Positive Payoffs. In the course of life some reinforcers will diminish or no longer be available. As some decrease we must replace them with others.

To experience reinforcers we must carry out behaviours which produce them. Boredom leads to a disinclination to perform such behaviours and this produces a vicious circle of decreasing performance leading to a reduction in reinforcers and less motivation to perform.

In general it is better to try to replace inappropriate Excitement Reinforcers – that is ones which are personally or socially harmful – with beneficial Excitement Reinforcers.

There are four major strategies for overcoming Boredom Stressers.

(1) Increase in Performance Stressers.
(2) Increase in Threat Stressers.
(3) The addition of random elements and chance to your Lifestyle.
(4) Mental exercises.

H*

PROGRAMME EIGHT – RCPs FOR – FRUSTRATION
LIFESTYLE STRESSERS

Frustration Stressers occur in situations where, whatever you do, your behaviour will not be followed by a positive reinforcement, or whatever you do will be followed by punishment. Stated more simply – whatever you do you will become a loser.

Situations in which this happens are called 'the double bind' and the following examples will make clear how these operate.

Suppose that in a bad marriage a wife wants and needs to have sex with her husband. But because of the way in which their marriage difficulties have developed she knows that if she makes sexual overtures towards her husband she will be rebuffed. Either he will plead fatigue or reject her so roughly that she will feel guilty and undesirable. Whatever approach she adopts in this situation will result in ultimately punishing consequences. If she asks for sex she will suffer the humiliation of a refusal. If she does not ask for sex the physical satisfaction she needs will never be provided. She will be a loser either way.

In a work situation the double bind often occurs through the need to serve two masters. For instance, an executive is given a firm directive by his board. But soon afterwards a union representative tells him that the employees are very unhappy with the consequences of this directive, and warns that unless it is changed there will be a crippling strike. The board refuse to change course. The executive is now confronted with two very undesirable consequences. He can either do as his directors want and risk a shut down, or yield to pressures from the shop floor and risk the sack.

Of course in both these examples the 'double bind' might have been avoided if the person concerned had taken a different and more assertive approach when faced with the original decisions. The use of assertion in preventing winner/loser situations and the inevitable frustrations they produce is a major strategy which will be discussed very fully in this Programme.

Perhaps the most frequent, and destructive Frustration

Stressers in modern life stem from confrontation with all forms and levels of bureaucracy – everything from the increasingly tangled web of governmental legislation to the obstructionist activities of surly doormen and rude receptionists. Encounters with tax officials, public administrators, medical and legal organisations and officials, local councils, policemen and traffic wardens can all place the individual in a double bind situation.

Typical symptoms of Frustration strain include:

Anxiety.
Mental confusion.
Irritation and anger outbursts.
Depression.

Anxiety and mental confusion usually arise in situations where, whatever choice is made for dealing with the situation, a Threat Stresser is likely to ensue; anger outbursts may well occur in interpersonal situations where someone with whom you are intimate is playing cat and mouse with you although these categorisations are by no means exclusive. Particularly interesting though is the response of depression to frustration which occurs typically when a person has been placed, for a long period of time, in double bind situations. The depression typically takes the form of 'What's the point of doing anything – I always end up hurt or in the wrong anyway'. This type of response will occur frequently with the person undergoing brain washing or interrogation procedures where the inquisitors are particularly skilled in placing blocks in front of the subject any time they attempt to explain themselves. The type of depression seen with this Lifestyle Stresser is similar to the one described in Programme Seven. But in this case it may have the added component of agitation and anxiety mixed with it.

Altering or Accepting

Frustration Stressers occur in double bind situations where we must inevitably lose out. The initial strategy for dealing with them is clearly to avoid so far as is possible, being placed in a situation where there are going to be winners or losers. There will always be a vast number of things in life which we dislike or disapprove of but which are beyond our powers as individuals to change. The alternatives here are either to accept them or to attempt to change them by joining an appropriate lobby or pressure group. This is becoming an increasingly popular and effective method by which people can band together to exert the sort of political, social or economic pressures which would be beyond them as individuals. There are now more than 600 such organisations in Britain concerned with making changes in society. They range from the National Council for Civil Liberties to the Trades Union Movement and deal with every-thing from race issues to sexual liberation, from saving the world from pollution to preventing a motorway from despoiling a particular neighbourhood. If you feel strongly about any issue it is almost certain there will be an association of like-minded people only too pleased to receive your help and support. It is certainly far more beneficial to do this than to sit at home and brood over the situation. Even if your group fails to achieve its aims you will at least have the satisfaction of giving the opposition a good fight.

In the same way it may help to relieve your feelings if you write a strongly worded letter to a local or national newspaper about some issue which frustrates you or complain bitterly to a company director or store manager about poor quality or service. Such letters may effect changes or result in an apology, they may have no effect at all on the larger issues. But they will give you a feeling that you have given them something to think about. In general it is better to come away from a situation with the view that: 'I gave them a piece of my mind even if they are too thick skinned to realise it . . .' than meekly to accept whatever life hands out and crawl away feeling whipped and dispirited. One word of warning about letters though. If you write an aggressive letter which could make a major change in your life inevitable, for example resignation in the face of a double bind situation, it is much better to wait twenty-four hours before posting it than to rush it into the mail. When you have calmed down and rethought the matter a more appropriate course of action may become clear. If resignation still seems the only answer then do not be afraid to take such a step. But control the situation rather than be controlled by your immediate fury.

A wise dictum to follow is to realise that in life there are some things which we must find the patience to accept and others which we must find the courage to change. Above all we need the wisdom to distinguish between the two.

If you are confronted with an insurmountable frustrator, perhaps through having to deal with faceless bureaucracy, then the resulting Stressers may leave you tense and anxious. In this case you should take measures to alleviate the effects of this frustration by learning how to control the anxiety build-up. Use the procedures taught in Programmes One and Six to help you. They will enable you to view the unchangeable in a more objective and calmer light and, perhaps, discover a different approach which will help to reduce some of the Stressers present.

In this Programme we want to deal mainly with procedures which will enable you to cope with frustrations at a personal level, in the four Life Areas, by providing the means to release pent up aggression, reduce anxiety and mental confusion and alleviate frustration-based depression.

1. Understanding the Assertion Habit

Double bind situations often occur simply because we allow them to. Because we are insufficiently assertive in our dealings with our environment. The assertion response is one of the most powerful weapons which you can develop against the disruptive effects of anxiety and depression arising from frustration situations. Basically it works because anger and its associated behaviours, such as shouting, being firm, and even exerting sudden muscular activity such as banging a table with your hand just as much as feelings of well being and its associated behaviours such as expressions of love, affection, friendship and admiration, is a parasympathetic response. This, as you will recall from Stage Two, is directly opposed to anxiety which is a sympathetic response. So, strange though it may seem at first sight, getting yourself outwardly angry, without holding back and doing it half-heartedly because of embarrassment, is an extremely valuable way of controlling anxiety.

Now we must define more closely what we mean by assertion and show how it can be developed by a series of structured exercises.

Let us first point out what assertion is not. Assertion is not tearing to shreds someone who is opposed to your views and showing them that you are a much better individual than they are. Assertion is not hurting someone because they have got on the wrong side of you. In short Assertion is *not* aggression.

In an aggression interchange there is always a winner and a loser, since the object is for one of the individuals to score points over the other, perhaps by making them feel stupid, embarrassed, anxious or just plain wrong. You may have been at either end of an aggression situation many times during your life – the one who scores the points or the one off whom the points are scored. There are some difficult consequences associated with being either the aggressor, people quite often grow to dislike you, or in being submissive, people can lose respect for you.

Now for what assertion is. Assertion is a forthright expression of your particular views or feelings about the matter voiced at the time that you develop them. They are conveyed to the other person or people firmly and without self-apology – whether they are positive comments or negative ones. They are an unashamed statement of what *you* feel to be right and just in a situation. And finally, and perhaps most importantly, they are information transmitting and promote a further interchange of information between the two participants. The assertive interchange is characterised by the fact that both or all parties to the interchange come away from it feeling that they have achieved their best rather than having beaten or been beaten.

This may seem a lengthy and tall order at first sight but we shall now give some simple examples of an assertive interchange and carry on to show you how you can develop the ability to produce spontaneous assertive responses through a series of exercises.

Imagine a situation in which one partner in a law firm is accusing another of unfair dealing over fees. He believes that he has been cheated of monies due to him and that inflated running expenses have been employed to reduce the overall amount which can be shared out. He comes blazing into his colleague's office and stands towering over him, one fist slamming down on the desk while brandishing sheaves of accounts – his evidence for the charge of double-dealing – in the other hand. He shouts and is clearly beside himself with rage. He is, at present, the aggressor in the situation and one of three things might now occur. First the other partner might become outraged himself and begin to return the aggression and escalate the row to a point where both storm out of the room with nothing resolved or where they take a decision, perhaps to dissolve the partnership, which both will later regret. The second possibility is for the attacked partner to become extremely defensive and finally be browbeaten into submitting to what may well be unfair demands. In both cases there will be losses for both sides as, sooner or later, mutual respect and confidence will be eroded and resentments will set in. In both cases Frustration Stressers will result. The third alternative is for the attacked partner to make an assertive interjection in the following manner. He turns in his chair to face his attacker and rises to his feet looking the attacking partner squarely in the eyes. When they are in a face to face position (and now physically equal with one another) he can say to his attacker: 'Look I can see you are clearly extremely angry (which demonstrates a sense of concern) but I do object to being spoken to in that way (a justifiable statement of his feelings of an invasion of his rights). Perhaps we could both sit down and look at the facts of the situation and put right any mistakes which may have been made (now leaving the situation wide open for further informational exchange, in order to clarify the truth of the matter, without either accusing his attacker of being wrong or accepting blame immediately himself).' By this assertive response the affair can be ventilated and both sides can reach what they feel is a fair settlement. Only in this way will the situation be resolved without either side feeling frustrated.

Lack of assertion in family and marital affairs is a common source of frustration. The two examples below, drawn from case histories, demonstrate what are probably the most frequent types of non-assertive or aggressive responses which lead, inevitably, to increased Frustration Stressers.

Consider a situation in which a ten-year-old boy wants a big increase in his weekly pocket money on the basis that his friend gets more than he does. The parents are not particularly well off and, moreover, do not feel that a child of that age should have excessive amounts of money. On the other hand they are very concerned to be 'good parents' and are worried over the damage which deprivation can do to children. They are afraid that he may feel that they are rejecting him or do not love him as much as his friend's parents love his friend. Such largely unfounded propaganda is usually disseminated by professional pundits whose income is in direct proportion to the number of worried parents trying to pick their way through a mass of contradictory statements on child rearing. Many children are wise enough to know that this situation exists and that parents do become anxious over whether or not they are adequately demonstrating their 'love'. Parents in this situation can respond in several ways. First of all the mother, who is probably approached initially as the 'soft touch', may simply pass the buck and tell the child that he must discuss it with his father, in which case a strained and frustrating period may follow. Secondly after much soul searching, her anxiety and irritation may spiral out of all proportion and she may yell at the boy to keep quiet and stop pestering her. This will lead to frustration and resentment on the child's side and eventual frustrated guilt feelings on hers.

Thirdly she may try to counter the guilt which her son is producing in her (by implying how much better his friend is looked after) by trying to produce guilt in her son for asking. She may reply: 'You do realise when daddy was ill two weeks ago he lost his money from his work and I am still trying to put by enough to pay for our holiday next year because we couldn't have one last year. . . .' This is designed, often with the quite knowing intention, to put down the boy's request by loading her difficulties onto his shoulders. Since he cannot do anything about these problems, this tactic will simply lead to frustration on the child's part and perhaps smouldering resentment. This is basically a dirty tactic and one which may well lead to an escalation of guilt-producing requests since the child may come back and say how unhappy he is getting and how insignificant he feels in relation to his friends. Mother and son may well end up trying to score more guilt points off the other than they are having scored off them.

A more effective approach with this type of request is the use of assertive behaviour called the *repeated refusal*. In this the mother should respond with some statement such as: 'I can see that things are probably a little tough for you (showing that she understands her son's predicament and giving some support in the situation) but the answer has to be no (asserting her right as one human being to another to refuse a request). We can't really afford it, and I am not sure how long this state of affairs will continue (not a justification for her refusal so much as a piece of financial information designed to be educative of the fact that the flow of money in any household is finite) so carry on doing your best to manage on what you get (another information transmitting statement).'

The child may then come back to ask in a more devious way or to demand how he can operate within his means but this statement on the part of the mother has effectively opened up a possible discussion point where she can help her son to work out ways, other than financial, in which he might put himself on a par with his friends and peers. On the point of his friend's parents being more considerate she might well, though certainly not defensively or apologetically, draw her son's attention to other ways in which he is probably better considered than his friend. Whatever the nature of these positive and informational interchanges, however, the mother should continue, if she really wants to refuse to say 'no'. The *repeated refusal* even in the face of tears and anger outbursts is her perfect right – and she should remember that if she capitulates in order to stop the child's tears then she will be experiencing negative reinforcement (as we explained in Programme Six) which will make it *more* likely that the child will use the tactic of tears and anger in future and increase the chances that she will give in to his demands.

For our third example let us look at a situation in which a young wife is being angrily attacked by her husband who considers that she has mismanaged her housekeeping allowance. He storms and shouts, working himself up into a torrent of excited abuse which spreads to other areas which he criticises. She feels that much of the criticism and abuse is illfounded. But he is clearly too angry to listen. What are the alternatives for her? First of all she might burst into tears and run from the room, which would leave her smouldering with resentment and in no way resolve the difficulties, with both husband and wife becoming frustrated that the other has not seen their point of view. Secondly she could stay where she was, keeping silent, and go into a sullen withdrawal which would probably lead to much the same result. Her third alternative might be to start a vituperative counter attack on some completely dissociated piece of her husband's behaviour and begin to criticise him in order to score points back. This again would simply lead to a frustrated non-resolution of the basic issues, as neither side *wants*, in such an encounter, to resolve anything but merely to demonstrate how much less reprehensible they are than the other. Her fourth option is the assertive one, in which she can both defuse her husband's anger and make her own feelings on the matter clear. Her reply might run as follows: 'You are obviously very angry with me (true and demonstrating that his anger is affecting her) and I wonder since you are so angry whether there is anything else that you are annoyed over and you want to tell me about (said with *no* sarcasm in the voice but simply asking for even more informational feedback and saying, assertively, that she realises that people sometimes build up resentments over a long period and she is prepared to listen. Shows understanding). Perhaps we can both sit down and discuss things (offering practical and informational opinion into what should now ensue).' This may seem, at first sight, as though the wife is making herself submissive and putting herself in the wrong by asking for even more criticism to be levelled at her. However, in general, an extremely rapid way of defusing another person's anger is to ask them to throw even more anger at you and accept that they too have a point of view and, indeed, a right to be angry. At the point where she suggests that they sit down and discuss it she should set an example by slowly taking a seat herself and perhaps by gesturing to another seat for him to sit down. It is obvious in this interchange that the choice has been given to the husband on how he should continue. He could carry on pouring scorn and criticism on his wife who should then simply sit and wait, giving him eye contact at the same time, for the tirade to blow itself out. The most likely result, however, is that he will almost immediately lower his voice, sit down and begin to discuss his own worries and anxieties about money and the way they are going to manage their affairs. Often, his anger will only have been a reflection of his own feelings of anxiety and insecurity about being a good provider. He will now have the chance to voice these insecurity feelings and he and his wife can work out strategies by which the anxieties can be reduced all round. In this case an assertive response will have facilitated a discussion about the key issues confronting the couple and lead to a non-frustrating interchange. As a final point, the wife, when the conversation becomes informational rather than resentful, has a right to state any misgivings and grievances which she has. But the couple should then work out a positive contract by which these can be resolved rather than embark on a points scoring exercise of: 'Well I only do that as a defence against your doing what you do. ...' For example, while he may object to her spending money on certain non-essentials, she may dislike his frequent late arrivals home after work. The way to approach this situation is by the positive direction of: 'I will try to cut down on luxury items which I buy and I would like you to try and reciprocate by having a few early nights at home with me.'

In these situations several different types of assertive behaviour have been demonstrated. It should be noted that the principles can be readily interchanged between the situations and incorporated into any other situations where they are relevant.

The assertion procedure helps to reduce or eliminate Frustration Stressers by either minimising or removing the 'winner/loser' situation. Like any other skill it demands certain basic knowledge and practice at implementing it. As with the acquisition of any skill, the initial stages may seem difficult or of doubtful value but we do urge you to persevere with the procedures. They have been found to be highly effective in clinical practice.

2. Becoming Assertive – Exaggerated Role Playing

For many people, especially those who have been schooled in not showing their feelings or making scenes, demonstrating any sort of disagreement may be so anxiety-producing that they cannot make a start on delivering the types of assertive responses which we described above. In such cases we have seen the fear of assertive interchanges lead to such extreme resolutions as a couple buying a new house with two bathrooms rather than try to resolve their problems of bathroom sharing for fear it would end in a row. In marriages this kind of suppression of feelings can often lead to restrictions on sexual expression and an inability to function in a spontaneous and enjoyable way. In business and social relationships it may well lead to strained interactions with everyone behaving in such a devious way in order to avoid a confrontation that important issues are never settled.

The most useful exercises with which to begin in this area of difficulty are practice sessions, where roles are exaggerated quite deliberately and exchanges impersonalised through feelings being ventilated by using a set phrase or *without the use of words at all*.

If assertion problems occur within marriage then couples can practise these exercises with one another. If they arise at work or in social areas then you have to find a suitable partner, perhaps a relative or close friend with whom to practise. It is essential to build up confidence in using these procedures in a familiar environment.

In these initial exercises the emphasis is upon recognising and accepting the feelings associated with anger. The behaviour patterns which it is important to build up are those common to expressions of anger:

Raising the voice and shouting.
Thumping a table or stamping a foot.
Exerting muscular activity.
Holding the body in an aggressive posture.
Maintaining tenacious eye contact.

a. Give Me the Towel! In this exercise the two people who are training grasp opposite ends of a strong towel and begin pulling in tug-of-war fashion against one another. At the same time they start shouting and screaming: 'Give me the towel!' and *nothing* else other than that. Very quickly both will begin to perspire and become red in the face and at this point the shouting should be increased to full volume as both people scream as angrily as they can 'Give me the towel!' Many people find it helpful to imagine that someone is trying to steal a valued possession from them and they are trying to wrench it back. Carry on the session only as long as neither participant is excessively fatigued and then collapse into chairs and relax as quickly and completely as you can. After a few minutes recuperation you may wish to have another go or you might prefer to leave it and try again later on. You may be surprised how difficult it is to get started with this exercise but do not be satisfied until you are able to hurl really full blooded shouts or screams at one another while practising and see how angry you can make yourself feel. It is very important to concentrate on this anger feeling and accept it.

We should point out here that, as with other exaggerated role playing exercises, if there is any particular medical reason why you should not engage in extremely strenuous physical activity then you should obtain the advice of your doctor before doing so.

b. The Number Game: This exercise is designed to enable the participants to express any kind of sentiment by voice intonation rather than by words. In this way a person can build up on the 'Give me the towel!' exercise by adding tonal expression to sheer quantity of sound. Tones expressing contempt, anxiety, disgust, sorrow, love, affection, admiration, disbelief and boredom can be integrated while still not actually expressing the sentiments in words.

The exercise is carried out with the participants standing about three feet apart and taking it in turn to voice a sentiment through a number. For example the first person may say: '83!' with the vocal intonation which clearly indicates: 'I hate you!' And then the second person may say: '12' with a vocal intonation consistent with: 'That's very hurtful.' The conversation might then continue through all sorts of intonations with the participants trying to coax one another, seduce one another or carry on any other type of emotive activity. During the exercise physical contact may be engaged upon and the parties can push one another or stroke one another – perhaps even end up making love with one another. We shall in fact talk more about 'making up' after one of the assertion exercises at the end of this procedure. Again this exercise should be carried out regularly so as to build up the ability to emote without feeling self-conscious or ridiculous. It is useful also in that it gives the person who is less verbally able to argue an equal chance with a partner who may always win a dispute when words are used.

c. Insults and Compliments: In this situation words and intonations are used and voice volume may vary between screams and shouts and quiet murmurings. The object here is to practise saying very basic things to one another which have been felt often but largely bottled up. Whether these are criticisms, insults, compliments or love making approaches, the ability to state them is equally important. The couple should sit or stand and take it in turn to send out an insult or negative evaluation or a compliment or positive evaluation. The person to whom the evaluation is sent should initially simply accept what has been said and not respond in any way. In each session there should be an approximately equal balance of positive and negative evaluations sent and received by each participant. During this exercise it is also important to say whatever it is you are feeling in as down to earth a way as makes you feel comfortable. For example, if in one of the insults you wish to say: 'I can't stand the way you fart in bed' – then say it like that and do not try to be polite by referring to 'rude noises and bad smells!' Similarly if you have, for a long time, been very turned on by a part of your partner's anatomy then you might say: 'I think you've got gorgeous tits', or 'I adore to touch your cock' rather than referring to the firmness of her breasts or his virility. Remember also that many couples find the use of earthy nouns to be particularly erotic and some experimentation with talking explicitly about sensations, secretions, anatomical detail and the actions of the organs involved may do a lot to remove embarrassment barriers and provide a highly information charged and erotic interchange. When carrying out this exercise you must never apologise either during or after the session for anything you have said. You *meant* them or you would not have said them. Equally there should be no recriminations for anything your partner has said, although later you can try to do something about the parts of your behaviour which were criticised and improve even further on the parts which were enjoyed.

When you have practised this exercise for some time you should go on to practise responses to insults or compliments but do so assertively – which means without justifying yourself. For example, in response to a negative evaluation or insult you might respond: 'I can see how that might annoy you' and in reply to a compliment you might respond: 'Thank you, that's very nice to hear.' All too often we are ready with some defensive snipe against a person who is critically appraising us or with some deflating comment in the face of a compliment. Responses of the type: 'Well you can take it or leave it . . .' or 'Oh, do you think so – it's just an old dress dug out from years ago' are both conversation stoppers and likely to prevent their unassertive senders from enjoying a productive interchange.

By the end of this period of training you should be well acquainted with the feelings associated with assertive respond-ing. It is likely that a lot of emotion will have been mobilised and while you are practising these exercises you should always try to capitalise on emotions which have been stirred up by following any productive line which seems to have emerged from the interchange – especially where sexual arousal may have occurred in an intimate partnership.

3. Making Up

In confrontations which are based on aggression a spiral or escalation of the aggression may have developed to a point where the participants are shouting at one another and scoring quarrelling points. At this sort of level it is very difficult indeed to stop the escalation as neither side will want to lose face and let the other have the final word. This sort of interchange can often last for hours or even days with continual sniping going on between the people involved. It is in this sort of escalating situation that it is very important to develop a strategy for end-ing the aggression, by making up, on some more productive basis.

It may be, if you have already developed quite an assertive relationship with the person involved, that you can decide on some signal to be used to indicate that you wish battle to cease and make up behaviour to begin. This signal may be slipping an arm around your partner or verbally saying that you would like to make up. At this point it is most important for the partner who has been approached in this way to respond co-operatively or the system will become considerably weakened. The use of such a signal does not mean that further discussion will not take place on the topic of disagreement but that it can do so without acrimony and personal sniping.

If you are in a situation where you cannot get your partner to agree to some such signalling strategy then you may have to carry out what is usually initially a much more difficult procedure – that of 'modelling'. In general if you carry out a piece of behaviour sufficiently frequently with a particular person then that person will come to recognise it and respond in a similar fashion. Aggression breeds aggression and children who are often beaten at an early age may learn to develop the habit of beating later in life. It is also true, however, that reconciliatory behaviour breeds reconciliations. On this basis you should make a decision, if you are frequently in a position of escalating aggression situations, to be the first to stop the escalation and to let your partner have the last word. But do this by saying something like: 'I really am very upset by this issue and I'd like to make up.' You are *not* apologising or admitting that you are wrong by doing this but making a positive and assertive move towards a more tenable situation. This may, as we say, prove very difficult to do in the early stages because you will feel as though you are doing all the work. But keep it up and you should reap the rewards later.

4. You are Entitled to Ask

Many frustration situations occur because something which is desired is not even asked for in the first place. Examples of this are frequently found in husband/wife relationships, especially in the area of sexual requirements, in dating and in work where privileges or better conditions are never sought because it is assumed that they will be refused.

In all these areas one major mistake is being made – and that is in not assertively letting others know that you have needs which you want to be fulfilled. If your spouse is unaware of certain desires on your part, if you walk past the person you wish to date each day without so much as a smile, or if the boss thinks that your working conditions are totally beneficial for you, then they cannot possibly realise that you want something and so cannot ever say yes.

The rule in this situation is always to ask. The secondary rule is not to mind if the person says 'no'. Clearly it is a pleasant bonus if the person says 'yes' but that is how you should consider it – as a bonus! It is not a terrible failure if they say 'no' since you will automatically have succeeded in being correctly assertive by asking in the first place.

So whether you are asking your spouse to make love in a new position, your boss for a pay rise or someone you have admired from a distance to go out with you to a film, you should evaluate only the actual behaviour of asking. As soon as you have asked, and before they have answered, you should use mental self-congratulation (as described in Programme Four). Remember that the more frequently you ask and the wider the range of things you ask for, the more likely it is that you will receive some positive responses. You will also become increasingly skilled in the way you ask for things in the future.

If you feel particularly anxious about asking for something then use Quick Relaxation (which you can learn in Programme One) to help overcome the feelings of physical tension which may make it difficult for you to speak fluently. Any mental confusion which you suffer can be reduced through the use of the procedures taught in Programme Three.

Remember that asking for things is a learned skill. Until you have gained practice at it you will not be able to do it without some effort and difficulty. But practice will eventually remove these problems and enable you to express your desires easily, thus removing a great many possible sources of Frustration Stressers.

5. Exit Skills

Many training manuals and popular books give advice on how to win friends and influence people. But there is little to guide the person whose privacy is consistently being invaded by people who want to impose on them for conversation, favours or merely attention. We have seen many examples of people in academic and business life who have had their entire day put behind schedule by having to listen to the dronings of a colleague or neighbour, sometimes for hours on end, while simply becoming more and more anxious that they are not doing what they should be doing without being able to do anything to bring the encounter to a conclusion. It also frequently happens that people who have stood up for their rights in a correctly assertive manner are faced with an unhappy end result because they have not walked away from the situation when they should have done. For example, a man has seen his employer and obtained a pay rise. Then instead of terminating the interview and leaving he has allowed it to continue and found himself agreeing to take on extra duties. It is essential in any confrontation to be able to extricate oneself effectively at the best possible point. Clearly the right moment to exit from a complete bore is *immediately*, while the best point in a negotiation situation is at the moment when you think you have achieved the maximum realistic gain.

Termination or exit skills can be seen most effectively in terms of 'stimulus control'. This means that the environment is contributing towards the undesirable situation and it is essential to change that stimulus if you are to exit successfully. Suppose, for example, that you are approached by your employer while working at your desk. He has nothing in particular to say to you but rambles on about a variety of quite unimportant topics and personal problems while you are trying to complete some important work. The thing *not* to do is simply bury yourself deeper in the piles of paper and hope he will take the hint and go away. If he intended to do that he would have done so within the first couple of minutes. The stimulus control must be changed. To do this the first thing is to push back your chair and stand up. This will probably produce a pause in his conversation during which you should say, firmly, something along these lines: 'Sir, I appreciate that you have your own difficulties but I would be grateful if you could leave me just at this moment to complete my work or the whole office is going to be put behind schedule.' During this time you should maintain eye contact. After this you should sit down and resume your work. If the person is a colleague or subordinate it may be even more effective to walk around the desk and gently touch the person's elbow while making a movement towards the door. Usually the person will follow you and exit.

Let us take a different situation. A busy housewife is caught by her neighbour while coming back from shopping. She has a dozen things to do against a deadline but the neighbour wants a good gossip. It will be quite useless for her to stand on one spot and make polite noises suggesting how busy she is or to try to edge towards the house. She must say politely but assertively that she has to get indoors as there are several urgent jobs needing her attention. She should then say goodbye and change the stimulus situation by moving purposefully towards the door. Any further attempts to delay her should be dealt with in a joking manner while still continuing to walk towards the door.

This is not being rude. It is matching your stated wish – to continue with your own affairs, against their stated wish – to command your attention, and assertively carrying out your wishes in the matter.

Summary

Frustration Stressers are associated with situations where, apparently, you are going to lose whatever you do.

It is important to determine whether frustrating situations are changeable or must be tolerated.

If the frustration is insurmountable then it is possible at least to reduce its effects by using Relaxation methods and Assertion responses.

The Assertive response is generally the best way of dealing with surmountable Frustration Stressers. It is effective in dealing with situations where certain needs are not being fulfilled, where people are creating too many demands on your time and capabilities, in situations where unrealistic demands are being made and when those involved find it difficult to engage in any emotional interaction.

It is possible to learn the Assertion response by means of structured exercises including exaggerated role playing, making up skills, demand and exit skills.

General Rules to be Maintained Through Any Assertion Interchange

(1) Maintain eye contact.
(2) Keep your body positions similar – either both standing or both sitting.
(3) Never apologise for expressing something which you honestly feel, but at the same time be prepared to accept justified criticism and show your regret over any real mistakes which you have made.

PROGRAMME NINE – RCPs FOR – BEREAVEMENT LIFESTYLE STRESSERS

Bereavement Stressers occur as a result of any situation which is assessed by the individual as a deeply felt loss. Many of these situations are obvious, and include death or permanent separation from a loved one, through emigration, and the loss of a marriage partner after a divorce. However, some of the circumstances which can give rise to this type of Stresser are less apparent as the list of common bereavement situations below will indicate.

Loss of a relative or close friend following a serious argument.
Loss of friends due to move to new area, or transfer at work.
Loss of a much loved pet animal.
Loss of a job through redundancy, retirement, closure or bankruptcy.
Loss of self-esteem following one of the above or any situation which results in demotion, dismissal from a club, society, social group, or team.
Loss of self-image following a disfiguring illness or handicapping accident.
Loss of self-respect following conviction for some crime.
Loss of sexual ability due to age or illness.
Loss of strength and agility with increasing years.
Loss of a deeply felt religious or political belief as a result of some dramatic disillusionment.
Loss of standing in family or community circles.
Loss of some cherished object.

It is a matter of common observation that the symptoms produced by Bereavement Stressers will usually be far stronger immediately after the loss has been suffered than they are after a passage of time. The duration of this mourning varies greatly according to the nature of the loss and the circumstances in which it has taken place. However, whenever any deeply felt loss has been suffered, especially after a death, the victim of these Stressers will have to work through a series of grief stages in order to come to terms with the bereavement and start to reintegrate their lives with the mainstream of the community once again. If these phases of grieving are not worked through, the Stressers arising from the bereavement will remain unresolved and are likely to produce handicapping difficulties which may prevent the person concerned from returning to a normal lifestyle. The symptoms listed below should, therefore, be regarded as a progression of feelings which will be experienced, in varying degrees of intensity by different individuals under different circumstances, over a period of days, weeks, months or even years following the loss. These phases of grieving have been established after many years research and clinical experience by our colleague Dr Ramsay of Amsterdam University. His work has indicated that there are seven major stages in working through a grief response and that these phases must be gone through in order for the bereavement to be resolved and removed. These phases are:

a. Shock
This response comes very quickly after the bereavement and can appear as a sense of numbness, apathy and withdrawal, an abnormal calm, an awareness of surroundings and feelings of unreality, mechanical responses and behaviours carried out in an automatic or detached way, physical pain or an inability to express emotions.

b. Denial
Although this is mostly seen in the early stages of the bereavement reaction, it is often found later when the bereavement is being worked through. The bereaved person acts as though the loved person or object was still there and that no loss had occurred. Sometimes the lost object is searched for or spoken to and it can appear as if the person is suffering from hallucinations.

c. Depression

As the person comes to realise that they really have been bereaved and denial ceases to work, they will experience despair, pain and a sense of great loss. At this point, if the person can cry, this emotional release will help in lowering the strain. Sometimes crying does not occur and again a sense of unnatural calm can appear.

d. Guilt

In this phase the person will often develop very pronounced guilt feelings over real or imagined negligence or harm inflicted on the lost person or object. The bereaved will often blame themselves for not having expressed more love or shown more care while the lost individual or object was there.

e. Anxiety

As the person realises the full implications of the loss panic responses may occur as they think of the changes which will take place and their lonely or disrupted future. At this point also there may be anxiety about suicidal thoughts, increased workload as they have to cope for themselves and for aggressive thoughts which begin to break through and which occur because they have been left behind to fend for themselves. The ferocity of these aggressive thoughts can sometimes be almost overwhelming and difficult to understand.

f. Aggression

In this phase the bereaved will often begin to blame other people bitterly for their loss. Ultimately they will also usually include themselves in the aggressive blaming behaviour. As they work through all the people who are left surviving in an aggressive way, the final aggression which they are faced with is against the lost person or object for the pain which has been inflicted on them by the loss. Usually the ease with which this last aggression, that towards the lost person or object, is experienced will depend on how close and integrated the person was with that which has been lost. The more intimate or valued the relationship the more difficult it usually is to give vent to this aggression.

g. Reintegration

In this phase the lost person or object has to be relinquished fully and a final farewell has to be said. The fact has to be accepted that life lies ahead with a set of problems and a set of new opportunities which do not depend on the lost person or object. The bereaved person then approaches this future life with the knowledge that the lost person or object will no longer be present. During this phase there may be some periods of depression around the anniversary of the loss, at birthdays, Christmas and so on, but these relapses are usually of short duration.

These stages are all essential to the grieving process. If there is any hold up on any of the phases then the person will not successfully work through to the Reintegration phase where life can be continued without the lost person or object.

In the majority of cases the stress of bereavement is *only* resolved with the passage of time and the working through of the loss. However, in cases where some hold up has occurred at any of the stages it may be necessary to take steps to ensure that the bereavement is resolved by moving through the remaining stages to Reintegration. The need to do this will depend on other factors, the main one of which being advanced age. Many old people who have lost their spouse will behave as though their partner was still present and will include them in conversations, lay places for them at the dinner table and even buy foods and other things which were their favourites. In such circumstances it is probably of little value to persuade them beyond this Denial phase since they derive comfort from this way of coping. But it is important in the majority of cases if you have been bereaved or are close to someone who has been bereaved that the seven stages of grieving are properly worked through.

The symptoms produced by any deeply felt loss are likely to be quite similar whatever the nature of that loss. However, the procedures by which they can best be resolved may vary

I

according to the type of loss which has been experienced. We have categorised loss situations into three main groups depending on the type of procedures which are generally most effective in dealing with the difficulties they produce. The first two groups can often be resolved by using procedures described in earlier Programmes. The third group, however, usually requires special procedures which are detailed in this Programme. It should be made clear, however, that one may have to work through the stages of grieving in circumstances other than a loss through death or permanent separation. The grief which arises from saying goodbye to old friends after retirement, or from the amputation of a limb as a result of an accident may equally need to be resolved by the procedures described here. Only *you* will know the intensity of grief stemming from a particular loss and understand the extent to which an inability to resolve grief is damaging to your health and happiness.

Group A
Losses which can be anticipated and planned for, if only a short time in advance. This group includes losses through retirement, redundancy, or a move to a distant part of the country, loss of strength and agility due to ageing.

Group B
Losses involving damage to self-esteem. These are not usually possible to plan in advance and can arise from a wide range of situations from illness to accident, and sexual dysfunction to demotion. Loss of self-esteem is often a component of the bereavement experienced after retirement or redundancy and it will be helpful, if this is part of your problem, to study the Programmes advised for both these groups.

Group C
Loss through death or the permanent separation from a loved one due to emigration. (Note that these procedures can also be used to resolve the grief which follows the death of a much loved

pet animal or the loss of some cherished object which has resulted in great feelings of grief.)

The symptoms produced in the first two groups include anxiety, boredom, depression, aggression, lack of confidence, frustration, an impairment in physical performance, lethargy and mental confusion. These have already been dealt with in previous Programmes where detailed RCPs have been given. In this Programme, therefore, we want to deal mainly with the problems arising from the third loss group, that is, mainly, bereavement as a result of death. However, in cases where the loss has occurred as a result of permanent separation from a loved one, for example through emigration, the same procedures may help to resolve the grief problems involved.

Procedures Needed for Dealing with the Three Loss Groups

Group A

If you can anticipate a loss it is usually possible to take steps to reduce or completely prevent many of the Stressers which will be associated with it when the time comes. This is especially true with retirement, where the right time to plan for the loss of a work routine and colleagues, a decrease in income and a change in home and social life is several years prior to the moment of parting with one's working life. As we explained in Programme Eight, many people choose the moment of retirement to move away from their old neighbourhoods and start a new life in the country or by the sea. Whether this is beneficial or not depends very largely on how much planning has gone into the change of lifestyle. Retired people who move to live amongst complete strangers in an unfamiliar part of the country are likely to encounter considerable adjustment problems. Threat Stressers may increase as the unfamiliar environment is assessed as being hostile, leading to anxiety and tension. Boredom and Frustration Stressers are likely to rise because the old routines, which helped to provide reinforcers, have vanished. It will be necessary to find new activities with which to replace these reinforcers in order to prevent boredom from becoming a major problem. In all these situations the most useful RCP Programmes to follow are:

> *Programme One* – To learn relaxation skills which will help combat anxiety.
> *Programme Two* – For reintroducing interest and excitement into your life.
> *Programme Six* – Which will train you to manage anxiety.
> *Programme Seven* – Which will explain procedures for combating boredom.

Group B

Where you have been bereaved of self-esteem, either by falling from favour at work, by being involved in a broken marriage or suffering a humiliating setback in an area of your life then it is important to appraise your situation realistically and discern how and where new and positive behaviours and attributes can be reintegrated into your lifestyle. The Positive Self-Talk procedures which we teach in Programme Two will be helpful here as will the Self-Reinforcement Motivational procedures of Programmes Three and Four. The most important step in reintegrating yourself with life is to establish a goal of attaining a new job, new marital status, new social position or whatever it is that has been lost. Remember that in regaining lost reinforcers it is much more effective where possible to obtain them from situations which are similar to the ones which were lost.

Group C

The procedures which we detail now may seem to be harsh and nearly impossible to carry out. This is a fair criticism. But they are not intentionally unkind and in justification we can assure you that they provide the most effective way currently known of reducing Bereavement Stresses in cases where it has proved impossible to come to terms with the loss. In the majority of cases where these procedures have been used bereaved people have been able to work through and resolve all the phases of grieving in as many days as it might otherwise have taken months or years – if indeed they would ever have been resolved.

There are two ways in which these procedures can be used. The first is in order to implement them yourself if you have suffered a bereavement through death or some other type of permanent separation. In these circumstances it will be of great value if you can enlist the aid of a friend to help you work through the procedures. Your friend must, however, first read through the procedures so that he or she understands what is involved and realises how painful, in the short term, implementing them will be for both of you. If you decide to embark on these procedures we must warn you that there will probably follow several days of intense unhappiness. The benefit is that at the end of this period you will have resolved your bereavement difficulties and be able to start living a more normal life again.

The second way these procedures might be used is to help a friend or relative who is suffering from bereavement difficulties. You should suggest that they read through the procedures carefully before asking if they would like you to help them along the lines we suggest. Again we should warn you that you must be prepared for a very difficult and painful period while the grief problems are resolved.

These procedures should *only* be used if there are genuine difficulties in reintegrating one's life after a bereavement and if the resolution of these difficulties will prove beneficial. For example, we have already mentioned the situation of an elderly person who refuses to accept that a loved one has died. The stages of grieving have clearly not been worked through in this instance and so Reintegration cannot take place. But against this the delusion that death has not occurred is clearly providing the old person with comfort and it would be both unkind and pointless to try and help them resolve their grief. However, in the case of a young person who is unable to pick up the threads of life many months after a bereavement, these procedures may be extremely beneficial and, perhaps, their only hope of starting to live a normal life again.

(i) Facing the Loss: For a period of time, which can be up to two or three hours in length in some cases, each day you should settle down and begin to think about the person you have lost. Picture them as vividly as you can and even begin to talk out loud to them, asking questions and remembering the old times in the conversation. During this stage it is valuable to use any mementoes to remind you of particular interactions which you had with them. Photographs, items of clothing, scrap-book cuttings, favourite objects and especially anything which was happening or important at the time bereavement occurred. It is important during this procedure to accept intense feelings of sadness and despair. It is completely natural that these should occur and you must go through a stage of weeping over your loss.

(ii) Feeling Sorry for Yourself: As you enter this phase of crying over your loss you should not be ashamed if you feel very sorry for yourself for this having happened to you. You have good reason to feel sorry for yourself and it is your right to express that grief. In Western cultures it is often felt to be more proper to keep a stiff upper lip in the face of such loss but this, in fact, slows down the whole process of working through bereavement. Cry with friends and relatives and get the sadness out of your system. When you are crying, really let yourself go and think about the saddest or most missed parts about your relationship. It is important at this stage to delve deeply into your memory and conjure up as vivid a recollection as possible of important events which happened between you. You should not hesitate to think gradually of more and more intimate parts of your relationship, from kissing and caressing through to the most private details of your love-making. Remember them and keep telling yourself that you will *not* experience them ever again. Allow yourself to feel as sad as you can. This probably runs contrary to every piece of advice you will have received

from society, where one is normally urged to start living again and to forget what has happened as completely as possible. You may also feel that by experiencing these deep memories you will be presenting yourself with situations of almost intolerable misery. But as long as you keep eliciting the memory and facing it the anxiety and sadness which it brings will gradually decrease and you will ultimately feel at peace with your loss. The hard fact is that after any serious bereavement you are going to experience pain, unhappiness and anguish and the choice is whether this should be spread over many months or years or condensed into a few painful hours or days.

(iii) The Relaxation Response: As you become deeply aware of your sense of loss and the sadness which you are exhibiting, it is likely that you will begin to feel very anxious about how you are going to cope with your future. Again this anxiety is natural and should be allowed to occur, although it is of great comfort and value to be able to use the Relaxation Response, as taught in Programmes One and Six, during this procedure. Set aside some time each day to practise relaxation and use it to help deal with your anxiety. In this case it will almost certainly not provide a complete answer but it will help to take the edge off your anxiety feelings.

(iv) Controlling Other Stressers: As you are now entering probably the most distressing phase of working through your bereavement, it is important, since this will be very stressful for you, not to put your general stress level too far over the OSL. For this reason we would advise you to try to reduce any other sources of stress currently in your life to a minimum. The ones most likely to arise are Frustration, Boredom and Physical Stressers. Any loss represents a decrease in reinforcers and during this stage of working through bereavement, you should accept any offers from friends and relatives for social inter-actions to help replace some of those reinforcers. This will also help ultimately with your Reintegration into a life which no longer includes what you have lost. Programme Seven will be of help to you here. Bereavements frequently lead to a loss of

appetite and sleep and a disinclination to take exercise. All these can reduce one's physical capacity and lead to stress and lowering of one's resistance to stress. Programme Ten should be consulted in order to avoid the worst difficulties which can arise.

(v) Dealing With Aggression: As you explore more and more the intimate interactions which you had with the dead person, there will be occasions when you feel angry towards others who might share some of the blame for your loss or towards yourself. This is quite natural and you should allow free expression of anger at such times. Ultimately you may also feel anger towards what has been lost and it is at this stage that many people will feel embarrassed and guilty about such emotions. But you must work with this emotion and use the argument that *you* are the one who has been left to pain and grief and that it is quite understandable to feel angry towards the dead person. At this point it may be useful to consult Programme Eight on dealing with Frustration Stressers and the use of the assertive response. Exaggerated role playing may be of particular value in giving vent to your aggression through shouting, or punching a cushion and finally directing your aggression at the person or object you have lost. Try to continue this procedure until you no longer feel guilty about these feelings and until you have become a little calmer in that you have put that which you have lost in perspective.

(vi) Saying Goodbye and Looking Forward: Now it is time to work on saying a final farewell to the lost person. You must tell yourself repeatedly that you will *never* see them again and that they will play no part in the rest of your life. By this time this will usually be a fairly easy last step which will leave you with a sense of fond memory of past occasions which you have enjoyed in their presence or in the lost situation. You should, of course, retain these fond memories. No one would suggest that you forget someone or something with whom there has been a good deal of important interaction carried out, but now the memories are of something past rather than still haunting you and you can go on to Reintegrate yourself back into a new

lifestyle. During this phase Programmes Four and Five may be useful.

Summary

Bereavement Stressers arise whenever something which is loved or highly regarded is lost.

Research has shown that there are seven major stages to pass through in resolving grief, these are:

Shock.
Denial.
Depression.
Guilt.
Anxiety.
Aggression.
Reintegration.

Unless these stages are worked through the grief problems will remain unresolved.

Where some types of loss are concerned, preplanning and the use of procedures detailed in earlier Programmes may be sufficient to alleviate or remove the major symptoms which occur. When a very serious loss has occurred, however, the person may be unable to resolve the grief which results. If this is restricting their life it may be necessary to use special procedures in order for them to face up to their loss and work through their grieving. These procedures are very painful in the short term but they offer the most effective and speedy method of resolving grief difficulties.

They should only be undertaken after a careful appraisal of the temporary unhappiness which they will produce and in those situations where a return to an integrated life is desirable.

Once the procedures have been started it is important that they are completed in order that the grief problems are fully resolved.

I*

PROGRAMME TEN – RCPs FOR – PHYSICAL LIFESTYLE STRESSERS

There are two groups of Physical Stressers. Those which occur as damaging elements, for example pollution and germs, in our external environment; and those which arise from changes, such as the process of ageing, within the body. It is virtually impossible to draw a clear line between these two categories since, for much of the time, they are intimately connected. For instance the rate at which a person ages is increased by such external factors as an inadequate diet, hardships and exposure to other Lifestyle Stressers. But even if one enjoyed a perfectly balanced and adequate diet, freedom from hardships and the ability to control all other forms of stress, ageing would still take place as the inevitable by-product of the metabolic process which keeps us alive. Similarly, cancers can arise which have no, as yet, apparent, external cause. But others are known to be associated with such external carcinogens as smoking and some forms of atmospheric pollution. There is, therefore, a constant interaction between the world beneath and the world beyond our protective layer of dead dermal cells. While most Physical Stressers can be measured quantitatively, as the amount of dust in the air or the lack of vitamins in the diet for example, there are others which arise subjectively from an attitude of mind. All psychosomatic illnesses come into this latter group.

Physical Stressers include:

Inadequate diet, whether the inadequacy is due to insufficient nutrition, as in most under-developed countries, or inappropriate foodstuffs as in the West.
Polluted water.
Excessive consumption of alcohol.
Smoking.
Lack of exercise.
Lack of sleep.
Atmospheric pollution – including dust, dirt, toxins, gamma

and high levels of ultra-violet radiation, some types of bacteria, viruses.

Meteorological conditions – such as extremes of heat or cold, great humidity, a lack of oxygen due to the altitude.

Ageing.

Working or living under conditions which artificially replicate the above situations.

Exposure to Physical Stressers not only raises the general levels of stress but it also reduces one's ability to combat stress from other Lifestyle Stressers. It is a matter of common observation that a person is less able to cope with stressful encounters after being deprived of sleep or if kept on an inadequate diet for an extended period.

Good health is something which many people regard as their natural birthright. But this is not so. To remain healthy, especially later in life, is a goal that must be planned and worked for. These days there is a dangerous tendency to rely on medicine, rather than ourselves, to maintain our health. Drugs and advances in surgery seem increasingly to be regarded as cure-alls which give us licence to abuse our bodies in any way we please. If we destroy our lung tissue with tobacco there is bound to be an operation or a course of drugs to clear up the problem. If we allow stress to control our lives and produce hypertension or heart trouble then we look to doctors to clear out the clogged arteries, replace worn heart valves with plastic and lower blood pressure with tablets.

In early Programmes we emphasised the need for you to treat yourself kindly. To reward yourself for achieving or attempting sub-goals in structured Programmes of change. To praise yourself for your efforts. Your attitude towards your body should be no less sympathetic. Few motorists would dare to treat their cars in the harsh and damaging way many people treat their physiology. If they did, then the vehicles probably would not last very long and few observers would be surprised when they broke down. Because our bodies have enormous reserves and recuperative powers they can tolerate abuse for many years without breaking down and with only a gradual impairment in performance. Their resistance is no justification for driving them into a state of eventual collapse. If you smoke, drink excessively, take insufficient exercise or go for long periods without enough sleep; or if you live and work in a polluted atmosphere, expose yourself to hardships and make no effort to control the Lifestyle Stressers then you are greatly increasing the speed and certainty of mental or physical collapse.

In mankind's recent history there have been many devastating epidemics. Millions have perished as cholera, dysentery, typhoid and tuberculosis swept across the globe. Today the majority of killer diseases are man-made. They can be directly attributed to the social, political and economic structures which we have created. In the under-developed countries these killer diseases are associated with nutritional deficiencies, in the affluent West they are mostly related to over-consumption in one form or another. They include cancers (especially of the lung), gastric ailments, hypertension and heart disease. Coronary heart disease is now a major slayer claiming the lives of 35,000 men under the age of 65 in Britain, and 700,000 Americans each year. In 1969 the World Health Organisation warned that heart disease could soon present mankind with the greatest epidemic it has ever faced, a prophesy which is rapidly being fulfilled.

A decade ago ulcers were looked on by many as a dubious status symbol of business efficiency, something the ambitious businessman achieved with the key to the executive washroom. Today a factory worker in his twenties is as likely to suffer from this disorder as a middle-aged company director. A young housewife can just as easily become the victim of a phobia or anxiety state as a woman at the menopause. The taking of tranquillisers is clearly one barometer by which to measure rising pressure levels in society. Here the figures show that dependence on prescribed tranquillisers has risen by 290 per cent since 1962, while by comparison the per capita consumption of alcohol rose by only 23 per cent.

The RCP Programmes presented so far will enable you to control and creatively use stress. But to use these effectively you must be as healthy as possible. This means combating as many of the Physical Stressers present in your life as you are able. There will be some Stressers which it is beyond your individual ability to remove. If your work demands that you spend hours in a very hot, cold, or dusty atmosphere, or if you have to live in the dirty air of a big city, then you may have simply to put up with considerable exposure to these damaging elements. The best you can do is to take certain precautions to minimise the damage which they will cause. Most of these are basic common sense. For example:

(1) Insist that correct precautions are taken whenever you have to work in an artificially polluted atmosphere. Safety masks, protective clothing and a strict observance of the regulations for handling toxic solutions, dangerous substances and forms of damaging radiation. In most industries precautions are observed and they are usually backed by legislation. The danger is that accidents can arise through carelessness on the part of those involved in the process because they have habituated to the routine and no longer give it their full concentration. We will look at this problem in Stage Six.

(2) Do everything you can to make your working environment as pleasant and safe as possible, either through direct action or union pressures. Ensure that there is sufficient ventilation in your office, for example, since a lack of oxygen can lead to rapid exhaustion and a lowering of concentration. Keep it as clean as possible to reduce the amount of dust in the environment.

(3) If you work in a dirt-laden atmosphere it is an act of biological madness to add to the dangers by smoking. Despite widespread warnings of the dangers of smoking there has been no decline in the number of cigarettes sold.

(4) Seize every opportunity to get out into clean, fresh air.

In addition to these general safeguards you should pay particular attention to getting sufficient exercise, to having enough restful sleep and to eating sensibly. These are the three main areas where Physical Stressers arise. They are also the ones most directly under our control. In this RCP Programme, therefore, we will concentrate on procedures for exerting such control.

In the procedures for taking more exercise and enjoying an adequate diet, we will provide a general framework of behavioural principles which will allow you to implement successfully any course of exercises or diet which you care to follow. So far as controlling insomnia is concerned we will describe a specific behavioural Programme which will enable you to increase your periods of restful sleep.

1. Exercise

Only your doctor, after a lengthy medical examination, can give you an accurate picture of your present state of health. Certainly before you embark on any Programme involving strenuous exercises you should consult your medical practitioner if there is the slightest risk that your heart may not be up to the strain involved.

Probably you have your own opinion on how fit, or otherwise, you are at this moment. Here are three checks, two quick and one involving a little time and effort, which you can make to give yourself a general idea of your state of fitness.

Sit in a comfortable chair and just stay still for a few minutes. Now take your pulse. The easiest way to do this is to locate the wrist pulse which is found just below the thumb ball. Place three fingers side by side on the wrist with the top finger just level with the base of the thumb ball. Now you should be able to detect the regular beat of the pulse beneath your middle finger. Using the second hand of your watch count the beats for one minute. An average pulse rate is just over seventy beats per minute.

Below that, sixty or fewer, is good. If the pulse rate is eighty or higher under these conditions then *you* are not in good condition. Since pulse rate varies, it is best to take a reading four or five times on different occasions, after a period of rest, before coming to a conclusion about your fitness.

Now repeat the pulse reading after taking some moderate exercise. Cardiologists use a standard exertion test known as the Masters two-step. The subject is asked to step up and down on a nine-inch high step for a minute and a half. You could try walking briskly up a short flight of steps, going down and repeating the exercise. Now take your pulse. The beat will clearly have increased but what you want to find out is how quickly it takes to return to the 'at rest' rate which you measured earlier. If it is still beating rapidly several minutes after this exertion this too is a warning that you are out of condition.

The final exercise is recommended by Dr Kenneth H. Cooper who has developed a theory about physical exercise he calls Aerobics. Dr Cooper's fitness test involves running or walking, or a combination of both, for twelve minutes to see how far you can get. Once again we must advise that you should only carry out this check if you are in reasonable physical health and have no history of heart trouble. If you are in any doubt then consult your doctor first. At the end of twelve minutes, stop and measure the distance you have travelled. If this is more than a mile and a half, you are in good shape. If you are male and have only covered one and a half miles then you are not as fit as you ought to be. Any man under fifty who only covers one mile or any woman under fifty who only covers three-quarters of a mile is in poor condition.

A business executive who strolls around the block with the dog every evening and plays a game of golf during the weekend may believe he is taking sufficient exercise. In fact neither of these activities does much good. A casual stroll which does not increase the heart or respiratory rate is useless so far as increasing physical fitness is concerned and the occasional game of golf, or tennis, however vigorous it may be at the time, is too intermittent to be much help. Weight lifting or chest expander exercises every morning may help to keep the body looking trim but they will not do much to help your overall fitness.

The most effective exercises involve what are termed endurance activities. They increase the rate of respiration so that extra oxygen is drawn into the bloodstream and steps up the heart rate helping to cleanse the arterial system through increased blood pressure. Endurance activities are the only exercises which can truly be said to fortify the body against Stressers. They include, in descending order of effectiveness:

Running, swimming, rapid bicycling, brisk walking, running on the spot, squash, handball and basketball.

All of these activities must be performed vigorously enough to work up a good sweat, to feel the chest rising and falling rapidly as air is drawn deep into the lungs, and to raise the pulse rate.

If, inspired by this advice, you decide to start on a brisk and extended Programme of endurance activities right away, it is almost certain that you will have given up the whole idea of physical exercise a few weeks from now. Overdoing it to start off with is the most common mistake made by people who suddenly feel the need for physical fitness. It accounts for a glut of second-hand static bicycles, barbells and chest expanders!

Structured Exercises

The first thing to establish is that you are fit enough to embark on any course of endurance activities. If in doubt, check with your doctor. He may prescribe an even more careful approach to maximum exertion than we advise here.

You may feel that one of the exercises suggested here would interest you sufficiently to sustain the essential motivation. Alternatively you might want to implement some other fitness Programme. There is a wide range of books on the subject which can give detailed help and advice. But whatever specific course you decide to embark on, there are certain general behavioural principles which must be applied if you are to carry on with such a Programme once the first flush of enthusiasm has passed. Below we describe a Programme which involves running as the endurance activity but the basic features can easily be adapted for use with any other type of physical exercise.

The preliminary step only involves exercising the writing hand. On a sheet of paper draw up a list of graded sub-goals leading towards the major goal desired. In this example our major goal is to run two miles after work each evening. In other instances it might be to complete a particular set of exercises, play a game of squash, swim a number of lengths of a pool or a certain distance at sea. This major goal goes at the bottom of the page, your current level of attainment at the top of the sheet. This may have to be determined by experiment. How far can you run at present without feeling uncomfortably short of breath? Do not overstretch yourself when carrying out this test. Stick within the distance which you can run comfortably so that your increased heart and respiratory rates soon return to normal after you stop running. Similar levels of current attainment can be determined for any other type of physical exercise. Between the current attainment and the desired goal you now fill in a series of sub-goals. These are levels of achievement you want to reach at certain times in your training Programme. Once again, do not overstretch yourself by taking on too large a jump between one sub-goal and the next. If you do you will be likely to fail and such failure damages motivation. The example below gives a series of graded sub-goals in a typical running Programme. Naturally, some of the sub-goals may have to be modified during the Programme if you are either attaining them too easily, and so losing motivation because there is insufficient challenge, or finding them too hard to reach and suffering from a lack of confidence in your ability as a result.

Structured Programme

Major Goal: To run 2 miles a day (3,520 yards).
Current Attainment: Can run 300 yards without undue discomfort.
Sub-Goal One: By end of first 6 days 600 yards without discomfort. This involves an increase of 50 yards per day for next 6 days.
Sub-Goal Two: By the end of 12 days to be able to run 1,200 yards per day without discomfort. This involves a daily increase of 100 yards per day for the next 6 days.
Sub-Goal Three: By the end of 18 days to be able to run 2,400 yards per day. This involves an increase of 200 yards per day for the next 6 days.
Sub-Goal Four: To be able to run 2 miles by the end of 24 days. This involves an increase of approximately 190 yards per day during the next 6 days.

You may find it more helpful to divide each sub-goal into six daily blocks on the Programme sheet and tick off each daily block as you achieve the target. This provides you with reinforcement for the achievement and a clear guide to your progress. Naturally, you will devise a series of graded sub-goals which cover a time period to suit yourself best. But be sure that the steps are neither too large nor too small between each sub-goal. In drawing up the structured exercise Programme it is best to build in some strategies for missed exercise periods due to such things as pressure of work, illness, really bad weather conditions or a trip away from home. If you make no provision for such likely setbacks you may feel guilty about missing out on a training day and lose confidence in your ability to reach the major goal. If you prepare for this kind of interruption to start with, you will have a strategy to take care of it. For example you might decide that a break of two days can be caught up with by a slight increase in the distance run, or the exercises completed, during the remaining period of that sub-goal. Providing that this does not make the jump in exertion too great, you should experience no problems. A long break may require more drastic revision of the schedule, perhaps dropping back to the sub-goal just below your current level of attainment. But do not go back too far or you may give up out of despair for the lost ground.

Now, having worked out your Programme, it is important to maintain your motivation while putting it into action. In RCP Programmes Two and Four, we talked about the value of the reinforcer, or positive payoff, in helping to establish desired pieces of behaviour. By writing out a timetable and pinning it up in a prominent place, perhaps on the door of the cupboard where you keep your exercise clothes, you will be able to give yourself a small positive payoff after completing your exercises. Just by ticking out another square on the timetable you will be providing concrete proof of attainment. But it is likely that larger payoffs will be needed to keep up the motivation, especially on days when you feel particularly sluggish or are late, or the weather is bad. A useful system here is to use the token method discussed in Programme Two. In this procedure you use counters, matches or small coins to attain a major payoff. This can be anything you find rewarding, from buying yourself a present, to sexual activity, to going out and watching a movie. Set a price on the desired payoff in terms of tokens. Now make a contract with yourself not to get that particular object or indulge in that particular piece of behaviour until you can 'buy' it using the tokens. Set a token price on every sub-goal. If you reach the sub-goal, pay yourself and collect the tokens towards buying your payoff. There is no need to wait until you have achieved the major goal. Indeed, if this is some days or weeks away, to try and do so may have adverse effect on your progress and motivation. Reward yourself after each session with a payment of tokens. At the end of, say, one week collect the tokens and get yourself the positive payoff.

The key points of this Exercise Programme can be summarised as follows:

a. Select the type of exercise which best suits your needs. Remember that many doctors believe that endurance activities, which increase the heart and respiratory rate, are more beneficial than other forms of fitness exercises.

b. Prepare yourself a *written* Programme to reach a desired major goal of exercise.

c. Write down your current attainment level in regard to that major goal. This may be determined by experiment. Be careful not to set your starting point too high.

d. Set down a series of sub-goals. Each sub-goal will demand the attainment of a slightly higher exercise target. Do not space the sub-goals too widely or you may fail to achieve the next one, but do not put them too close together or each will be achieved too easily. In both cases you will lose motivation.

e. Sustain motivation by using the payoff system. Do not rely on the satisfaction of having carried out the exercise alone to motivate you to continue.

2. Sleep

For many people, the inability to get sufficient restful sleep is a major Physical Stresser. After only a couple of hours of uneasy tossing and turning they wake up in the cold light of early dawn with no hope of going back to sleep again. Or they may lie resentfully awake for hours after going to bed, their bodies stubbornly refusing to allow them the sleep which they crave. Usually such sufferers turn to drugs to help them, but drug-induced sleep is never as satisfactory as naturally occurring rest.

The average need is eight hours per night, but we all have different requirements which, typically, change at different periods of life. Some people may need ten or twelve hours sleep every night to remain in peak condition while others manage just as well on three or four hours. As we get older there is a tendency to need less sleep.

One of the difficulties facing people in sedentary occupations is that their minds may be exhausted while their bodies, which have done little more exhausting than sit in a chair and push a pen or lift a telephone receiver all day, are hardly fatigued at all. If this is happening in your case, some brisk physical exercise after work will probably help a great deal. There are other things which you can do too, to help promote sleep. Avoid drinking coffee or tea within several hours of going to bed. If you want a beneficial nightcap then a glass of milk, laced with a spoonful of whisky or rum if you prefer, is recommended. Make sure that the bedroom is well ventilated and not too warm. Empty your bladder just prior to going to bed, particularly if you are past middle age, as otherwise a build up of urine will often wake you up before morning. Take a hot bath and prepare for bed in a calm and leisurely fashion. Make a routine of getting your milk ready, selecting a book, washing and undressing. Allow yourself to wind down slowly. Try to banish worrying or irritating thoughts from your mind – we will tell you how to deal with persistently stressful thoughts in a moment – and concentrate on the pleasant aspects of the day. Move slowly and anticipate the pleasure of lying between warm blankets on a comfortable mattress. Making love or masturbating are also physiologically sound ways of preparing the body for sleep.

If you have carried out some or all of these procedures you may find that you drop off to sleep quite quickly. Your chances will further improve if you use the Deep Muscle Relaxation exercises taught in RCP Programme One once you are in bed.

But suppose that you have done all that we have suggested and you still cannot sleep. Here is what you do.

a. **Get out of bed:** You should allow yourself a certain amount of time, say fifteen minutes, in which to fall asleep. If you are still wide awake at the end of this period, and by setting yourself a time limit you actually increase the chances of falling asleep, do not stay restlessly turning in bed. By doing so you come to associate bed with insomnia rather than with sleep. After several occasions, during which you have remained in bed for hours on end without being able to sleep, you will come under stimulus control from the bed. The very act of getting into bed will make you feel anxious and wide awake.

b. Having got out of bed, spend ten minutes doing some small routine chores, finish the washing up, dust the room, or sit in a chair and listen to some soothing music. It does not matter *what* you do so long as it is undemanding on your mental and physical energies. Now return to bed. Give yourself another fifteen minutes in which to fall asleep. If you still remain wakeful at the end of this second period, get out of bed again. Spend fifteen or twenty minutes in the same way as before and then go back to bed. If you have suffered from insomnia for an extended period you may have come under very strong stimulus control from the bed. In such cases it is not exceptional for you to have to get in and out of bed half a dozen times before you finally drop off to sleep. But this will only happen for a very few nights. Your body soon learns to associate bed not with staying awake, as before, but with sleep. The number of journeys in and out of bed swiftly decreases and at the end of a week or ten days you will probably find that you fall off to sleep within the first fifteen minute period.

c. While you lie in bed trying to sleep, ideas may circle restlessly in your mind. Your brain seems to be on fire with thoughts, fears, worries and plans. You hold lengthy conversations with yourself or with others. You vividly conjure up scenes in which you confront people with an injustice you have suffered, criticise an aggressive colleague or neighbour, lay down the foundations for a career which will make your fortune, or go through every incident of the day. There is only one way to deal with these circling thoughts: get them out of your system. If, at the end of the first time period, you are still lying awake with your mind racing then make the chore which you carry out, once you have climbed from the bed, one of writing down those thoughts. Empty them from your brain onto a sheet of paper. Scribble down every idea at random as it comes to you. Use the ideogram method explained in Programme Three. If answers to problems or schemes for overcoming difficulties occur to you then write those down as well. When you read them in the cold light of day they will probably turn out to be rubbish – but never mind. The object of this exercise is not to preserve some great idea for posterity but to liberate it from your brain by externalising it.

These strategies for sleep have now been used extensively in behavioural psychology approaches to the problem. *Stresswatch*, in its research programme, has developed a cassette course to combine the strategies with sleep-inducing sound combinations and this has been found to speed up the acquisition of effective sleeping habits.

The procedures for combating insomnia and enjoying a restful night's sleep can be summarised as follows:

a. Prepare for your sleep before you ever go to bed. Avoid coffee or tea. A better nightcap is milk, perhaps laced with a *little* alcohol. If you have been exercising your mind rather than your body during the day then take some physical exercise during the evening.
b. Get ready for bed in a slow, routine way which starts to wind down your system for rest. Avoid working on mental problems prior to going to bed.
c. In bed use Deep Muscle Relaxation to help you drop off to sleep. Remember that relaxation can often be enhanced through sexual outlet whether with your partner or by masturbation. But set yourself a time limit of, say, fifteen minutes for dropping off to sleep. If you are still awake at the end of this period get out of bed.

d. Away from the bed carry out some routine chores which involve little mental exertion, read an unstimulating book or listen to some quiet music. A better alternative, especially if you have thoughts chasing through your brain, is to sit down and pour out every idea in your head onto paper, using the ideogram method.

e. Get back to bed and use relaxation again to help you sleep. If you are still awake at the end of the determined period then get out of bed again and repeat the chores or write out more of the ideas in your head.

f. Repeat this procedure until you finally fall asleep within the period you have set yourself. Only in this way can you avoid the bed becoming a stimulus control which helps to keep you awake. At first, especially if you have suffered from insomnia for a considerable period of time, you may have to get in and out of bed several times. But your body will soon learn to associate bed with sleep and you will rapidly drop off in the first period of time.

3. Diet and Weight Control

In order to combat Stressers and maintain yourself in the best possible physical health your diet must not only be sufficient for your needs but it must be balanced. Overeating is as much a harmful Physical Stresser as is insufficient nutrition. It is also one of the most prevalent complaints in the affluent West. One in five male American adults are too fat. Ten per cent of the United States' population is overweight. Obese people not only suffer from the Physical Stressers which arise from their bodies' efforts to handle the excess fat but also from other Lifestyle Stressers stemming directly from their weight problems. These frequently include some or all of the following:

Performance Stressers – carrying out tasks which were simple when they were slim can present increasing problems to overweight sufferers.

Threat Stressers – most overweight people are painfully aware of the risks they run from their problem.
Boredom Stressers – they are not able to take part in as many activities as the person of normal weight.
Frustration Stressers – these arise because of their inability to perform physical activities which others take for granted.
Bereavement Stressers – these occur as they mourn for their departed slim selves.

Even when people maintain themselves at around the correct weight for their height and body type, diet inadequacies can still present problems. An insufficient supply of the proteins, fats, carbohydrates and vitamins needed by the body to sustain active life can lead to rapid fatigue, an inability to concentrate or perform strenuous physical activities for an extended period and a lowering of resistance to illness. Severe vitamin deficiencies can cause various ailments, such as scurvy (deficiency of Vitamin C), nerve disorders and loss of appetite (deficiency of Vitamin B1-Thiamine), poor bone and tooth development, dental decay, rickets (deficiency of Vitamin D). It may be thought that such problems are found only in under-developed countries but, as any doctor working in the poorer areas of large Western cities will testify, vitamin deficiencies are by no means a rarity. This is not because foods which will provide these essential diet elements are unavailable but through ignorance of nutritional requirements which causes them to be ignored.

If you are interested in living as healthily as possible then you should read a good, basic book on nutrition and learn what sort of foods are valuable and which ones you can well do without. Money is all too often spent on such things as candy bars, fizzy drinks, and cream cakes which are harmful, when it could be spent on, say, fresh fruit which would be beneficial.

A common mistake, when it comes to meals, is to distribute the food intake unevenly throughout the day. Typically, a busy person will begin the morning with a hastily snatched cup of coffee and, perhaps, a slice of bread or a little breakfast cereal. Lunch may be no more than a sandwich or a snack, while the evening meal, to compensate for the small amount of food taken during the day, will be heavy. The result of this schedule is that the necessary energy-producing foods are seldom readily available to the body at the times when they are most needed. During the morning, when energy consumption is normally high, the body has an insufficient blood-glucose level because of the meagre breakfast. During the afternoon it may be able to pick up some energy from the light lunch but it is not until the evening, when it is usually least needed, that the body is provided with a really adequate supply of energy. Unless this energy is worked off prior to going to bed, and this does not usually happen, the blood-glucose level remains high during the hours of sleep and, in the morning, it is still so high that the person has little appetite for breakfast. So the blood-glucose cycle is repeated. A far more sensible arrangement is to eat a large breakfast which contains a good mixture of protein and carbohydrates. This will release glucose into the bloodstream at a steady rate during the day. Lunch should be a proper meal, not just a snack, so that the depleted energy levels can be topped up again for the afternoon's exertions. Dinner, by comparison, should be a light, easily digested meal. This will not only help you to sleep better but it will ensure that, by morning, your blood-glucose level is low enough for you to have an appetite for a hearty breakfast.

The average Westerner consumes around 3,000 calories per day. If you were to eat no more than 2,600 calories per day you would still have sufficient energy available for all but the most strenuous physical activities.

Your correct weight depends on body build and height. Table One gives average weights for adults of different heights. Ideally you should be lighter than these averages by up to 7 lb. Your mirror will prove an effective weight increase guide to augment the unarguable readings of the bathroom scales. If you are still in doubt about whether or not you have unnecessary layers of fat, try this test. Pinch up a fold of skin at the back of the upper arm, the triceps and measure it. Repeat the exercise with the flesh just below a shoulder blade. Finally take a measurement below the rib cage. None of these folds should measure more than one inch across. Of the three areas it is most likely that the flesh below the rib cage will be in excess of the vital inch. This is because the thickening of the tissues frequently starts in this region.

TABLE TWO – *Weight and Height Averages*

| | *Men* | | | | *Women* | | |
| *Height* | | *Weight* | | *Height* | | *Weight* | |
ft.	*in.*	*st.*	*lb.*	*ft.*	*in.*	*st.*	*lb.*
5	0	9	0	4	8	8	0
5	1	9	2	4	9	8	2
5	2	9	4	4	10	8	4
5	3	9	7	4	11	8	6
5	4	9	10	5	0	8	8
5	5	10	0	5	1	8	10
5	6	10	4	5	2	8	12
5	7	10	8	5	3	9	1
5	8	10	12	5	4	9	5
5	9	11	2	5	5	9	8
5	10	11	7	5	6	9	12
5	11	11	12	5	7	10	2
6	0	12	4	5	8	10	6
6	1	12	10	5	9	10	10
6	2	13	2	5	10	11	0
6	3	13	8	5	11	11	3
6	4	14	0	6	0	11	7

Weight includes light clothing and no shoes.

Height measured without shoes.

If you are much overweight the chances are that you have, at some time, tried to go on a diet and failed. Do not be discouraged by this failure, or failures. Statistics show that the vast majority of overweight people who start on a diet revert to their old weights, or even add a few pounds on top of them, within twelve months of starting out with high hopes and good intentions to slim. From a behavioural point of view this is not surprising. We have already explained that activities which are followed by reinforcement rapidly become established as pieces of routine behaviour. We have also said that the more immediate the reinforcement the more firmly and rapidly the behaviour is established. Food is one of the most basic and powerful reinforcers. Usually the reward follows the moment a morsel of food is pushed between the lips. There is the satisfaction of having the mouth full, of experiencing the texture and taste of the food and finally the comfortable feeling of a full stomach.

When you start a diet you diminish, to some extent, this type of reinforcer while the positive payoff for slimming, a reduction in weight, may not occur for several days or weeks. This makes the downward pointer on the bathroom scales a very delayed reinforcer and, as such, an ineffective one. To diet successfully you must reinforce the slimming behaviour far more immediately as you work through a structured dieting schedule which allows you to progress from one sub-goal to the next easily and surely.

The following behavioural Programme for reducing weight should be used in conjunction with whatever diet scheme most appeals to you. Remember we are only providing the basic framework of psychological principles. It is up to you to fill in the details from whatever diet book or article you please.

As a first step you must prepare on a sheet of paper a structured Programme of sub-goals which lead to the ultimate goal. This will be the weight you wish to have reached by the end of the Programme. This major goal is written at the bottom of the page. At the top of the page write your starting point which will be your present weight.

Now write down a series of sub-goals for weight loss. These will probably be weekly reductions in weight. Refer to the particular diet which you intend to follow in order to see what loss can reasonably be expected. Do not try and lose too much weight over too short a period. If you do then you may well fail and lose confidence in your diet schedule. On the other hand the weight reduction must be realistic enough to keep you encouraged and motivated.

Next, prepare a list of reinforcers as we explained in Programme Two. These payoffs will be used to establish the slim eating habits. The reinforcers can include anything – with the exception of food of course! – which you find pleasant. They must be such that you can make use of them immediately after you have completed a piece of desired behaviour. Equipped with these lists, you can now go ahead with the main part of the weight control Programme.

The pieces of desired behaviour which you should now incorporate into your eating habits are the crucial building blocks with which to erect a pattern of eating behaviour which will lead to a reduction in weight. For this reason it is these behaviours themselves which should be reinforced and the weight loss considered as an almost inevitable consequence of eating in this new way. These behaviours have all been found, by observational research, to be those consistent with the 'thin eater'. Thin eaters and fat eaters behave quite differently in the presence of food and the object of this Programme is to produce, in the obese person, a method of eating which exactly parallels that used by the thin person and so leads to a decrease in weight. We shall present these behaviours as a series of ten tactics which you should reinforce every time you have the opportunity to put them into operation.

a. Rediscovering Taste

The overweight person will, typically, eat food quickly without tasting it. The result of this habit is that foods which the person may not even like are often shovelled down the throat along with the rest of the meal and the person has no time to make a choice as to whether they wish to carry on eating the particular food in front of them. An exercise which should be carried out daily throughout the entire weight control Programme and which will help in relearning how to use the sense of taste is as follows:

Break one small corner from a bar of chocolate and draw it slowly into your mouth after placing it on your tongue.

Smell and taste the chocolate as you do this and when it is in your mouth press it against your teeth and roof of your mouth and let it dissolve without swallowing.

Feel the chocolate coating your mouth and teeth and increase this coating by moving the tongue around your mouth.

After savouring the chocolate for as long as you can, allow the sweet mixture to be swallowed in small amounts at a time.

Clean your mouth completely by licking with your tongue and, at the same time, think about the sensations of just eating the chocolate.

Now ask yourself whether you want a further piece of chocolate. If the answer is yes then carry on and repeat the exercise. But almost certainly the reply will be no, as your craving will have been satisfied by the way in which you ate the first piece.

Repeat the same exercise with an apple, the first bite of which will provide very different sensations from those you obtained from the chocolate.

b. Expand your Eating Time

Learn to develop the habit of being the last person to finish, or if eating alone, of trying to double or treble the amount of time you usually take to eat a meal. Chew the food very slowly and savour it as we have just described. While chewing the food put down your eating utensils and concentrate on chewing and tasting. After you have swallowed the food, stop for a few seconds, possibly sipping a drink or talking briefly to your companion. Then take another mouthful and so on.

By eating slowly your stomach will have a better chance to relay to your brain that it is full and each time you finish a mouthful you will have more chance to exercise your control over the choice of whether to continue eating or not. This provides a guard against the fat eating habit of gorging quickly and giving the stomach insufficient chance to let the brain know that enough food has been ingested until there is a sudden, uncomfortable feeling of engorgement.

c. Into the Waste Not Onto the Waist!

Typically, the fat eater will be unable, perhaps through harsh training in childhood, to see food thrown away. The thin eater though will often leave food which is actually unrequired for effective bodily functioning. Although it may initially be difficult, you should learn how to throw away food and lower the anxiety which this produces in the early stages by repeating the practice frequently. All sorts of arguments against this practice may come to mind but, essentially, there is no valid argument against the fact that if the food is of no particular use to you (and after the feeling of hunger has gone this is the case) then there is no point in continuing to push it into your mouth.

d. Rediscover Hunger

The overweight person hardly ever experiences pangs of hunger. Eating is usually carried out in response to depression, anxiety, loneliness or excitement. Or maybe it has just become an associated learned habit which you perform when carrying out other behaviours such as watching television or making a phone call. You must, therefore, learn to associate eating with feelings of hunger and the later cessation of such feelings. To do this you must make yourself hungry by refraining from eating for a sufficiently long period (something like twelve hours is enough for most people) and understand how it feels to alleviate the hunger by the exercises we have already outlined. You will be surprised to find that it may only take four or five mouthfuls of food to remove your hunger pangs completely.

e. Count Up the Calories

In order to eat anywhere without having to carry around food scales, you should learn how to assess calorie content by sight. Each time you weigh food in the early stages of a diet to find out the calorie content, note how large the portion is by comparison with some easy standard such as the length of your finger, the size of your hand or the volume of your fist. Learn to compare mixtures of food on sight with these standards and balance your plate, when eating out, accordingly.

f. Stimulus Control

Overweight people often eat in irregular environments and at irregular times. You should establish a fixed stimulus situation in which to eat all your meals. At home, whether alone or with others, you should lay a table properly and eat while sitting down. Prepare meals so that second helpings are not available. Do not carry out other activities, apart from talking, while eating. At work, eat in a certain room or a certain corner of your desk if you cannot leave the office. In other words learn that the only times to eat are when you are under your particular stimulus control.

g. Exercise

This is generally important, as we pointed out earlier in this Programme, to tone up flabby muscles and you should try to build up a Programme of exercise along the lines previously described.

h. Assessing Yourself

Take a note of your weight every day and look at yourself naked for some time in front of a mirror. Concentrate on those areas where improvement can be seen and, as time passes, accept the fact that, because of bone formation which is unchangeable, some areas will remain much the same. Concentrate your attention on those areas which are changeable and remark on them constantly to yourself. As positive changes take place, accentuate them by taking more interest over your style of dress, hair and any other ways in which you can enhance your appearance. Pamper your body and devote time to bathing, grooming and tending to your appearance. Do this daily and learn to love your body.

i. Build Up Your Social Life

As your figure begins to improve, start to go into social situations which you have previously avoided through self-consciousness. Occasionally give yourself major reinforcers by holding parties at home and, as frequently as you can, go into varied social situations and build up a more pleasurable lifestyle to make the whole weight control process worthwhile.

Also begin to act much more assertively when faced with pressure to eat more at social functions. Tell those who prevail upon you to 'have a second helping' that you have enjoyed what you have eaten so far, so much that to accept more would be an over-indulgence and might spoil your pleasure. Programme Eight may be of great help in developing these assertive habits.

j. Choosing When to Overeat

Everyone, fat or thin, overeats from time to time. The difference, however, is that overweight people usually become excessively guilty and depressed when they do so and often resort to more overeating to comfort themselves! You should, therefore, actually plan overeating periods into your life so that you can gorge yourself without guilt. You can then build other meal times around the periods of gorging so that your overall calorie intake does not become excessive. For example, a businessman may overeat at two expense account lunches during the week but plan for these by undereating at some other meals. A woman may plan for a family celebration meal in much the same way.

K

The best way of dealing with such temptation is to give into it – but on your terms.

Using these tactics will basically give you one important privilege which, as an over-eater has not previously been available to you. That privilege is the exercise of choice. Whether at a second by second level of choosing to go onto another mouthful or at a week by week level in deciding whether to have a gorge you can now plan on a rational basis rather than take the almost inevitable risk of over-indulging.

Summary

Physical Stressers increase the level of stress present in two ways: by causing damage themselves and by lowering resistance to other types of Stressers.

The two major sources for Physical Stressers are largely uncontrollable factors in the environment and largely controllable elements within our own behaviour.

We have dealt primarily with the controllable factors in this Programme and in particular physical fitness, sleep patterns and weight control.

Remember that physical good health is not your natural birthright. It is something which you have to work at and strive for.

Stage Five

A Ten Day Training Programme

CONTENTS

Stage Five

A Ten Day Training Programme

INTRODUCTION

In this Stage you will find a structured ten-day-long Training Programme designed to help you make a start with any of the first eight Programmes from Stage Four.

Two Programmes, Nine and Ten, have been excluded from this structured schedule for the following reasons.

Where Bereavement Stressers arise from events other than a loss by death, you are directed, in Programme Nine, to appropriate RCPs within the first eight Programmes. These can then be implemented, if you want to do this, using the system described in this Stage. However, where the Stresser has occurred as a result of death it is inappropriate to try and work through the RCPs at any pace other than that dictated by your own feelings. The pace should be dictated by the speed with which the grief problems can be resolved.

In Programme Ten, we outline three structured RCPs for getting more exercise, improving sleep and controlling diet and weight and these should be carried out in the way described in that Programme.

You may feel that simply having acquired the information appropriate to changing your handling of Stress for the better is sufficient for you to be able to go on and put into effect the procedures which we have described. If this is the case then you should do just that. If, however, you feel that you need a more supportive and directive schedule by which to begin implementing these procedures, or if having started on your own you encounter unexpected difficulties, then this Stage of the book will provide you with the necessary thrust to engage yourself fully in your RCPs.

This schedule will be maximally effective if you go through it in the order and at the rate which we suggest. At the end of the ten days for which it lasts, you will have had a good deal of practice in the initial implementing of your new Response Control Procedures and will be in a position to continue to develop your own self-managed Programme from that point on.

Note that in this Stage we are working from day to consecutive day. It may not prove possible, when it comes to putting into practice some of the procedures described and in working towards major goals, to fit them into our ten-day timescale. If, for example, your major goal is to learn a new action sport in order to control Boredom Lifestyle Stressers, it will be almost impossible for you to achieve this within ten days. What you should do, in such a case, is ensure that you are working steadily and consistently through the sub-goals leading up to a long-term major goal during the Ten Day Programme.

DAY ONE – SELF-RECORDING CHARTS

These instructions should be followed no matter which of the eight RCP Programmes you intend to implement during the next nine days. The first task today consists of starting to compile a series of records concerning the particular Stressers or Negative Responses which you have identified in Stage Three. To do this you will need a small notebook or pad with pages marked out as in Diagrams Seven, Eight and Nine. Under each of the headings you will be making notes about the stress situations and your responses to them. You will also be collecting reinforcers, that is situations or pieces of behaviour from which you derive pleasure. Note and include in your list any items which occur fairly frequently and are of short duration, as well as infrequent and lengthy pleasures. The shorter and more frequent items will later be used to reinforce behaviour directly, ·

DIAGRAM SEVEN – *Record Keeping Chart showing the general type of information to be gathered under each of the three headings*

Lifestyle Stresser(s) Being Monitored:

Date:

Stimulus	*Response*	*Reinforcers*
Surroundings in which you encountered Stresser.	What you did.	Pleasurable activities and situations experienced during the day.
Time of day.	How you felt.	
People or objects present relevant to Stresser.	How long it lasted.	
Activities carried on by you and others.	Effects on behaviour. What you thought.	
(Use shorthand if necessary but maintain accuracy of Record Keeping)		

Total Number of Negative Stress Responses experienced:

DIAGRAM EIGHT – *Example of records kept for Threat Lifestyle Stresser*

Lifestyle Stresser Being Monitored: Threat.

Date: 26th July.

Stimulus	Response	Reinforcers
In office. Noon. Manager comes in to discuss target figures. Working on urgent task. Cannot find appropriate files. He gets angry. Others in the office watching me.	Tried to find files. Got very tense and confused. Could not remember where they had been put. Felt heart racing and began to feel slightly sick. Went red. Stammered. Felt foolish and ineffectual etc. . . .	Smoking. Eating bar of chocolate. Buying Hi-Fi magazine. Eating sandwich in the park. Watching girl in office across the street. Spending time in radio store looking at latest equipment. Buying new tuner. Buying new jazz cassette. Going to concert.
At station. Rush hour. Mislaid ticket. Others pushing past me. Train about to leave.	Felt sick with panic. Tried to argue with ticket collector. Searched frantically through all pockets. Soaked with sweat. Thought everybody must think I was a fool. Terrified would miss the train etc. . . .	

K*

DIAGRAM NINE – *Example of records kept for Boredom Lifestyle Stresser*

Lifestyle Stresser Being Monitored: Boredom.

Date: 8th September.

Stimulus	Response	Reinforcers
10 a.m. At home in kitchen with children. Pile of cleaning and clearing to do. Washing in sink. Drink coffee and think about making a start. Consider going over to see friend on other side of town.	Feel lethargic. So much work to do it seems impossible to know where to start. Have slight headache. No enthusiasm. Think about long bus journey and decide to stay in. Read newspaper without any interest.	Going to parties. Holding coffee mornings. Having a chocolate cake at mid-morning. Lying on bed nude and thinking about sex. Watching TV. Reading new magazine. Buying some new clothes. Having hair done. Chatting to friends on the phone.
Lunch time. Need to make meal for children. Afternoon seems to stretch endlessly ahead. Consider going out shopping.	Prepare some food for children. No appetite myself. Have a snack. Sit for a long time. Feel anxious about work to be done still. Go into other room to avoid mess in the kitchen.	

298 THRIVE ON STRESS

whereas the less frequent or lengthy ones may have to be obtained through cashing in tokens or points which have been collected throughout the day or week as a result of carrying out part of your Programme.

Examples of Short Term Reinforcers: Making a phone call, having coffee, buying or reading a magazine, relaxing, having an alcoholic drink, or a sexual outlet, including masturbation.

Examples of Longer Term Reinforcers: Going to the cinema or theatre, going out dancing, going away for the weekend, buying yourself an expensive gift, booking a holiday.

There will be many more reinforcers in your own repertoire and they should be gathered, no matter how small, trivial or intimate (as in the case of sexual activity) they might seem. The only important thing is that you find them pleasurable.

DAY ONE

Programme One

Read through the Deep Muscle Relaxation Procedure and make sure that you have learned the mnemonic for the muscle groups. Find your comfortable relaxation area and carry out a thirty-minute Deep Relaxation training session. Try and do this without too much reference to the book, since the activity of reading and turning pages will disrupt your relaxation. But take care not to miss out any of the major muscle groups.

Programme Two

Write down the Lifestyle Stresser which you are going to use to build up your stress level to the OSL. Pick some goal within that Lifestyle Stresser which will provide you with a taxing situation.

Programme Three

Select two or three congestion points during the day and make
out a priority list of things which you have to do at these times.
Remember to note especially the times at which congestion
occurs on your self-recording chart.

Programme Four

Note particular times of Negative Stress Responses during
self-recording. If you have difficulty filling in the reinforcement
column in your self-recording chart, try to look, in as much
detail as possible, at your behaviour, as you are sure to find
something which is pleasant if this is only breaking the
monotony of doing nothing. Make sure you understand the
difference between a strategy and a tactic as explained in the
Programme and try to develop an overall goal at which to aim.

Programme Five

The first day should be spent just keeping records and trying to
determine which goals you should specify in particular Life Area
activities. Special consideration should be given to specifying
the goals in a positive and accurate way.

Programme Six

Start self-recording and Deep Relaxation training as in Programme One.

Programme Seven

Concentrate on gathering reinforcers and building up your Programme of self-recording, noting particular areas of special difficulty.

Programme Eight

Begin Relaxation training as described in Programme One. As well as normal record keeping try to list other Frustration Stressers from memory.

DAY TWO

For All Programmes

Continue with self-recording. Pay particular attention to noting down Negative Stress Responses. Try and increase the amount of information available to you about how, when and where these responses particularly occur. Note the number of occasions during the day that these occur. Add to your list of reinforcers. Do not be afraid to put down anything and everything which gives you pleasure.

Programme One

Repeat the Deep Muscle Relaxation training session as in Day One but today try and find time for two thirty-minute sessions.

During this session concentrate particularly on the feeling of letting your muscles unwind and of trying to visualise each muscle group in turn as they relax completely.

Programme Two

Construct a hierarchy between your present level of performance and the goal which you chose on Day One. Remember to keep the sub-goals equally spaced so as not to make too large or too small a jump between each.

Programme Three

Repeat your graded priority lists to gain practice and if you have noted any negative self statements begin to develop Positive Self-Talk statements based on them.

Programme Four

Try to motivate yourself to continue record keeping by carrying out one of your reinforcing behaviours every time you make an entry on your record sheet. Establish a series of tactics, or sub-goals, by which your overall goal or strategy developed in Day One may be reached.

Programme Five

List a number of situations which you encounter which present you with Performance Stressers. From this list extract two or three with which you wish to deal initially.

Programme Six

Use the records and your memory to build up a hierarchy of Threat situations. Continue to follow Programme One to learn Relaxation skills.

Programme Seven

Develop a goal from one of the RCPs designed to reduce the certainty in your life. Decide on a high-level goal which you might not attain or some risky activity which you can build into your leisure time. Jot down possible sub-goals which will have to be completed in order to increase the Chance or Risk factor in your life.

Programme Eight

On the basis of your records from Day One, try to pinpoint particular Frustration Stressers. Select a specific type of Frustration Stresser from one of the Life Areas to work on for a time. Carry on with Relaxation training.

DAY THREE

For All Programmes

Continue with self-recording and the collection of reinforcers. You should find it easier now to identify those times of the day when the Stressers which you are recording occur and the responses they produce. Be certain to keep a daily total of Negative Stress Responses. File away earlier record sheets carefully as you will be able to use them to assess your progress in controlling and creatively using Stress.

Programme One

Repeat the Deep Muscle Relaxation training on two further occasions of thirty minutes duration. Concentrate on letting the muscles unwind and, this time, adding and focusing on the key word 'Relax' each time you breathe out. Use your regular and even breathing to encourage the relaxing effects.

Programme Two

Attempt the first of the sub-goals in the list which you have constructed and use positive reinforcers from your list to reward yourself. Start to look around your environment for ways in which to change it so that it becomes more agreeable or interesting.

Programme Three

Note congestion points again and begin trying to predict when they are likely to occur during the day. Test your predictions against reality as recorded on the chart. Practise using 'positive coping statements' to combat negative self-talk.

Programme Four

Today you should begin to construct your Thought Tank. Do not worry if it is not very full to start off with but at least try to make one on a subject of your choice.

Programme Five

Having accurately developed particular goals of increasing Performance you should now construct a series of sub-goals which can be used in order to acquire or consolidate the skill with which you are having difficulty. Make sure that the sub-goals are carefully spaced so that they offer neither too great a challenge nor too little difficulty in their accomplishment. Today you may not get beyond random jottings concerning possible sub-goal skills.

Programme Six

With the help of a friend begin to practise Tension Control and the recognition of the initial Anxiety Surge. Think about the first item on your list of Threat Stressers and build up a Positive Self-Statement about it. Carry on with Programme One.

Programme Seven

Order the sub-goals which you noted yesterday into a logical sequence with sufficient space between them to make reaching each of them slightly stretching. Make a start on the first sub-goal.

Programme Eight

Begin practising assertion skills by exaggerated role playing. Carry out just one of the exercises. Continue to develop Relaxation training.

DAY FOUR

For All Programmes

Continue with self-recording and, if possible, add to your list of long and short term reinforcers. Make certain you note the total number of Negative Stress Responses at the end of each day.

Programme One

Two further periods, each of thirty minutes, should be set aside for Deep Muscle Relaxation today. Use the key word 'Relax' together with even breathing to help you really unwind and let go. Try during these two sessions to develop your passive concentration and allow the feelings of relaxation to take over. Examine your record keeping and notice whether there is any change in the total number of Negative Stress Responses experienced.

Programme Two

If you have started to put the first sub-goal into effect note any difficulties which may have arisen, then either attempt the next sub-goal or repeat the previous day's sub-goal if you are not happy about how you performed. Use positive reinforcers to increase motivation.

Programme Three

Using your priority lists look to see whether the same problem reccurs frequently. If so try to form a strategy to get rid of that problem, such as memorising particular facts and figures, better organisation of files, refusing to accept calls at that time and so on. Carry on noting congestion points during the day.

Programme Four

Attempt one of the sub-goals or tactics leading to the overall goal (strategy) which you developed on Day One. Remember always to debrief on the outcome of such an attempt and build up on self-image by praising yourself for a positive attempt. Carry out another Thought Tank exercise on a different subject.

Programme Five

Make sure your sub-goals are correctly ordered and sensibly spaced. Practise the first sub-goal and use positive reinforcement in order to motivate yourself to attain it. At this stage it is important to concentrate on consistency of practice. If the skill is physical in nature you should look into Relaxation training in Programme One to see if it might help. If it is a mental skill you should read the procedures in Programme Three to see if they are relevant.

Programme Six

Use the first item in your hierarchy to engender a small amount of anxiety while you are carrying out your Relaxation training. Bring down the anxiety by using the Relaxation Response and use Positive Self-Talk developed yesterday to help you to do this. Continue Programme One. After you have finished reinforce yourself for your efforts.

Programme Seven

Continue to work through your sub-goals towards the overall goal. Start to build up a list of activities which you can build into the 'taking a chance' procedure.

Programme Eight

Practise the exercise on exaggerated role playing but add one or two of the other exercises. Carry on with Relaxation training with the schedule for Programme One.

DAY FIVE

For All Programmes

Carry on with self-recording as on the previous four days. A study of the data now available to you should start to reveal a pattern of Stressers and Negative Stress Responses. As you start to implement the procedures being taught in your Programmes, you should begin to notice a decrease in negative stress effects. Whenever a new source of reinforcement, whether long or short term, presents itself, be sure to note it down. Nothing is too trivial or elaborate to include providing it gives you pleasure.

Programme One

Carry out another two sessions of Deep Muscle Relaxation training. Today we want you to start including a pleasant image in your thoughts which you can dwell on and which you can allow to relax you even more deeply. If you are finding it difficult to sustain your efforts to practise relaxation then begin to use some of the positive reinforcers which you have gathered so far in a contract with yourself so that you give yourself a reward at the end of each practice session.

Programme Two

Continue to work through your graded list. Note whether any increases in stress are making life more interesting for you and helping to limit negative responses.

Programme Three

Plan today to pace yourself and use your available energy quanta evenly through the day. Between the congestion points guard against using any energy quanta unnecessarily. By the end of this period you should be concentrating on the skill of allocating channel capacity at congestion points to problems which confront you according to your priority lists.

Programme Four

Have another go at the same sub-goal or try the next one if you managed well yesterday. Develop another Thought Tank, and, today, add this to the other two and begin constructing a hyper-Thought Tank. In debriefing yourself try to look at positive and negative aspects of your behaviour and try to develop Positive Self-Talk.

Programme Five

Practise the same sub-goal again or, if you are happy with this, move onto the next one. Continue to work on any Relaxation or mental skills which you feel are appropriate.

Programme Six

Go through the next one or more situations in your list of Threat Stressers, again using Anxiety Management with both Relaxation Response and Coping Statements to control the Anxiety Spiral after you have felt the first surge of anxiety. You should begin to control the build up of tension and anxiety in imaginary situations.

Programme Seven

Continue to work through the sub-goals towards your taxing overall goal. Play your first game of Chance with the die and the list of alternatives.

Programme Eight

Practise exaggerated role playing and Relaxation. If appropriate practise Making-Up skills. Use positive reinforcement to motivate you after each attempt.

DAY SIX

For All Programmes

Continue to self-record and, whenever possible, add to your list of reinforcers. About this time in the schedule some people tend to get bored with noting details on their Stresser charts. But it is important to carry on with the record keeping at least until the end of the Ten Day Training Programme. Very often the simple act of putting down information about Stresses can help to control and use them.

Programme One

Today you should have one practice session of Deep Relaxation and one of Quick Relaxation training. Try to concentrate on the key word 'Relax' to enable you to do this and try to use passive concentration. Use reinforcers, if necessary, to sustain motivation in the training.

Programme Two

By now you should have made a good start on your graded sub-goals and be well on your way to adding additional stress and more and more taxing behaviours each day. Remember that while the distance between the sub-goals should not be impossibly large, you should feel stretched when progressing from one to the next.

Programme Three

Practise building up Coping Statements and Positive Self-Talk to deal with any anxiety situation where you get confused. As you allocate your quanta proportionately to the congestion points, reinforce yourself after dealing with each point of congestion by taking a few minutes to do something relaxing and pleasant.

Programme Four

Construct another Thought Tank and add it to the rest. Continue to construct a list of positive thoughts and attributes about yourself and extract some key positive feelings which you can keep repeating in order to build up Self-Image.

Programme Five

Note particularly whether you are carrying out practice consistently. You should try to practise each sub-goal as often as you reasonably can each day. Move on to the next sub-goal in the series only after you have completed the previous one satisfactorily.

Programme Six

Finish off working through the Threat hierarchy in imagination. Spend some time debriefing on how you managed to cope with the situation in imagination. Increase your list of Positive Self-Statements and reinforce yourself each time you work on the problem. Carry on with Programme One.

Programme Seven

Play another game of Chance with the die and carry on working through your sub-goals to your overall goal. Start producing your Mind Bender Concept Cards.

Programme Eight

Practise Exaggerated Role Playing, Relaxation and Making Up skills. Now carry out these skills in your imagination and in mock situations with a friend.

DAY SEVEN

For All Programmes

We hope that you are managing to sustain interest in this schedule and that you are really *working* at the RCPs. Time and effort invested during these ten days will pay off handsomely for the rest of your life. No longer will you be the victim of Stress, but its master. The self-recording charts should be kept up and a note made of all the Negative Stress Responses experienced during the day. These should now start to diminish as you gain greater and greater control over your Stress Responses. Add to your list of reinforcers when you can.

Programme One

Carry out two more sessions of Quick Relaxation today and try to relax even more quickly each time you do this. Have at least one Deep Relaxation training session.

Programme Two

The effects of increased stress should now start to make themselves felt. Check your list of sub-goals to make sure that these are not too closely spaced. If you feel progress has been slow then rewrite the list with a greater distance between each of the sub-goals.

Programme Three

Today add Ideogram practice to your schedule and spend fifteen minutes or so developing your first one. Carry on practising pacing, listing priorities, and reinforcing your progress.

Programme Four

Develop another Thought Tank and add it to the rest. Continue to work through your tactics towards your overall strategy. At this point it may be useful to assess your progress and decide whether your tactics should be modified in any way in the light of experience. Perhaps you can speed up progress towards the overall goal by reducing the number of stages needed to work through?

Programme Five

Check your self-recording charts and see whether you notice any decrease in Negative Stress Responses in your Performance. It may be too early to detect major ones at this stage but try to look for any positive gains which you have made. Carry on to work through the sub-goals until the skills become internalised.

Programme Six

Go through all the items in the hierarchy in imagination while relaxed and imagine yourself carrying out the activities while controlling Anxiety and using Positive Self-Talk. Continue to practise Quick and Differential Relaxation skills.

Programme Seven

Continue to build up your Concept Cards and to use the die for increasing Chance factors. Carry on working towards your overall goal.

Programme Eight

Continue to practise Exaggerated Role Playing and Relaxation and Making Up skills. Try asking for something in real life in an assertive way and use self-reinforcement to praise yourself *immediately* after having asked and before you get a response. Remember that asking is the important thing.

DAY EIGHT

For All Programmes

Your self-recording charts should now start to indicate the beneficial changes, however small, which are taking place as you begin to master Stress Responses and gradually learn to control and use Stress. Do not be worried if the early gains are slight. Remember how you learned to ride a bicycle or swim? Within a very short space of time of having mastered the initial skill, progress was swift and your confidence increased rapidly. The same thing will happen in learning to control Stress. Continue with the self-recording and use reinforcers from your list to motivate you. Reward yourself for making every attempt towards acquiring a procedure or achieving a goal. Add to your list of reinforcers whenever you can.

Programme One

Today have one session of Quick Relaxation and one of Deep Muscle Relaxation. If you feel that you are able to relax deeply and quickly without difficulty then carry on and practise Differential Relaxation. Use reinforcers to reward yourself after each session if these will help you to sustain your interest.

Programme Two

Continue working at your sub-goals. At this stage you may feel like introducing another Stresser. If so write down a goal and a series of graded sub-goals as we did on Day Two.

Programme Three

Practise pacing, listing priorities, Coping Statements and Ideograms. Also include the procedure for dealing with temptation if loss of concentration has been a problem. Remember to reinforce these new behaviours each time you do them by carrying out some pleasurable activity.

Programme Four

By reference to your self-recording chart check how many Negative Responses you arc now experiencing. It should be possible to detect a decrease at this stage. If this has happened then add your ability to control Stress, in this constructive way, to your Positive Self-Image Statement. If no progress has been made debrief on why not and go through some of the previous day's assignments again.

Programme Five

Continue to work through the sub-goals and use reinforcers to help motivate you. If you are progressing well towards one major goal start considering other goals, perhaps selected from the list you made on Day One, and work out sub-goals by which they might be achieved.

Programme Six

Brief yourself, first in imagination, for dealing with the first item on your Threat hierarchy and then practise in real life. Remember WASP. When you return home go through a period of Relaxation and debriefing. Reinforce yourself for having made the effort. Continue with the Relaxation training.

Programme Seven

Try to finish off your Concept Cards. Build up the number of alternatives which you use with the die, making these increasingly taxing and stressful. Remember that you *must* obey the dictates of Chance when playing this game or the whole point is lost. Carry on working through your sub-goals. Use reinforcers to help keep you motivated.

Programme Eight

Examine your record sheet to date and see if you can identify any decrease in Negative Stress Response due to Frustration Stressers. Continue to practise all the skills which you have been developing, including Relaxation.

DAY NINE

For All Programmes

You are nearly at the end of this structured schedule. By now, procedures which may have appeared rather complicated and hard to put into effect on Day One should seem more natural and easily applied. Do not worry if certain procedures still strike you as rather mechanical. Remember that until a skill has been internalised it is bound to require effort and thought. Compare learning to control Stress with the skills needed to carry out any other piece of behaviour, from using a typewriter to speaking a foreign language, and you will begin to see how much practice is necessary in order to achieve effortless performance. Still keep on with the self-recording charts and continue to add to your list of reinforcers.

Programme One

Carry out two sessions of Quick Relaxation training, more if you have the time or feel the need for further practice, and one period of Differential Relaxation training.

Programme Two

Carry on working through the sub-goals. Check progress and again assess how well you have graded these. Use reinforcers to sustain the new, stressful behaviour.

Programme Three

Continue as for Day Eight by practising all the procedures which you have so far begun. You should now be able to note some alleviation of Negative Responses and be able to predict accurately when congestion or confusion points are going to arise.

Programme Four

Carry on working towards the overall goal. Build up your hyper-Thought Tank and try to prepare for any periods during the day when any Negative Responses occur. Develop specific Positive Self-Talk Statements to see you through these crisis periods.

Programme Five

Some of the earlier sub-goal skills should by now have become internalised and you should continue to practise to consolidate these. You might now include another Life Area or some different goal in your schedule. As before start work on the first sub-goal and do not proceed to the next until you are confident of having internalised it.

Programme Six

Brief yourself in imagination and attempt the next item on your hierarchy using Positive Self-Statements derived from yesterday's attempts. Again debrief on your return home and practise Relaxation training as before. Use reinforcers to help establish this new approach to your Threat Stressers.

Programme Seven

Check your record chart. You should be able to note some improvement in Negative Stress Responses resulting from Boredom Stressers. Play the first game with your Mind Bender Concept Cards.

Programme Eight

Practise the skills which you have already established and include in today's exercises some practice with Exit skills. Use a member of the family or a friend in a mock situation so that you can discover which type of exit line suits you.

DAY TEN

For All Programmes

With today's exercises you will have completed the structured schedule. But this must not mean an end to your practising procedures. Ten days was selected, on the basis of clinical experience, as the time which most people need to start them moving effectively towards mastery of the necessary RCPs. It

L

should not be regarded as a complete Programme of Stress Control in itself but rather as a starting point from which you can develop an increasingly flexible and personalised approach to controlling and using Stress. Remember that it is only by consistent practice that the necessary skills can become internalised and so carried out as 'second nature' in any situation. You may care to continue with the self-recording charts. As you grow more and more skilled in your handling of Stress these charts will provide interesting and revealing reading. After a few weeks of using RCPs in your life you should be able to look back, almost with astonishment, at the difficulties once presented by situations with which you now cope easily. Always bear in mind the importance of reinforcers in helping to establish new pieces of behaviour.

Programme One

By now you should be able to relax deeply and quickly and also have begun to move around in a relaxed way. Continue to practise these skills, possibly increasing the number of practice sessions each day but reducing the time spent for each session.

Programme Two

There should now be a beneficial change in your life with far fewer Negative Stress Responses. A check with your record keeping chart will tell you if the Stressers which you introduced into your environment have been effective. Review the whole Programme at this stage and make any adjustments you feel necessary. In the weeks and months ahead continue to use Stress in this creative way. Regular monitoring of your OSL in the four Life Areas will ensure that the Stress does not rise dangerously high at times when external Stressers increase for any reason.

Programme Three

Today begin predicting when confusion or congestion points will arise and try to approach these points by conserving your energy before they occur. Prepare to use more energy at certain points by storing it at others.

Programme Four

Continue to work on the Hyper-Thought Tank and to make progress towards the overall strategy. If this work has gone well you should start to think about new overall goals and the necessary tactics by which to attain them.

Programme Five

From now on you should have a structured approach towards Performance Stressers which will enable you to maintain mastery over them whatever new activities or changes arise in your life. Continue to practise consistently as you work through hierarchies of sub-goals and to reinforce yourself for doing so.

M

Programme Six

Attempt the next item on your hierarchy and consolidate the first one after you have briefed yourself for it in imagination. Debrief as usual after carrying it out. Continue to work on consolidating Relaxation skills. From this point on you should be quite capable of going through the graded list of Threat Stressers while controlling Anxiety Spirals.

Programme Seven

Continue to play Mind Bender games whenever you get the opportunity. If you have achieved the overall goal then you should notice a steady improvement in Negative Stress Responses as your Stress level starts to come up towards the OSL.

Programme Eight

Practise the skills you have learned so far and, after a mock situation of Exit skills, purposely get yourself involved with somebody from whom you have to make an exit quite firmly. After you have done so, debrief on how well you were able to leave without being apologetic or offering excuses. From today onwards you should continue to build up practical experience in using Assertion to combat Frustration Stressers.

Stage Six

Stress and Society

In the foregoing Programme we have described a variety of Response Control Procedures which enable individuals to control Stress and use it creatively. By putting these RCPs to work for you the Six Lifestyle Stressers can be regulated and the internal Strain which they produced kept at a beneficial level. But, of course, while Stress is frequently a destructive force for the individual suffering from its uncontrolled effects it is not unique to individuals. On the basis of many years' observation and extensive clinical experience we believe that whole societies respond to uncontrolled Stressers in much the same way as do individuals. Indeed we believe that it is possible to measure the Stress levels in society as a whole by examining the tactics which are most widely used in order to combat them. The tactics are, as we explained in Stage One, largely those of escapism. Once the level of Stress and the major Stressers present in any society have been determined, however crudely, it should be possible not only to suggest the most effective methods of reducing this Stress but also to predict how that society will respond to external challenges and changes. If this hypothesis is correct, and the empirical evidence resulting from our investigations and experience suggests that it is generally accurate, then it raises important and far-reaching issues.

For example, it is often suggested that man is violent by nature and largely unpredictable in behaviour. The inherent aggression instinct to fight for survival which many sociologists and anthropologists detect in mankind is not, in our view, caused by an ineradicable blood lust. It is a learned response to environmental Stressers and it can be switched off by applying environmental control over those Stressers. Nor do we believe that behaviours are irrational and unpredictable. They are, in fact, rather depressingly predictable. Hooliganism, vandalism, urban crime, civil disorder, international warfare and the atrocities perpetrated in the name of some political or religious dogma are not surprising aberrations but the entirely logical and, indeed, inevitable outcomes of uncontrolled Stressers. Such dangerous and potentially globally fatal behaviours cannot be replaced with socially beneficial responses by either pious words or increased forms of repression. They can only be effectively eradicated by learning to regulate Stress in a constructive way and through eliminating the destructive consequences of Negative Stress Responses by manipulating the environment.

It is commonly, and in our view correctly, assumed that man lives under greater Stress today than at any time in his history. An examination of our six major Lifestyle Stressers in relation to social changes makes it clear why this should have occurred and why, unless high-level changes of attitude take place, it is likely to continue to spiral out of control.

Performance Stressers have increased because tasks have become increasingly difficult to perform. The level of skill needed to work in almost any technical or managerial occupation, from the skilled artisan to the sub-atomic physicist has risen at an almost exponential rate since the last war. Today's technicians, even at the most basic level are, of necessity, far better trained and educated than their pre-World War II equivalents. Increasing specialisation has meant that tasks have become more and more refined so that a point has been reached where it is impossible for the general public to understand the intricate details of many technologies. It is even almost as difficult for another specialist working in the same general field, unless he undergoes specific training, to appreciate fully all the implications of a piece of advanced research. Commercial competition has resulted in intense pressure on scientists, technicians, engineers and, indeed, all types of specialists to stretch their Performance skills to the limit. It is becoming harder and harder to keep up with the expansion of knowledge let alone remain in the front of the race. Under these circumstances the rise in Performance Stressers, at all levels of society above the most unskilled, is hardly surprising.

Threat Stressers have grown equally rapidly. Not only is the world a far more dangerous place in which to live than half a century ago, thanks mainly to the strenuous efforts of all the major powers to 'defend' themselves with a growing armoury of chemical, biological and nuclear weapons. But what is just as important, we are far more aware of the dangers, on a global scale, than at any time in our history. Television, radio and the news media can speed information about a conflict in Southern Africa to a hundred million front rooms almost as the conflict breaks out. The more sensationally deadly developments in the arms race, in genetic engineering, in naturally occurring hazards are the daily fare of almost everybody. Threat of a local nature, such as crime, communal disturbances, outbreaks of dangerous diseases, the escape of violent men and women from prisons flood into every home at the flick of a switch or the turn of a page. On all sides our survival appears to be menaced by imminent destruction. Many of the dangers are real enough, but a great deal more sensationalism results from the need for newspaper companies to sell more copies than their rivals and TV stations to gain high audience ratings from the news. Of course journalists and television reporters do not make bad news, but editorial emphasis and selection can present any number of pictures of society and it is an undeniable fact that bad news sells papers and that, perhaps, a majority of people do like to read about violence and study the more gloomy prophesies of the specialists. If we consider this need for 'bad news' in the light of the escape mechanisms from Stress which we discussed in Stage One, it becomes less surprising. News has now become a branch of entertainment and the vicarious excitement which can be gained from reading about dangers from the security and comfort of the front room provide a temporary relief from Boredom. But, of course, many people are unable to deal with the anxieties which such reports produce and so the level of Threat Stressers in their lives rises to a dangerous level.

Boredom Stressers are the inevitable consequence of production lines, routine jobs at home and in industry, bleak, uninspired architecture, lack of facilities for sport or other leisure pursuits and a lifestyle restricted by lack of money, education or opportunity. Boredom Stressers have increased not simply because of the rapid industrialisation of society, although this has provided the means for making millions bored, but ironically, by the greater level of general education. The illiterate peasant who has never known any other life may derive great pleasure and stimulation from the quiet contemplation of a rural landscape and we would not criticise him for these bucolic delights. But once the horizons have been broadened and the index of possibilities made available to the people in school, subsequent attempts to restrict their lifestyle to fit the economic and social 'requirements' of an industrialised nation are recipes for disaster. Strikes, go slows, work-to-rules, acts of vandalism and hooliganism are regarded with horror by the media and comfortable middle-class society, which, taking considerable care to produce Boredom-removing strategies and facilities in its own environment, is promised increasingly punitive and harsh measures with which to deal with such deviancy. Our view is that far from holding up its collective hands in horror at such outbreaks, the legislative and social system should regard them as promising evidence of man's resilience in the face of socially created Boredom. Strikes, whatever the economic merits or demerits, can be seen in behavioural terms as highly reinforcing activities providing both short term immediate payoffs and longer term rewards. The interruption in a monotonous routine, such as the arrival of a car body in your working area every 1 minute 55 seconds during an eight hour day, is the first reinforcer. Then comes the welcome change to meetings and discussions which, however tedious many of the participants may feel them to be, are certainly more entertaining than production line work. If the strike is a large one there will be media attention, television cameras at the gates and journalists eager for the opinions of the rank and file as much as of the leadership. The individual has thus asserted himself in an environment which normally provides little scope for individuality. Not only are Boredom Stressers removed but many Frustration Stressers are similarly alleviated. Finally, usually, there comes an increase in pay or an improvement in working conditions. But even if these were not the ultimate reward, indeed if the strikers were forced back on the same or even inferior terms, the act of striking would still have been reinforced by the immediate consequences of the behaviour which were to escape Boredom. In this way it would become more likely, however positive *or* adverse, the return to work conditions, that a further strike would occur. The more adverse the conditions of a return to work, the more vindictive the response of a victorious management, the more likely it may appear that a second strike will follow. But while the Frustration and Threat Stressers which would arise from this sort of situation must clearly influence the decision to strike, in the main striking can be regarded as a piece of behaviour separate from any negotiations which follow it or any terms achieved. The act of striking is established by the reinforcer of a release from the Boredom and Frustration Stressers built into the production line. One would predict, from behavioural principles, that the incidence of strikes must therefore increase – no matter what levels of pay are achieved – so long as Boredom Stressers remain unrelieved. This prediction is, in fact, being born out in practice since in many industries strikes continue no matter what material advances are achieved.

Frustration Stressers arise from many of the causes which produce Boredom Stressers and frequently from the Negative Stress Responses of the Boredom itself. They are also engendered by the proliferation of government and local authority legislation. Frustrations are also a product of increased education and a greater awareness of the possibilities of life. If you want to cage a tiger and never run the risk of its trying to escape then you must do so from birth and ensure that the beast never gets a taste of the world beyond its cage. If it does then it will become more and more dangerous to confine. People now know what might be achieved, what happiness and fulfilment they could discover in their lives and they are less and less inclined to endure the restrictions placed on them by society as a whole. Since, in most cases, they can do very little but accept and endure, the rise in Frustration Stressers is inevitable.

Bereavement Stressers have probably not risen as fast as the other Stressers save in so far as more people now have greater goals and higher ambitions. The trappings of success are probably better publicised than in the past and the chances of the ordinary individual reaching the heights has increased, if only marginally. The boy from the slums can now make it as a pop singer, clothes designer, writer or actor in a way which was next to impossible twenty years ago. But at the same time the chances of failing, of watching the glittering prizes of social or commercial success slip from eagerly outstretched fingers have also greatly multiplied. For this reason many more people fail and suffer the Bereavement Stressers resulting from a lost job, lost wealth and status, and a loss of self-respect.

Physical Stressers, despite the enormous increases in expenditure on medical research and the expansion of the health services, are probably greater than at any time in our past. The plagues and epidemics which swept across Europe and the United States have been replaced, as we noted in Programme Ten, by the modern Stress-related epidemics of coronary heart disease and so called mental illness. Noise, dirt, dust and atmospheric pollution, processed and packaged food strained and drained of essential nutrients, and urban living which limits healthy exercise are part and parcel of twentieth-century man's lifestyle.

We said at the start of this discussion that the types of Stresser most prevalent in any society could be largely determined by examining the tactics which that society used to divert itself from the resulting Negative Stress Responses or to prevent the most socially undesirable consequences of those responses. To carry out a detailed analysis requires considerable research and would need a book length explanation to describe and justify the procedures employed. In general it can be said that Boredom Stressers may be measured by the level of vandalism, petty crime and outbreaks of 'senseless' violence and, in a democratic society which tolerates these expressions of discontent, by the level of strikes, work-to-rules or go-slows. In a totalitarian society they can be measured by the intensity of the repressive laws needed to prevent the kind of behaviours described above. Thus society in Britain can be judged to be suffering from just as high levels of Boredom and Frustration Stressers as can the black population of South Africa. The difference is that because a certain amount of vandalism and outbreaks of hooliganism occur, alongside industrial disputes, there is a certain safety valve. The brutality and repression of the South African government and police against blacks means that when the Stressers spiral out of control the explosion must, inevitably, be excessively violent and destructive.

Of course it would be quite wrong to imply that Boredom Stressers alone are responsible for vandalism and crime. Frustration Stressers play their part, as we have described above, and so, too, do Threat Stressers as people feel their survival threatened, by the forces of law – which they regard as being the tool of an antagonistic establishment – by unemployment, by bad housing and little hope for the future.

The level of Threat Stressers in society can be measured not only by the number of tranquillisers prescribed but also by the levels of vicarious violence needed. The rise in screen violence, in the cinema and on the television, is not a causal factor of environmental violence in our view but a reflection of a need to sublimate the effects of Threat Stressers in a socially acceptable way. The greater the Stresses produced by Boredom and Threat, the more directly violent these distractions are likely to prove. In eighteenth-century Britain, when the mass of people lived lives of considerable Boredom, coupled with Threat through disease, famine and harsh civil laws, accepted forms of entertainment included public executions, bear baiting and cock fighting. The continuing attraction of reality violence in today's society can be seen from the numbers of people who are drawn to disasters such as floods or fires as well as to motor car and train accidents.

We are not, of course, suggesting that Stressers alone were responsible for changes in social attitudes towards such obvious suffering. Nevertheless, our research has shown a clear connection between the type and levels of Stressers most prevalent in society and general attitudes within that society towards what are regarded as socially acceptable manifestations of violence.

In this book we have dealt in detail with procedures which can be used by individuals to control and utilise Stress. We would like to conclude our Programme by suggesting, in broad terms, how this approach towards Stress might be applied on a far wider scale to eliminate or reduce two of the more socially damaging consequences of Negative Stress Responses, vandalism and industrial disputes.

Vandalism

Nobody in Britain or America can deny the extent of this problem in many areas, nor the hard cash costs involved. It has been estimated that vandalism costs the United States $200,000 million every year. This includes $100,000 million worth of damage to schools which are a prime target for the vandal, with destruction ranging from smashed up rooms to arson which razes whole blocks.

In Britain there were nearly 80,000 cases of criminal damage exceeding £20 in 1975, a ten-fold increase over 1965. Repairing the damage caused by vandals cost the Post Office £426,000 between 1971–2, the last year for which figures were available. London Transport spends around £200,000 annually patching up and putting right their trains and buses after the wreckers have been at work. British Rail spends in excess of £1 million a year, the same sum that Liverpool spent clearing up, cleaning up or, in some cases, pulling down vandalised houses.

The conventional response by authorities faced with this massive problem is intensified security, stronger and less easily vandalised equipment or buildings and stiffer penalties for those caught. In the view of many sociologists the real culprits are less the vandals themselves the architects and developers than who constructed the gaunt high rise estates where there is no individual ownership of property and, consequently, nobody prepared to take responsibility for protecting commonly shared facilities. Oscar Newman, an American expert, has suggested that the impact of modern architecture is such that it triggers off destructive impulses. These views are, in our opinion, quite correct. But they do little more to provide a practical and effective answer to the problem than the harsher penalty cure proposed by the law-and-order advocates. It is hardly realistic, however desirable many people would consider this, to urge that we tear down the high rise blocks and replace them by less socially inoffensive buildings. The mistakes have got to be lived with at least for the next generation.

The answer, in our view, lies in a behavioural approach towards the problem. The vandal damages and destroys because it is reinforcing behaviour. It is exciting and stimulates the flow of adrenalin at a level which can give pleasure. It is interesting to watch the effects of bricks turning rather tedious acres of glass into abstract designs. It is physically satisfying to expend energy breaking things up. It is an expression of individuality to spray messages and slogans on uniformly bleak walls. Instead of trying to prevent these manifestations through punishment, the energies involved should be channelled into socially constructive uses. This does not mean regimented work forces of young people being employed to clean up canals and collect litter, but a realisation that there is a need to work off physical energy and generate adrenalin which will not be met by offering table tennis in a converted church hall or providing parks where football is forbidden. Large sums of money, not a token gesture, must be spent on creating adventure areas which offer genuine challenges rather than a few planks, some old barrels and a rubber tyre on a rope! There should be facilities for as many types of action sport as possible as well as areas where people can simply mess around without any regimentation and with as few restrictions as are compatible with physical safety.

This would certainly demand a large financial investment but much money could also be saved through a reduction in wanton damage, and the social consequences would be extremely desirable. Legislators must also break themselves of the habit of looking at risk sports only with an eye to eliminating their risks. The recent interest in hang-gliding in Britain provides a good example of the excessively protective role which the state is now adopting. After some fatalities, a very small number by comparison with the total number of those taking part, pressures were exerted to limit or even prohibit the sport. Certainly any dangerous sport should only be learned and practised under qualified supervision so that unnecessary risks are eliminated. But it is no part of the state's function to tell its citizens what risks they should take or how and where they should be taken. Providing, always, that only the participant is endangered then the freedom to kill yourself should be absolute.

Research in America has shown that vandalism of property most frequently occurs when no individual ownership of that property is apparent. For this reason we believe that tenants of council owned property should be encouraged to buy their houses or apartments. The purchase price could be kept low since such a transaction must not be regarded as a profit-making exercise but simply a way of transferring, into private care, some publicly owned piece of property. Generally it is only when an individual has ownership of a house or apartment that he or she will invest time and trouble in protecting and preserving it.

In behavioural psychology there is a concept called 'learned helplessness' which means that people develop the habit of being unable to look after themselves because they are never given the opportunity of practising this necessary behaviour. Without denying the gains and benefits of a welfare society we must also say that 'learned helplessness' is increasing in Western society and will continue to increase until responsibility for the way in which we live and develop is returned to each individual. Only in this way can the Negative Stress Responses of lethargy and aggression be effectively eliminated.

Industrial Disputes

We have already discussed the reinforcing nature of strikes and go-slows. But even in the absence of these difficulties, production line working produces Stressers which can lead to carelessness, shoddy production and needless accidents through the habituation of the task.

In Kalmar, south-east Sweden, the Volvo car company have a purpose-built factory which offers one solution to the Stressers resulting from an ever-rolling production line. They have abandoned the concept of a chain-driven line which was devised by Henry Ford more than half a century ago and, in doing so, they have not only produced better cars but happier and more enthusiastic car workers. It is now accepted in Scandinavia that if you buy a Volvo P242 or P244 which have been assembled at the Kalmar plant you will get a first-class vehicle. Before they constructed their plant Volvo consulted the views of the employees about what was wrong with their job. A large number said, quite simply, that they wanted to have some pride in the end product. In under three years a factory incorporating their wishes was designed and built. Consisting of four linked, hexagonal units it is unlike any car factory anywhere else in the world. There is no continuous belt feeding the vehicle under assembly to a line of workers each responsible for some small addition. Instead there are computer controlled trolleys whose speed can be varied according to the wishes of the workers. If they want a faster rate of vehicles through their hands the trolleys can be speeded up, if a hold-up develops they can be slowed. Assembly is carried out by 25 construction teams each containing about 15 members, which has been found to be the ideal number. Each of these teams has its own workshop area, rest-rooms, showers and sauna. The team members arrange their own work schedules in consultation with a foreman who looks after two workshop areas. While the teams do not make the whole car they are responsible for completing an entire process. There are various other refinements as well, for example working heights can be varied at the touch of a button to bring assemblies into the easiest position. The plant has a fully equipped medical unit and there is a bonus payment for every employee who loses no more than one day in three months through sickness. As a result of all these changes and improvements Kalmar produces 620 high-quality cars each week from a workforce of 600. By comparison it takes 6,600 British car workers at British Leyland's Cowley factory to turn out 5,100 far less complex vehicles. The industrial history of the British car industry is, to say the least, an unhappy one while at Kalmar absenteeism and disputes are non-existent and production losses through sickness are negligible. Gosta Blomberg, the factory's information officer, says that the system could be adapted for the mass production of any item and many industrialists agree. But whether they will have the imagination to adopt the Kalmar production line methods remains to be seen.

Individual involvement and responsibility for the product, coupled with the best possible working conditions and the highest viable rate of pay for the job are sound procedures for controlling and using Stress in any industrial or commercial setting. In Britain some smaller factories have experimented with switching around workers so that everybody gets a chance to do the more interesting and complicated tasks while also taking a turn at the duller, more routine chores which are essential for production. Such a revolutionary approach to work routines requires considerable co-operation between management and unions, but it can pay handsome dividends.

The general principles for controlling Stressers in an industrial or commercial setting can be summarised as follows:

(1) Give every individual as much personal responsibility as possible.

(2) Organise work forces as small teams, around the size of a football team is ideal, and give each team responsibility for completing some major part of the assembly or production process.

(3) Make the work as varied as possible and increase Performance Stress, if this can be done, so as to prevent habituation. To give one example of how this can be beneficial, an extremely important task in military aviation is watching radar screens. This is also, for most of the time, a tedious chore which, nevertheless, demands a high degree of concentration. It was found that if a rogue blimp was deliberately created on the screen at random intervals the radar operators were kept far more alert and interested than they would otherwise have been. This random element in what was otherwise a routine task provided sufficient interest to prevent the behaviour being habituated.

(4) Working conditions should be as clean, interesting and comfortable as the task permits. Only if the lighting, heating and ventilation are correctly adjusted will Physical Stressers be reduced to a minimum.

(5) In order to prevent Frustration Stressers from building up, every worker should have a direct line of communication to management so that petty disputes and small problems can be eliminated or resolved before they grow out of all proportion.

(6) Opportunities should be provided for getting rid of physical energy, if the job is a sedentary mental one, or of relaxing if the work requires great concentration combined with physical or mental exertion. In our view the concept of a tea or coffee break should be replaced by a *Stress Break*. During this time employees would be able to refresh themselves, but, at the same time, get the opportunity of adjusting levels of Stress back to their

OSL. For example people with very routine, low Performance high Boredom Stresser jobs would have a chance to do something which they found interesting either physically or intellectually. Ideally there would be areas set aside for physical exertion as well as for relaxation.

Perhaps such suggestions strike you as out of touch with industrial and commercial reality. Where is the money to come from for the non-essential 'luxuries'? it may be asked. Why should companies provide such facilities in any case? others may argue. The purpose of a factory is to produce goods and provide jobs. The responsibility of management is to manage, that of workers to work. The answers can be found in the days lost through strikes, sickness and absenteeism, in the increasing damage caused by vandals and hooliganism. Only when society faces up to the root cause of such problems and seeks to deal with the Stressers which produce them will the situation improve.

Stress can destroy a society as effectively as it can cripple and kill an individual. Controlled and used creatively, it can transform the nature of that society as beneficially as it can improve and revitalise your own life. Negative Stress Responses are the root cause of almost every social ill which confronts us today. We must learn to eliminate them through imaginative Stress control procedures rather than continue on our present suicidal course of attempting to repress them or divert attention away from them.

Only in this way will modern society, like modern man, discover that it is possible to Thrive on Stress.

NOTE

In this book we have referred to procedures of relaxation and stress control which can be made easier by using cassette courses and biofeedback equipment developed by the authors.

The main cassette courses for use with this book are: **Relaxation**, which teaches the skills of deep, quick and differential relaxation; and **Stress Control**, which builds upon the skills learned in **Relaxation** by teaching you how to recognise and use the early warning signals of stress effects within the body.

The main piece of equipment for use with this book is: **The Stress Watch**. This is a biofeedback machine which enables you to see at a glance, on a meter, how your response to stress is changing. It is pocket sized and for use is simply held in the palm of the hand.

For details of these items and other new developments in the field of stress control write to: Dr Robert Sharpe, P.O. Box 4AR, London W1A 4AR.